# RAILWAYS OF CANADA

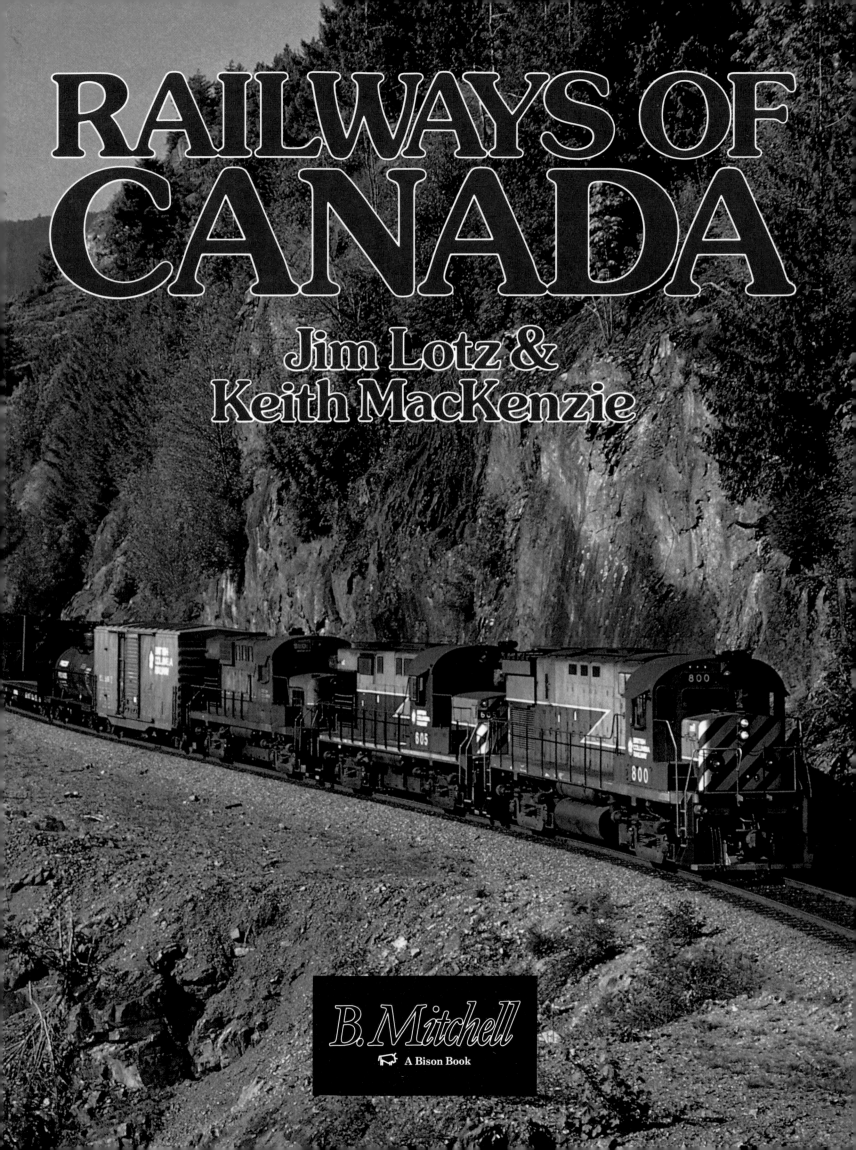

# RAILWAYS OF CANADA

## Jim Lotz & Keith MacKenzie

**B. Mitchell**

A Bison Book

This edition published by
W H Smith Publishers, Canada.

Produced by
Bison Books Corp.
15 Sherwood Place
Greenwich, CT 06830
USA

ISBN 0-88665-479-3

Printed in Hong Kong

*Page 1:* The second largest of Canada's railways, the Canadian Pacific (now CP Rail) is an important transporter of raw material and manufactured goods. Here, powerful CP Rail diesel road switchers speed a long coal train through Canada's picturesque countryside.

*Pages 2–3:* A trio of British Columbia Railway road switchers with the old green paint job (now changed to red, white and blue) haul a mixed freight along the rails near Howe Sound, in Beautiful British Columbia. BC Rail Ltd, the latest evolution of the company, is the third largest Canadian railway.

*These pages:* An EMD passenger diesel fronts this Canadian National passenger train of 1954, in the days before VIA Rail assumed the bulk of Canadian rail passenger service. Canadian National is the largest Canadian railway.

Edited by Thomas G Aylesworth, Pamela Berkman, Timothy Jacobs and Bill Yenne

Designed by Bill Yenne and Tom Debolski

# Contents

# INTRODUCTION

With the second largest land area of any nation on Earth, Canada possesses a vastness which could, in the nineteenth century, be brought into human scale only by rail transport. Indeed, this huge and rugged country was first defined as a nation by its railways.

Canada is today home to the only two railways—Canadian National and Canadian Pacific—which truly span the entire North American continent. They each cover roughly 75 degrees of the Earth's circumference, while Australia's continent-spanning India Pacific and America's great Southern Pacific span barely 35 degrees. Even the great Trans Siberian Railway in the Soviet Union—the longest railway in the world—spans only 85 degrees. As in the Russian Empire of the nineteenth century, Canada's vast horizons cried out for the power of steel rails to bind its cities, outposts and wilderness into a single great civilization. The tiny Champlain and St Lawrence Railroad Company, the first of the building blocks that would become CN, was the first-ever steam railway in the country, making its maiden run in 1836.

A little over 100 years ago Canada was not yet truly a nation. The Canadian Confederation, created in 1867, consisted of only four provinces: Quebec, Ontario, Nova Scotia and New Brunswick; British Columbia in the far west remained a crown colony. Between the burgeoning provinces of the east and the growing settlement on the Pacific coast was a vast, virtual wilderness, unknown and sparsely populated. By 1871, only 23,000 of Canada's 3.5 million inhabitants lived west of Lake Superior. With all the available arable land gradually being occupied in the United States, some American politicans and settlers spoke of annexing the prairies to the north; these virtually unprotected territories had yet to become part of Canada. Sir John A Macdonald, prime minister of Canada from 1867 to 1873 and again from 1878 to 1891, had long been concerned about pressures; and in response, the fledgling Canadian govern-

*Below:* **Three Canadian National EMD diesel road switchers highball a 'grain extra' across the Thompson River at Lytton, British Columbia.** *At right:* **Replete with old Canadian Pacific colors and logo, the CP** *Dominion* **was photographed as it refueled near Field, British Columbia. Locos like this have been phased out in favor of road switchers.**

ment drew Manitoba and British Columbia into the Confederation in 1870 and 1871, respectively.

If Canada was to become a strong, progressive and united country, a network of railways to bind it together—from the eastern provinces to the Pacific Ocean, from the arctic wastelands to the fertile prairies—was necessary. When the last spike of the Canadian Pacific Railway was driven at Craigellachie, British Columbia, on 7 November 1885, Canada gained a new world image and a new sense of identity. This new railway was more than just two ribbons of steel—it was an instrument of national unity, and later a source of friction. Canadian National is just as much a part of Canadian history. These two railways now control 80 percent of the rail miles in Canada.

This book is an overview of today's Canadian railways. It details the histories of the various companies that played important roles in the development of Canada as a modern nation. In particular, large, separate sections are devoted to Canadian Pacific and Canadian National, whose stories are directly linked with that of the nation of Canada. The story of Canada's railways is indeed the story of Canada herself.

*At right:* **A Canadian National freight speeds past, near Oshawa, Ontario. A close look at this train reveals boxcars, grain cars, a tank car, hopper cars and a couple of auto parts cars—the kind of mixed haulage that keeps Canada's railways healthy.**

# Canada's Railways

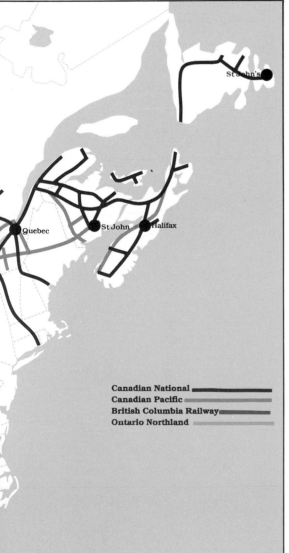

## Canada's Railway Companies

| Company | Miles | Locos | Cars |
|---|---|---|---|
| Canadian National Railways[*] | 34,220 | 3272 | 94,133 |
| CP Rail (Canadian Pacific) | 15,500 | 1200 | 58,000 |
| BC Rail | 1389 | 103 | 10,000 |
| Ontario Northland Railway | 754 | 34 | 1060 |
| Dominion Atlantic Railway | 277 | — | — |
| Cartier Railway Company | 260 | 50 | 1315 |
| Esquimalt & Nanaimo Railway | 195 | — | — |
| Toronto, Hamilton & Buffalo | 110 | 17 | 608 |
| White Pass & Yukon Corporation[**] | 110 | 23 | 450 |
| BC Hydro Rail | 104 | 20 | 264 |
| Greater Winnipeg Water District Railway | 97 | 6 | 130 |
| Devco Railway | 88 | 16 | 635 |
| Roberval & Saguenay Railway | 54 | 14 | 193 |
| Canada & Gulf Terminal Railway | 30 | 1 | — |
| Napierville Junction Railway | 28 | 2 | 29 |
| Essex Terminal Railway | 24 | 6 | 5 |
| Grand River Railway | 16 | — | — |

## US railroads with track mileage in Canada

| Company | Mileage operated in Canada | Percentage in Canada of their total mileage |
|---|---|---|
| CONRAIL | 328 | 2.4 |
| Norfolk & Western | 322 | 4.0 |
| Chesapeake & Ohio Railway[***] | 201 | 1.2 |
| Burlington Northern | 181 | .72 |

All data current as of 1987 excepted as noted

[*] Included in Canadian National's mileage are the Central Vermont Railway, with 375 miles in the US, and the Duluth, Winnipeg & Pacific Railway, with 165 miles in the US.

[**] as of 1982 when operation was suspended
[***] as of 1984

Canadian National
Canadian Pacific
British Columbia Railway
Ontario Northland

# Part One: Railways of Canada

## British Columbia Railway (BC Rail)

O n 27 February 1912, the Pacific Great Eastern Railway (PGE) which would become BC Rail was founded by industrialists who had the grand and ambitious plan to build a railway from Vancouver to northern British Columbia: it seemed only logical that the sleeping wealth of central and northern British Columbia should be tapped with a railway. Investment money for the project came from Great Britain—indeed the company's founders had named their project after Britain's Great Eastern Railway to attract English investors. A freight deal had even been worked out with the Grand Trunk Pacific Railroad, under which the PGE was to carry all of the Grand Trunk's freight between Vancouver and Prince George—then named Fort George.

The PGE's first locomotive, built by Manning Wardle of Leeds, England in 1874, was acquired when the company bought the Howe Sound & Northern Railway in 1912. Another famous locomotive of the early period was PGE Number 51, the first locomotive bought new by PGE and, despite its number, the third locomotive acquired by the railway. It was built in Canada by the Montreal Locomotive Works in 1913. This locomotive and its sister, Number 52, saw service until being retired and, sadly, scrapped in 1954.

Despite its promise, and the enthusiasm of its backers, the good times were not to last for PGE. Soon after it was founded, a severe and long-lasting recession hit British Columbia and the provincial government took control of a bankrupt PGE in 1918. The government thus acquired a political liability that would plague successive administrations for decades: keeping the railway was difficult to justify, but shutting it down would be political suicide.

Construction, however, continued on the railway until 1921, resulting in a popular, if unprofitable, passenger line running from the foot of Lonsdale Avenue in North Vancouver to Whytecliff in West Vancouver, and a main line that ran from Squamish to Quesnel.

For the next several decades the PGE was the object of great affection—from tourists, employees and the people who lived near its tracks—while being the object of ridicule by others. 'Neither Pacific, Great nor Eastern,' intoned the more witty of its detractors. The railway limped along with a very small operating budget and a lot of heart. Nails were straightened and reused, while machinists spent a lot of time rummaging around in the scrap heap. Even the popular North Shore passenger service closed in 1928.

However, by the late 1940s, the British Columbia economy was better. The province's interior had a new product that made the supporters of the railway gloat: lumber. The government wanted further construction to be done on the line. Soon the PGE had scores of modern diesel locomotives and the latest in microwave communications, and by 1952, the railway had reached Prince George. In 1956, the Howe Sound section was completed, and by 1958, the railway reached the Peace River district. In 1971, the line to Fort Nelson was completed. Despite this expansion, the British Columbia Railway continued to lose money— owing to an ambitious construction schedule and deficit financing. By 1976, the finances of the railway and its relationship with the provincial government became a matter of a Royal Commission of Inquiry. The Commission, among other things, recommended that the railway con-

centrate on operating as a business, rather than as a developmental agent of the government.

Another change for the railway was a new name. In the late 1960s and early 1970s, with nationalism sweeping the country, it was obvious that the name PGE had little to do with British Columbia. In addition, as the road and its business grew, PGE cars began showing up in various North American rail yards during this time and it was soon obvious that PGE's initials conflicted with those of the Pacific Gas & Electric utility company. PGE's name was changed to BC Rail in 1972—and was once more changed in 1984 to BC Rail Ltd.

Some of the locomotives of this more prosperous period were the Budd models RDC-3 (cab forward, with baggage compartment) and RDC-1 (cab rear, straight coach). These were built by the Budd Corporation of Philadelphia and delivered new in 1956. In the meantime, seven self-propelled Budd passenger cars were purchased by the railway to replace its aging coach fleet. (BC Rail now has nine Budd cars.)

Other newer locomotives include a 30-locomotive block of the MLW 700 Series, 3000-hp units featuring Alco 251

*Below:* **Two 6000 hp BC Rail Ltd GF6C electric locos (built by General Motors of Canada) head a 98 car train on the Tumbler subdivision north of Prince George.**

16-cylinder turbocharged engines which were purchased between 1969 and 1973.

The company also acquired 17 General Motors diesel electrics from General Motors Canada under the designation SD-40-2. The first of these, Numbers 751 and 753, were both delivered in October 1980, while the last of the series, Number 767, was shipped in July 1985. Seven General Motors electric traction locomotives of the GF6-C class were built to haul coal on the 129 km Tumbler sub-division north of Prince George. Number 6001, delivered in December 1983, was the first built; while the last, 6007, was delivered in August 1984; these units generate 6000 hp and were also built by General Motors Canada.

Today, the British Columbia Railway is a corporation which is vital to the economy of the province, with assets in excess of 1.2 billion Canadian dollars. Its 50-kV electric coal line at Tumbler ridge is recognized as one of the most advanced of its kind in the world.

Between 1981 and 1987, the railway achieved six years of substantial profits—returns to the province of its long-held investment. BC Rail Ltd is now the third largest railway in Canada, with about 1300 miles of track. Its head office, BC Rail Centre, is located at Lonsdale Quay in North Vancouver. The railway's early visionaries—and the successive governments that stood by it—have been proven right.

## BC Hydro Rail & Power Authority

Owned by the Province of British Columbia, the British Columbia Hydro & Power Authority (BCHPA) supplies electric power and gas to much of British Columbia and Victoria. The rail service was reorganized from the BC Electric Railway Company Limited (BCER), an electric inter-urban and street railway that began operations in Vancouver and its surrounding areas in 1897, when it took over public transit in Vancouver, Victoria, North Vancouver and New Westminster—the principal cities of the province. Along the Fraser Valley, BCER provided a vital link between towns isolated from one another by distance and the absence of good roads.

The BCER's electric rail cars brought dairy and other produce to market regardless of weather, supplied farmers with feed, machinery and supplies, carried logs to the mills in return for lumber and shingles and supplied convenient transportation for the settlers and their families when they visited the cities.

A major setback for BCER came in 1913 through competition from jitneys—small buses and motor cars which were independently owned. These offered extremely flexible schedules and routing—and were often enclosed against the weather, whereas the BCER's city streetcars were not. Dr Adam Shortt, who investigated jitney competition in 1917, noted that many people rode them for pleasure and social contacts. He pronounced them 'an irresponsible service' with no permanent commitment to meet public transit needs. In 1918 the Vancouver city council declared them illegal, ending the competition that had almost crippled regular transit service.

Though sturdy and dependable, the rail cars fell victim to progress. Vancouver's first motorbus line went into operation in 1923 and, from that time, the electrical rail cars were replaced gradually by motor and trolley buses, but BCER's freight service inherited much of the existing right-of-way, and most of it is still in use.

No one, however, could negotiate with the weather. On Sunday, 20 January 1935, a freak snowstorm dropped between 19.7 and 25.6 inches of snow on Vancouver, stopping the streetcars. Some were mired for hours on the streets until crews came to dig them out. The city was isolated because transcontinental trains were stopped by snow in the mountains, and most power and telegraph lines were down: these services were not fully restored for several weeks. On the coast, the snow turned to sleet, then to rain. In six days, Vancouver got as much rain as normally fell in three months!

The storm affected the company in a very painful way: BCER Vice President John Hewall became ill through overexertion in snow removal; he died on 3 February of that year.

World War II brought women into service as BCER conductors for the first time because most young men were in the military. Maintenance crews had to exert maximum efforts to keep the rolling stock serviced and running because no new cars could be bought.

After the war, the 12 mph speed limit for BCER vehicles was raised to 18 mph, and 15 mph in school zones. In the early 1950s, BCER carried out a 'Rails to Rubber' program. City streetcars were replaced by trolley coaches and buses, and interurban passenger cars were replaced by buses of Pacific Stage Lines, now Pacific Coach Lines.

Prior to 1950, the greater part of eastbound freight carried was from the forest industries. Then, as additional industries were established on the Lower Mainland, the railway freight business became more diversified. Through the years, heavier rail was installed to accommodate powerful diesel locomotives and the diversified cargo. This new 115 pound rail replaced the 85, 70 and 60 pound rail used in earlier times.

The rail service, now concentrated on freight handling, was acquired by BC Hydro Rail & Power Authority (BCHPA) when it was formed in 1962 by the amalgamation of the BCER and the BC Power Commission. The first annual report of BC Hydro reported that the rail freight service had carried 1,567,000 tons in the year ended 31 March 1963. In 1965, BC Hydro Rail completed the 21 acre marshalling yard in Burnaby, outside Vancouver—it was large enough to store 450 cars. Good building soil had become scarce in the area; the yard was built partly on a peat bog with 20 to 25 feet of soft organic silt beneath wet peat, which was from five to 25 feet in depth. Use of sawdust and other fill, with new drainage methods, brought about sufficient settling in 10 months to permit construction to proceed. In

*Opposite:* **A BC Rail Ltd passenger train, with Budd motive power, heads north through snowy countryside near Garibaldi.** *Above:* **A freshly painted BC Rail MLW 3000hp road switcher is one of a string of such hauling BC Rail Ltd freight through the beautiful scenery near Darcy.** *Below:* **With the old British Columbia Railway paint scheme, this MLW road switcher leads freight past Howe Sound.**

1967 a new repair and service center was completed at the same location.

Significant changes came with the introduction of the computer. A computerized car control and information system— introduced in 1979—has been very successful in improving customer service, locating and dispatching rail cars, and preparing customers' bills.

In 1980, the provincial government reorganized the passenger transportation system, and the service is now a responsibility of BC Transit. The BCHPA, as of 1984, operated a diesel-powered freight service between Vancouver and Chilliwick carrying automobiles, food and forest products. Still a small railway—104 miles—BC Hydro now owns approximately 20 locomotives and 264 cars.

## Ontario Northland Railway

Owned by the Province of Ontario, the Ontario Northland Railway operates primarily from North Bay to Moosonee. There are branch lines to Timmins, Iroquois Falls, Noranda, Elk Lake, Dane and Sherman Mine.

Originally chartered as the Temiskaming & Northern Ontario Railway (T&NO) in 1902, the line was built northward from North Bay to open up an area of isolated settlement. Construction began the same year, with the first segment starting public operation in 1905 to New Liskeard, 112 miles from North Bay. By 1908, construction had reached Cochrane, 252 miles from North Bay, where the line met the National Transcontinental Railway. As the province's rich natural resources were discovered, branch lines were built to exploit them. Small branches were built from Cobalt to Kerr Lake, from Englehart to Charlton and from Porquis to the Timmins area. In 1927, a 60 mile branch east from

Swastika to Noranda, Quebec, was finished to tap the gold mines of Kirkland Lake and the copper at Noranda. Meanwhile, the 186 mile Cochrane to Moosonee line, which had begun in 1922, reached its destination in 1931. The line was seen as having wood pulp transport prospects, with Moosonee being thought of as an iron ore terminal and even as a seaport for exporting farm products.

The T&NO was renamed as the Ontario Northland Railway in 1946, both because the new name better described the area it served and also to avoid confusion with the other T&NO—the Texas & New Orleans Railroad.

Today, the ONR interchanges with Canadian National Railway at Cochrane, Rouyn and North Bay, and the Canadian Pacific Railway at North Bay. Minerals and forest products make up a large percentage of ONR's carload and freight movements, and newsprint is a major source of freight revenue. The Ontario Northland Railway also operates a passenger service between Toronto, Timmins and Moosonee.

## Toronto, Hamilton & Buffalo Railway

Located on the far west shores of Lake Ontario, almost equidistant to Toronto and Buffalo, New York, the TH&B serves the busy area in the southern Ontario peninsula between Port Colborne and Waterford, via Hamilton, with 17 locomotives and 111 rail miles. The railway was incorporated in 1884. In 1895, the line opened for business and, in that same year, was bought by a consortium comprised of the Canadian Pacific, the New York Central (through its Michigan Central affiliate) and Canada Southern. In 1977 the New York Central merged with the Pennsylvania, transferring its interest to the Penn Central, while the Canada

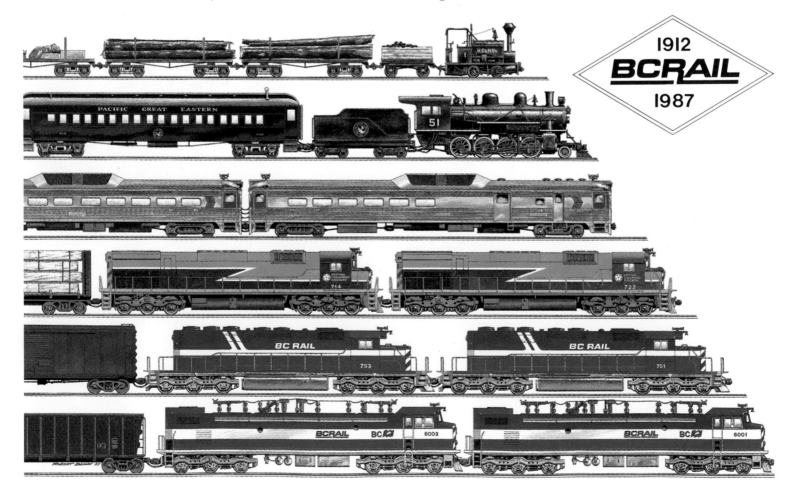

Southern interests were bought by CP. CP wholly absorbed the TH&B in 1987. As part of the larger road, it carries fertilizer, chemicals, iron and steel.

## Dominion Atlantic Railway

Dominion Atlantic Railway, whose equipment is owned by CP Rail, covers 277 track miles through Nova Scotia's farm land. It is headquartered in Kentville, Nova Scotia, near the Minas Basin and the Bay of Fundy.

## Cartier Railway

The Cartier Railway Company is located on the banks of the St Lawrence River and headquartered in the town of Port Cartier in northern Quebec. Although much smaller than Canada's 'Big Three' railways, Cartier, the country's sixth largest, plays an important role in servicing the surrounding area. Cartier operates 50 locomotives, 1315 cars, and owns 260 miles of track.

## White Pass & Yukon Corporation Ltd

Construction began on the White Pass and Yukon Corporation Ltd in 1898, and the last spike was driven home on 29 July 1900 at Carcross. The company had been created in the wake of the Klondike gold rush—to build a rail link across the coastal mountains between Skagway, Alaska, and Whitehorse, in the Yukon Territory. Over this route flowed both men and materials headed for the newly discovered Klondike goldfields. The little railway prospered

*Below opposite, from top to bottom:* The motive power, name changes and paint schemes in the history of BC Rail Ltd. This lineup corresponds exactly to the text on pages 10–12 (please see). *Above:* Three of the Cartier Railway's 50 locomotives lead a long train in northern Quebec (see text, this page). *Below:* An Ontario Northland 3000hp EMD GT40TC road switcher. Please see text, page 14.

*Above:* A BC Hydro Rail (see text, pages 12–14) mixed freight winds through lower British Columbia. *Below left:* A White Pass & Yukon Railway passenger train rounds Lake Bennett. *Above left:* White Pass & Yukon Railway antique steam engine Number 73 during the summer of 1982, just prior to the suspension of WP&YR rail operations.

during the gold rush, but when mining production declined, the WP&Y itself went into decline, and eventual reorganization. It became a carrier of varied freight consignments, a passenger hauler, and the main mover of ore concentrates in the area.

However, World War II and the new Alaska Highway brought new business to the railroad: war materials and defense supplies for northern North America. Because the increased traffic was too much for the WP&Y to handle, the US Army took over its operations, and supplied several locomotives purchased from US lines. After the war, WP&Y went back to business as usual.

It was no exaggeration to call the 110 miles of narrow gauge railway between Skagway and Whitehorse an essential connection between the Yukon and the outside world. While in operation, the railway hauled more than 600,000 tons of freight and carried some 65,000 passengers a year. Manufactured goods, foodstuffs, construction materials, industrial equipment and gas—all of which are vital to the homes, mines and industries of the north country—moved north via the WP&Y. Southbound, WP&Y trains carried silver, lead, zinc and copper concentrates bound for North American and overseas markets.

In the early 1900s, the company, recognizing the need for a coordinated intermodal transportation system, started stagecoach and riverboat services which interlocked with its rail facilities. In time, the WP&Y comprised a varied group of wholly-owned and interrelated companies. By 1982, it operated a facility for the export of bulk mineral concentrates, had a mining and exploration division and marketed petroleum products, tires, batteries and accessories.

In that same year, however, economic conditions in the Yukon Territory had become such that there were not enough freight and ore concentrate shipments to keep the railway in operation. Since then, a road has been built between Whitehorse and Skagway—and freight in that area now moves by truck.

Nevertheless, the possibility of resuming passenger operations has been considered and it is hoped that a summer tourist operation connecting the railroad with cruise ships at Skagway might become a reality—renewing a trade that began in the early 1900s.

## VIA Rail Canada

VIA Rail Canada was created by the Canadian government in 1977 as a passenger subsidiary of Canadian National and today it manages all former passenger rail service in Canada except for commuter trains. Canadian National's and Canadian Pacific's passenger equipment was in turn taken over in March and September 1978, respectively.

During this reorganization, combinations and discontinuations of trains occurred. In September 1978 the two major transcontinental trains in Canada, Canadian National's *Super Continental* and Canadian Pacific's *Canadian,* were combined east of Winnipeg. A notable discontinuation occurred when Canadian National's *Montreal-Halifax Scotian* was replaced by an extension of Canadian Pacific's *Montreal-St Johns Atlantic Limited* to Halifax. Although the *Atlantic's* route through northern Maine provided a faster route than the earlier CP one, it was nevertheless discontinued in 1981.

In 1981 and 1982 VIA took delivery of the first group of Canadian-built LRC (Light, Rapid, Comfortable) locomotives and cars. LRC locomotives and cars, equipped with automatic attitude-tilt mechanisms, are designed for operation at speeds up to 125 mph.

*These pages:* A Canadian National diesel passenger train speeds along under gorgeous Canadian skies, in the days before VIA Rail took over all such passenger traffic.
*Overleaf:* The Canadian National's famous *Continental Limited* climbs to the heights in the glory days of the CN's passenger service. British Columbia's Mount Robison provides a magnificent backdrop for this nostalgic scene.

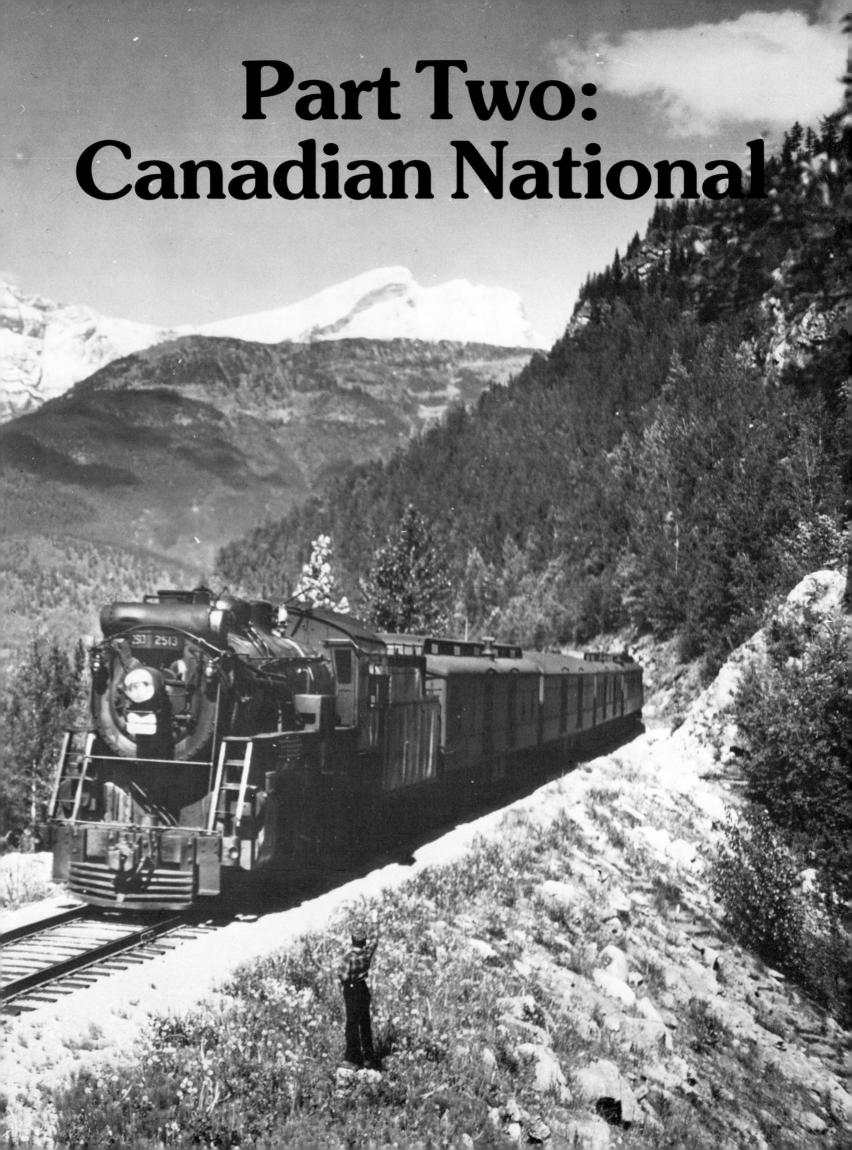

# Part Two:
# Canadian National

# The Early Years

## The First Railway in Canada

In the early 19th century, British North America was very different from today's Canada. There were fewer than two million settlers in a land of almost ten million square kilometres of dense forests, vast swamps, and spectacular mountain ranges. The established colonies were Nova Scotia, Prince Edward Island, New Brunswick, Newfoundland, Lower Canada, and Upper Canada. Between the latter and the great mountain ranges far to the west lay Prince Rupert's Land, owned by the Hudson's Bay Company. This fur-trading company also controlled the coastal strip beyond the mountains, but there were few settlers there.

Life was challenging. Long winters brought bitter cold and blizzards. Narrow dirt roads linking settlements often had stumps sticking up right in the middle of them, and countless potholes. Rain and spring thaws turned them into impassable quagmires, so that travellers—whether on foot, horseback, in wagons or stagecoaches—sometimes had to wait several days for a road to dry before they could go on.

Rivers and lakes served as main thoroughfares, the highways of the nation. Halifax, Quebec City, and Saint John, New Brunswick were the most important ports, bustling with people and activity. Ships from Europe and the United States could sail 800 kilometres up the St Lawrence River to Montreal. They carried linens, chinaware, fashionable clothes, machinery, and many other goods needed by settlers scattered across a young country. But Montreal was as far as ships could go, because of the Lachine Rapids.

Above the rapids, boats carried passengers and freight between cities and towns on the Great Lakes. There also was a chain of rivers and lakes leading westward from Montreal which made it possible for men using canoes—long, wide ones, each big enough to hold 10 or 12 persons with cargo and supplies—to reach the Prairies and beyond.

Yet travel by water also posed problems. For five or six months a year, ice prevented travel and business slowed down while people waited for the spring break-up. In summer, rapids and waterfalls caused many difficulties and delays, so in some places canals were built to bypass them. They helped but, because there were many locks and they were small, travel was slow. Still, where there were no canals, people had to unload their goods from ships or canoes, and either carry both their goods and their boats or use wagons or carts along primitive roads.

Businessmen in Upper and Lower Canada and the Maritimes knew that for their trade to prosper and the country to develop, faster and better ways of moving people and goods would have to be found. They were very excited, therefore, when in the mid-1820s railways using steam-powered locomotives appeared, first in England and later in the United States.

By 1832, a group of Montreal businessmen called 'The Company of Proprietors' began planning Canada's first railway. The Champlain and St Lawrence Railroad opened for business on 21 July 1836 with a celebration attended by hundreds of people. Among those who took the first train ride in Canada were the Governor General of Lower Canada Lord Gosford, and French Canadian 'patriote' Louis-Joseph Papineau.

*Below left:* This artist's rendition of Canada's first locomotive, the *Dorchester*, depicts the locomotive's maiden run on 21 July 1836. Note the similarity between this loco and its prototype, the Stephenson *Rocket* (above). Early locos were skitterish, but proved a point.

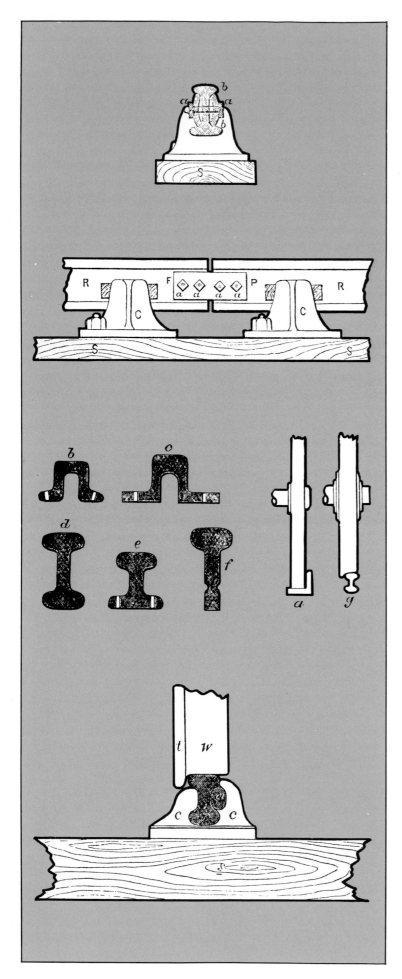

Early railroad inventors went wild with rail designs, and early Canadian railroads used nearly all such designs—some of which are depicted *above*. The brouhaha ended when the American Robert Stevens invented his 'inverted T' rail. *Opposite:* An early express engine. which bears design similarities to the *Dorchester*. but on a larger scale.

The line was 14 miles long, and ran between La Prairie on the St Lawrence River near Montreal and Saint-Jean (then St Johns) on the Richelieu. It was built to replace a road which served as the northernmost link in the traffic route between Montreal and New York City, and which had itself been built to circumvent rapids in the Richelieu which prevented boats from sailing between the St Lawrence and Lake Champlain.

The Champlain and St Lawrence Railroad was a big success. Its little locomotive regularly ran its trackage in less than an hour, reaching the amazing speed of 30 mph. Even in good weather, it took a stagecoach three hours to cover the same distance by road.

Because everyone wanted to use 'the iron horse,' a steady flow of passengers and freight soon made the line profitable.

Early railways were quite different from those of today. Their tracks were of wood, with long strips of iron spiked along the tops. Because heat and cold made the iron expand and contract, the strips often came loose and curled up at the ends. When a train passed over such 'snake rails,' as they were called, the ends tore the undersides of the coaches, and made holes in water tanks behind locomotives.

The first locomotive used in Canada, the *Dorchester,* was imported from England. It was 13 feet long and, like almost all early locomotives, burned wood to make the steam which powered it. (Today's locomotives are about 90 feet long and use diesel fuel to generate the electricity which runs them.) The *Dorchester* also had a very tall smokestack, to prevent large sparks from flying into the air and setting fire to trees and grass beside the tracks.

Railway journeys could be like carnival rides. For example, at the opening of the Montreal and Lachine, another early railway, the Scottish engineer was so proud of his Scottish-built locomotive that he pulled the coaches filled with very important passengers at 60mph. Not only were they terrified, but the bumping and jolting squashed many expensive top hats and hoop skirts, and sparks shooting from the smokestack burned large holes in ladies' dresses. The engineer very nearly lost his job on the first day!

Railways changed the lives of many Canadian settlers. Before there were trains, earning money wasn't easy for people in rural areas. But railways paid local men to lay tracks and once a line was opened farmers could use trains to ship their produce for sale far from home. Eggs, butter, milk, fruit, chickens, rabbits—all were sent off to city markets, and dollars came back. What's more, farmers were paid to provide wood for locomotives, and while a train was stopped, local craftsmen had a chance to sell their wares to passengers.

Thus a new rail line always meant prosperity and growth. In fact, more than one small town actually moved to a new location to be closer to where the trains ran. The arrival of the train was the highlight of a day. A crowd would wait at the station to stare at wealthy travellers and chat with passengers who got off to take a stroll.

Railways also built telegraph lines to send messages from one station to another, warning their workers of problems along the line or informing them of train movements. Naturally, the telegraph began to provide services to communities as well. In emergencies, its operator could wire for help, and important news arrived much faster by wire than by mail. Trains also provided the means for people in small places to feel closer to the rest of the world, as they brought newpapers and letters in a few days rather than in weeks or months as stagecoaches had done.

## Government Help for Railways

In 1841 the British Parliament, on a recommendation by Lord Durham, joined Lower and Upper Canada into one Province of Canada. The need to tie the new province together with rails was making itself felt. But making money in the railway business in Canada was not easy to do. By 1850, although about 40 companies had been granted permission by the government to build rail lines, only six, including the Champlain and St Lawrence, had actually laid track. Of the six railways that did lay track, three were short lines bypassing obstructions in water routes: the Champlain and St Lawrence; the Montreal and Lachine Railroad, 8 miles long, skirting the Lachine Rapids in the St Lawrence River; and the Erie and Ontario Railway, 11 miles long, built to bypass the Niagra Falls. There were 80 miles in all.

The problem was a lack of investment capital. Before any money could be earned, much had to be spent on surveying routes, clearing and levelling land, determining how best to cross streams and swamps, laying rail, and then importing locomotives and passenger and freight cars from England or the United States.

Businessmen in the young colonies simply were not wealthy enough to provide the necessary funds. Investors elsewhere were reluctant to put money into a railway in British North America because they thought the population was too small to make it pay.

By the end of the 1840s British North America was realizing both the need for railway expansion and the difficulty of financing it. British and American contractors discovered the virgin field awaiting them. The example set in the United States was powerful. Massachusetts had guaranteed bonds of local roads to the extent of $8 million, and though New York's experience had been more

varied, the successes were stressed and the failures were plausibly explained away.

It was clear that, if Canada was ever to have a reliable rail network, the government would have to help companies find money to pay for building it. Francis Hincks, merchant, journalist, and politician, moderate reformer, and Canada's first notable finance minister, took the initiative. As inspector-general in the second Baldwin-La-Fontaine cabinet, he brought down the first installment of his railway policy in 1849. He had drawn up two memoranda—one suggesting that the crown lands in the province might be offered as security for the capital to build the road within the province, and the other urging the Imperial government to undertake the road from Halifax to Quebec. Financiers gave no encouragement to the first suggestion, and the British government had not replied to the second by the end of the session of 1848–49. Accordingly, in April 1849 Hincks brought down a new policy, based upon a suggestion of the directors of the St Lawrence & Atlantic. The proposal, called the Guarantee Act of 1849, was to guarantee the interest, not exceeding 6 percent, on half the bonds of any railway over 75 miles long, and whenever half the road had been constructed the province was to be protected by a first charge after the bondholders' lien.

Even with this aid construction did not proceed swiftly. It was still necessary for the companies to complete half the road before qualifying for government assistance. This the St Lawrence road effected slowly, in face of quarrels with contractors, repudiation of calls by shareholders, and hesitancy of banks to make advances. The Great Western did not get underway until 1851, when American finan-

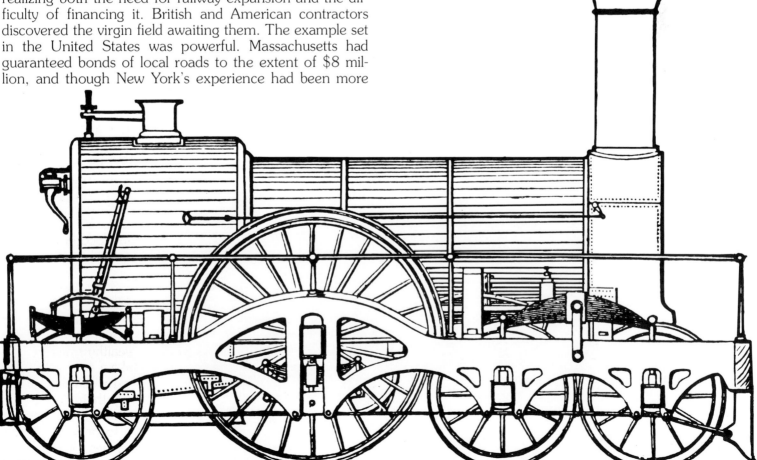

BAGGAGE ROOM

CANADIAN EXPRESS CO.

G.T.R. STATION, STRATH...

*These pages:* The Grand Trunk Railway's St Williams, Ontario station is shown here on a fine 19th century day. In evidence are baggage facilities (left end of building), express and telegraph service signs, train schedule (the chalkboard above the seated man in the bowler hat) and gentlemen and ladies in all their travelling finery.

ciers connected with the New York Central took shares and a place on the directorate. In the same year the Toronto, Simcoe & Huron, later known as the Northern, began construction.

Not surprisingly, many new lines were now begun. In fact during the next 65 years some 34,915 miles of track were laid between the Atlantic and the Pacific Oceans, uniting a new nation. Especially between 1850 and 1860, many small lines were built to link groups of neighbouring towns, and longer, more expensive networks were developed to connect major centers.

The 8 or 10 years which followed 1849 are notable not only for a sudden outburst of railway construction and speculative activity throughout the provinces, but for the beginning of that close connection between politics and railways which is distinctively Canadian. In this era parliament became the field of railway debate. Local politicians discovered the cash value of votes and influence. Statesmen began to talk of links of Empire and began to press the claims of their constituencies for needed railway communications. Cabinets realized the value of the charters they could grant or the credit they could pledge, and contractors swarmed to the task.

## In the Maritimes

Meanwhile, suggestions from the Maritime Provinces had brought still more ambitious schemes within practical range. These led Hincks to take the second step in his policy of aid to railways.

In the Maritime colonies, starting railways was more difficult. From 1835 to 1850, many railways had been projected, but, with the exception of a small coal tramway in Nova Scotia, built in 1839 from the Albion coal mines to tidewater, not a mile was built before 1847. As early as 1827 there were plans to build a line from St Andrews on the Bay of Fundy to Quebec City. In 1835 a railway association was formed in St Andrews, an exploratory survey was made and the interest of lower Canada was enlisted. In the following year New Brunswick gave a charter to the St Andrews & Quebec Railroad, and the Imperial government agreed to bear the cost of a survey, but it was speedily halted because of protests from Maine. There was no clear border between the future New Brunswick and the United States, and the American Government protested that the line would run through what they claimed was part of the United States, so to avoid bad feelings the British Government abandoned the railway project. In 1842 the Ashburton Treaty assigned to the United States a great part of the territory through which the line was projected, and the promoters gave up.

In 1845 the railway mania in England brought a revival of all colonial schemes. Sir Richard Broun took up the plan for a line from Halifax to Quebec. This discussion revived the flagging hopes of St Andrews, and a beginning was made by a railway from St Andrews to Woodstock, the New Brunswick & Canada, for which ground was broken in November 1847. In 1853, a company was formed to build another long line, this time between Portland in Maine, and Halifax. However, after only a few miles of track had been laid the company ran out of money.

The provincial legislature concluded early that it would be impossible to induce private interests to build an intercolonial road unaided. They were unanimous also, not yet having emerged from colonial dependence, in wanting to throw the greater burden of such aid on the British government. In the absence of a colonial federation the United Kingdom was the main connecting link between the colonies in British North America and was presumably most interested in matters affecting more than a single colony. The British government, however, had by this time decided that the old policy of treating the colonies as an estate or plantation of the mother country, protecting or developing them in return for the monopoly of their trade, did not pay. It had reluctantly conceded them political home rule; it was soon to thrust upon them freedom of trade; and it was not inclined to retain burdens when it had given up privileges. Mr Gladstone, secretary for the Colonies, agreed, however, in 1846, to have a survey made at the expense of the three colonies concerned.

This survey, the starting point for the controversies and the proposals of a generation, was completed in 1848, under Major Robinson and Lieutenant Henderson of the Royal Engineers. 'Major Robinson's Line,' as it came to be known, ran roughly in the direction eventually followed by the Intercolonial—from Halifax to Truro, and thence north to Miramichi and the Chaleur Bay, and up the Metapedia Valley to the St Lawrence.

After the plan of a northern route to Quebec was abandoned, interest shifted to the Portland connections. The building of the road from Montreal to Portland added further strength to the claims of this route. The name of the proposed road, the European & North American, expressed the hope that the road from Portland to Halifax would become the channel of communication between the United States and Europe, at least for passengers, mail and express traffic.

In July 1850 a great convention assembled in Portland, attended by delegates from New Brunswick and Nova Scotia as well as from Maine and other New England states. The delegates from the Maritime Provinces returned home full of enthusiasm, but increasingly uncertain about the securing of the necessary capital. At this stage Joseph Howe came to the front. He proposed to seek from the Imperial government a guarantee of the necessary loan, in order that the province might borrow on lower terms. The Colonial Office, while expressing its approval of the Portland scheme, declined to give a guarantee more than a cash contribution. Not daunted, Howe sailed for England in November 1850 and in spite of Cabinet changes in London secured the pledge he desired.

Howe returned triumphant. The British government would guarantee a loan of $35 million which would build the roads to Portland and to Quebec and perhaps still farther west. This railway's importance lay in the fact that it provided a short route between the Province's largest port on the Atlantic and towns on the Bay of Fundy.

Then suddenly the bubble burst. The Colonial Office, late in 1851, declared that Howe had been mistaken in declaring that the guarantee was to extend to the European & North American project. The British government had no objection to this road being built, but would not aid it. The officials of the Colonial Office declared that they never meant to promise anything else. The whole plan thus fell to the ground. The consent of the three provinces was essential, and the New Brunswick would not support the Halifax & Quebec project if the Portland road,

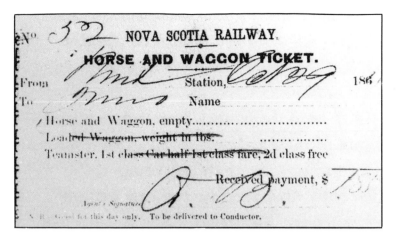

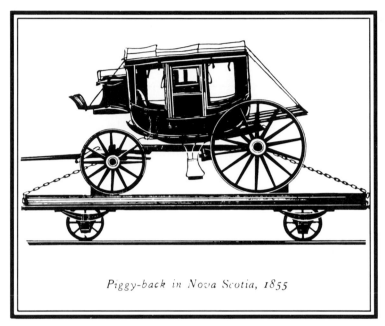

*Piggy-back in Nova Scotia, 1855*

Piggybacking is nothing new—the ticket *at top, above,* and the illustration *above* clearly show that carrying wagons and their attendant horses was normal for 19th century Canadian railways. Today's piggybacks haul truck trailers and other intermodal containers.

running through the most populous and influential sections of the province, was to be postponed indefinitely. Finance Minister Hincks was determined to save the situation. Accompanied by John Young and EP Taché, he visited Fredericton and Halifax early in 1852, and hammered out a compromise. New Brunswick agreed to join in the Halifax to Quebec project on condition that the road should run from Halifax to St John and thence up the valley of the St John River; Nova Scotia agreed to this change, which made St John rather than Halifax the main ocean terminus, on condition that New Brunswick should bear five-twelfths as against its own three-twelfths of the cost. It remained to secure the consent of the Imperial government and Hincks, Chandler and Howe arranged to sail for England early in March. Upon a peremptory request from Hincks for a definite answer within a fortnight, the British Cabinet, in spite of the previous promise to consider the route an open question, declined to aid any but a road following Major Robinson's line. The negotiations broke off, joint action between the provinces failed, and each province switched to its own separate track.

It was on 13 June 1854 that the first sod was turned for the construction of the Nova Scotia Railway—a beginning made at last. The road was to run from Halifax to Truro, with a branch to Windsor. Progress was slow, but

by 1858 the 93 miles planned had been completed.

The line's track was somewhat unusual in that the iron rails were shaped the same top and bottom; when the top became worn, they were turned upside down.

They also carried an unusual kind of traffic. Before the railway, farmers living near Windsor and Truro had taken produce to Halifax by horse and wagon. To attract them, the Nova Scotia Railway offered to load horse, wagon and driver onto a flat car. In the capital's station, they were unloaded and the wagon went off to market. (Today, railways carry highway trailers on flat cars in a similar type of service called 'piggyback'.)

A halt in progress came when reality succeeded the glowing visions of the prospectus, the service proved poor, and the returns low. Nine years later an extension from Truro to Pictou was constructed.

New Brunswick had a more variable experience. After the collapse of the Halifax & Quebec project, her efforts were confined to the road running north from St Andrews and to the European & North American.

## Rail Travel in the Mid-1800s

The first 'age of iron—and of brass' came to an end before 1860. Between 1850 and 1860, the mileage of all the provinces grew from 66 to 2065. By 1867 it had increased only 213 miles. In two of the intervening years not a mile was built. A halt had come, for stock taking and heart searching.

A person—or package—could travel by train all the way from Riviére du Loup in Quebec to Sarnia in Ontario. People who did so found the journey long and tiring. Most rails were only 18 feet long and there was quite a gap between the end of one and the beginning of the next (to prevent the 'snake rails' mentioned previously). As wheels crossed the gaps, cars jolted and passengers bounced. Cushioned seats made first-class travel a little more comfortable, but everyone in second class sat on plain wooden benches. Trains stopped at mealtimes because there were no dining cars. They also stopped for the night, because there were no sleeping accommodations on board, and passengers had to find rooms in hotels.

The first sleeping car in the world was designed and built in Hamilton, Ontario, by the Great Western Railway. It looked like a box car fitted with long benches, and each passenger was given a rug and a pillow. They certainly weren't comfortable, but at least trains could keep rolling through the night, so the journey took less time.

Locomotives used wood for fuel then and, because it burned quickly, trains had to stop every 50 miles to pick up another load, supplies by farmers. When a train was running late, passengers were asked to help bring the wood aboard.

If the trip was difficult for passengers, it was extremely so for train and locomotive crews. The fireman had to keep throwing heavy logs into the fire box and, whenever he had a chance, climb outside onto the engine to grease bearings. It was also his job to load the wood at each stop, and clean ashes out of the fire box.

There were compensations, though. The crews were very popular in the towns they passed through, because they brought news and gossip from other points along a line. Engineers especially were admired. They were idols for children who were learning in school how big the world around them really was, and dreaming of seeing it.

# The Building Blocks

## The Grand Trunk

The most important railway company established between 1850 and 1860 was the Grand Trunk Railway Company of Canada. Its name stemmed from its purpose: to operate a long, important main line which other, smaller lines would join.

By 1851 the St Lawrence, the Great Western and the Northern were under way, and more ambitious schemes proposed. The Guarantee Act of 1849 was proving inadequate, and the government was considering an extension.

In 1849 Hincks had argued against government ownership; now he argued for it. The new act, passed in April 1852, marked the second or Grand Trunk phase of his gradually shaping policy. The next move was to arrange terms with the other provinces and secure the promised Imperial guarantee.

It is clear, however, that the British government was unwilling to consider anything but the unacceptable Major Robinson line. Hincks was justified in looking elsewhere for capital, but he was not justified in binding himself to one firm of contractors, however eminent, which is what he had done.

Hincks returned to Canada in the summer of 1852 with a tentative contract in his pocket. To Canada, too, came Henry Jackson, a partner in the Brassey Company, the railway-building firm with whom Hincks had associated himself. The supposition of the government was that the English contractors would simply subscribe for the bulk of the stock in these companies, but the Canadian promoters were not willing to give up their rights so easily, and they subscribed for the full $3 million which was authorized. Hincks met this move by bringing down a bill

*At right and above right:* These Grand Trunk 4–4–0 coalburners were typical of North American motive power in the 1880s. Such engines were often used for both passenger and freight hauling, though their large driving wheels were conducive to building up speed, while engines with comparatively smaller wheels developed better traction.

*At left:* This 1870s-era smoke belcher is surrounded by its very proud-looking crew. These fellows were privileged to operate the most advanced means of propulsion available on the planet in their time. The Grand Trunk had tough going in its infancy, but struggled on to do its mother country—Canada—good service. *Above* is an early company logo.

to incorporate a new company, the Grand Trunk Railway Company of Canada, and the rights of the rival claimants came before parliament for decision.

Hincks became alarmed at Montreal interest arrayed against him, and proposed as a compromise that the Grand Trunk should absorb the St Lawrence road and build the bridge at Montreal on the condition that the opposition to its westward plans should be abandoned. Upon this all parties agreed, and the English and Canadian promoters joined forces.

Negotiations were completed in England early in 1853. As yet the Grand Trunk Company was but a name. The real parties to the bargain were many. First came John Ross, a member of the Canadian cabinet, but representing the future Grand Trunk, of which he was elected president. The Barings and Glyns, eminent banking houses, had a twofold part to play, as they were closely connected to the contractors and were also the London agents of the Canadian government. The contractors themselves, Peto, Brassey, Betts and Jackson, had spent a year studying the Canadian situation and put in anxious weeks hammering out the details of the agreement and the prospectus to follow it.

A glowing prospectus was drawn up. The amalgamated road would be the most comprehensive railway system in the world, comprising 1112 miles, stretching from Portland and eventually from Halifax (by both the northern and the southern route) to Lake Huron. The whole future traffic between west and east must therefore pass over the Grand Trunk, as both geographical conditions and legislative enactment prevented it from injurious competition. It was backed by government guarantee and Canadian investment, and its execution was in the hands of the most eminent contractors. The total capital was fixed at $47.5 million.

A M Ross was appointed chief engineer, and S P Bidder general manager, both on the nomination of the English bankers and contractors. Plant was assembled in Canada, orders for rails and equipment were placed in England, and workers came out by the thousand. At one time 14,000 men were directly employed on the railways in upper Canada alone. In July 1853 the last gaps in the

*These pages:* A freight train stops for water at Coopersville in 1890. Such stops cost time, and were one of the factors that would eventually do in steam locos, as diesels—whose development would follow the scene shown here by some 40–50 years—needed no such stops.

# Great International Route.

## GRAND TRUNK
### Broad Gauge Railway.

---

## 1377 MILES UNDER ONE MANAGEMENT!

---

### THE GREAT DIRECT CANADIAN
## MAIL AND EXPRESS ROUTE
### BETWEEN THE
## Eastern and Western States.

---

### THE CHEAPEST AND BEST ROUTE TO ALL POINTS EAST AND WEST,

Close Connections. made with all Connecting Lines, and Through Tickets issued to all important points.

☞ For San Francisco, Sacramento, Salt Lake City, Omaha, and intermediate places on the Pacific Railway, the Grand Trunk is the most direct route.

---

**Splendid Palace Sleeping Cars are now run between Chicago and Sarnia without change.**

---

*From Passengers holding Through Tickets, American Money is received, at par, for Sleeping Berths and Refreshments.*

BE SURE AND ASK FOR TICKETS VIA THE GRAND TRUNK RAILWAY.

C. J. BRYDGES, MANAGING DIRECTOR.

*Thomas Edison's printing press could have produced the ad* above *and the ticket* below *(see caption. facing page) but the young inventor was busy publishing the first newspaper on wheels (see text at right).*

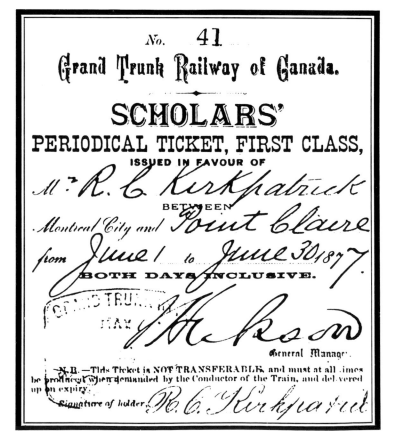

No. 41
Grand Trunk Railway of Canada.

SCHOLARS'
PERIODICAL TICKET, FIRST CLASS,
ISSUED IN FAVOUR OF
Mr R. C. Kirkpatrick
BETWEEN
Montreal City and Point Claire
from June 1 to June 30, 1877.
BOTH DAYS INCLUSIVE.

General Manager.

N.B.—This Ticket is NOT TRANSFERABLE, and must at all times be produced when demanded by the Conductor of the Train, and delivered up on expiry.

Signature of holder R. C. Kirkpatrick

St Lawrence & Atlantic had been filled up, though not permanently. In 1854 the Quebec and Richmond section was opened; in 1855, the road from Montreal to Brockville and from Lévis to St Thomas, Quebec; in 1856, the Brockville to Toronto and Toronto to Stratford sections.

Thousands of people from Toronto, Quebec, Boston and Portland poured into Montreal for the giant party celebrating the completion of the line from Montreal to Toronto in 1856. The city held a parade one morning and gave a banquet for more than 4000 guests. They sat at over 1000 yards of tablecloths and used 88,000 knives, forks, and spoons. The following evening there was a ball but, according to newspaper reports, the hall was so crowded that no one had room to dance until one o'clock in the morning, after some of the people had gone home.

Not until 1858 was the western road completed as far as London. The year 1859 saw the completion of the Victoria Bridge across the St Lawrence at Montreal. Over a mile long, it had only one track when it was opened in 1859, but a second was added during major reconstruction 40 years later. The extension from St Mary's to Sarnia, and a new road on Michigan, running from Port Huron to Detroit were also completed in 1859. Coincidentally, also in 1859, Thomas Alva Edison, inventor of the incandescent light bulb and originator of a host of technological innovations in the fields of telegraphy, sound recording and electricity, began his career on the Chicago, Detroit & and Canada Grand Trunk Junction Railroad as a newsboy and 'candy butcher' or candy seller.

Hired at the age of twelve, Edison worked from morning to midnight on the Port Huron to Detroit run, using spare time during layovers to experiment in baggage car chemistry laboratory. He removed the lab in 1862 after a phosphorous fire set the car ablaze but substituted a printing press for his chemicals. He wrote and printed the first paper ever published on a moving train—The Weekly Herald—and charged three cents a copy.

Success was mixed with tragedy and heroism. An accident while boarding a moving freight on the Port Huron left the young inventor partly deaf. In 1862, Edison's quick action saved the life of Jimmie Mackenzie, the 3-year-old son of the Grand Trunk stationmaster in Mt. Clemens, Michigan. Edison snatched the boy from the path of an oncoming train, and the grateful father, J U Mackenzie, an experienced telegrapher, rewarded him by teaching him to be a telegrapher. This was a turning point in the life of a young Edison. The telegraph key on which he learned his craft is now in Greenfield Village, Dearborn, Michigan. (J U Mackenzie later joined Edison at his New Jersey Menlo Park laboratory and aided in a number of inventions.)

Edison was a telegrapher at the railroad's Stratford Junction, Ontario Station, staying there until 1864, when he resigned. His telegraphy experience created an interest in elementary circuitry that led to his first inventions. Grand Trunk was an impetus toward a great career.

In his biography, Thomas Edison tells of handling the controls of a steam locomotive when he was 15 years old. His unauthorized stint as an engineer was made on The Arab in 1862. On several occasions, the regular crew let Edison handle the controls between Port Huron and Mount Clemens, Mich. so they could sleep. The so-called 'Edison line of the Grand Trunk' was the Chicago, Detroit

*Above:* A Grand Trunk woodburner (note the flaring smokestack) stops at Durand passenger station in the 1880s. *Above opposite:* An early ad touting the GT's Canadian rail connections. *Below opposite:* A student fare ticket, good for one month's travel between two points, of 1877.

& Canada Grand Trunk Junction between Port Huron and Detroit built by Grand trunk in 1858–59.

The Grand Trunk was complete from Lake Huron to the Atlantic in 1860. In the 10 years that followed, working expenses varied from 58 to 85 percent of the gross receipts, instead of the 40 percent which the prospectus had foreshadowed; not a cent of dividend was paid on ordinary shares.

The prophecy that operating expenses would not exceed 40 percent of earnings, based on English experience, failed partly because earnings were lower, but more because operating expenses were higher than anticipated. The company had more than its share of hard luck from commercial depression, and from loss on American paper money in the Civil war. Differences in gauge, lack of permanent connections at Chicago, lack of return freight, rate wars with the American railroads which had been built west at the same time or later, the inferiority of Montreal to New York as of old in harbor facilities and ocean service, the failure of Portland to become a great commercial center—all meant hope and dividends deferred.

The Grand Trunk did Canada good service, however. In 1850 there were only 66 miles of road in all of the provinces. In 1860 there were 2065. The Great Western and Northern were pushed forward under the provisions of the earlier Guarantee Act; roads of more local interest were fostered by municipal rivalry. Their building brought new activity in every branch of commerce.

## The Great Western

In Ontario, The Great Western railway started building two lines, one from Hamilton to Niagara Falls and the other from Hamilton to London. The company had actually been formed in 1834, but it was not until the government promised to help that the Great Western could afford to begin laying track.

By 1858, the company was operating 360 miles of rail lines, from Toronto to Windsor, Niagara Falls, and Sarnia. These lines were very important to Canada because they opened up the rich farmlands of southwestern Ontario. As well, they provided rail links with the United States.

The Great Western was a very progressive company. For example, it was the first railway in the world to sort mail *en route*. Later on, special 'Railway Post Office' cars were built, and remained in use until 1971. (Since then, most Canadian inter-city mail has been moved by air.) The Great Western also built the first railway suspension

*These pages:* The Great Western's early motive power is evident in this vintage photo of the *William Weir*, half out of a station shed. The GW was financially far more successful than the majority of early railroads; perhaps that's why these gents look so pleased with themselves.

W^M. WEIR

bridge, opened to traffic in 1855. Spanning the Niagara River just below the Falls, it was 820 feet long and considered an engineering marvel of the times.

The Great Western came nearest of any early road to being a financial success; alone of the guaranteed roads it repaid the government loan, nearly in full.

## The Intercolonial

In 1857, Queen Victoria named Ottawa as the Capital Province of Canada, and during the next decade serious talk about political union of all the British North American colonies began.

Leaders of the four Maritime colonies met in Charlottetown in 1864 to discuss uniting them. A few months later, another conference was held in Quebec to discuss a larger federation, of the Maritimes with the Province of Canada. Railways were not only an important topic at both meetings, but New Brunswick and Nova Scotia refused to participate in the larger plan unless they were promised a rail link with what would become Quebec and Ontario.

Railways were also important to the provinces that joined the Confederation after it became a fact on July 1, 1867, with John A MacDonald as prime minister.

Two years later, Canada bought Prince Rupert's Land from the Hudson's Bay Company and marked out what are today's three Prairie Provinces and the Yukon Territory and Northwest Territories. Manitoba entered Confederation in 1870. Beyond the Rocky Mountains, British Columbia joined in 1871 because it was promised a rail link with the rest of the country—otherwise, it would probably have joined the United States. And Prince Edward Island decided to become a part of Canada in 1873 when it ran out of money to finish building its own railway.

The outstanding achievement of the period after confederation, however, was the building of the Intercolonial. It had been projected largely in order to make closer union between the provinces possible, but, as it turned out, it was Confederation that brought the Intercolonial, not the Intercolonial that brought Confederation.

After the breakdown of negotiations in London in 1852, each province had turned to its own tasks. Each in building its own roads provided possible links in the future Intercolonial chain. In Canada the Grand Trunk ran to a point 120 miles east of Quebec; in New Brunswick, St John was connected with both the east and west boundaries of the province; in Nova Scotia, a road ran north from Halifax as far as Truro. A gap of nearly 500 miles between Rivière du Loup and Truro remained. To bridge this wilderness seemed beyond the private or public resources of the divided provinces. Unanimous on one point only, they once more turned to the British government. In 1857 and 1858 dispatches and deputations sought aid, but sought it in vain. When the Civil War broke out in the United States, official British sympathy was given to the South. In 1861 the British sent 8000 troops to Canada in response to an incident in which Captain Wilks of the Union forces had seized two confederate officers from aboard a ship named *The Trent*.

*At right:* The Great Western's Great International Railway Suspension Bridge, connecting the United States and Canada—and the New York Central and the Great Western Railways. Opened in 1855, this bridge was the first railroad suspension bridge. Niagra Falls is in the distance.

*Above:* The Fathers of Confederation —who represented the Maritime colonies in effecting a confederation with provincial Canada on 1 July 1867—held rail-road building high on their list of priorities. *At right:* The first locomotive built at Moncton, New Brunswick. Railways provided a vital binding for the nation that would become modern Canada.

The Trent Affair, as it came to be called, showed how near Britain and the North were to war, a war which would at once have exposed isolated Canada to attack. The military argument for closer connection then took on new weight with the British government, and it proposed, to a joint delegation in 1861, to revert to its offer of 10 years earlier—to guarantee a colonial loan for a railway by an approved route. During the progress of the survey negotiations for the union of the provinces had begun, and when Confederation came about in 1867, the building of the Intercolonial at the common expense of the Dominion, with an imperial guarantee to the extent of $15 million, was one of the conditions of the union.

The construction was entrusted in December 1868 to a commission of four, and six years later the minister of public works took over direct control. At last, on July 1876, nine years after Confederation, the 500 miles between Truro and Rivière du Loup were opened for traffic throughout. As branch lines were completed small companies sold their trackage and equipment to larger ones, and thus the Intercolonial acquired the line between Rivière du Loup and Lévis, across the St Lawrence from Quebec City.

In the meantime the Dominion had taken over the Nova Scotia, New Brunswick, and Prince Edward Island government roads. In 1876 there were in all 950 miles of railway under the control of the Dominion government, as against 4268 miles of private lines.

## The Canadian Pacific

Unlike most Canadian railroads, the Canadian Pacific was never absorbed by the Canadian National Railway. It remains in business to this day and is now the second-largest railroad in Canada. Its story, however, is important to the history of all Canada's rails—indeed, it is important to the history of all Canada. The construction of the Canadian Pacific opened up the western provinces to many of the smaller lines and industries that eventually became part of CN.

After the coming of the locomotive, one needed only imagination and a map to see all British North America clamped by an iron band. Engineers like Bonnycastle and Synge and Carmichael-Smyth wrote of the possibility in the the 1840s. Promoters were not lacking. But two things were needed before the dreams on paper could become facts in steel—national unity and international rivalry. Years before Confederation, such far-seeing Canadians as William M'Dougall and George Brown had pressed for the annexation of the British territories beyond the Lakes. After Confederation, all speed was made to buy out the sovereign rights of the Hudson's Bay Company. Then came the first Riel Rebellion, to bring home the need of a western road, as the Trent Affair had brought home the need of the Intercolonial. The decisive political factor came into play in 1870, when British Columbia entered the federation.

The other factor, international rivalry, exercised its influence about the same time. In the United States the railway had rapidly pushed westward, but had halted before the deserts and mountains lying between Mississippi and the Pacific. The rivalry of pro-slavery and anti-slavery parties in Congress had deadlocked all plans of public aid to either southern or northern route. Then the Civil War broke the deadlock: the need of binding the West to the side of the North created a strong public demand for a Pacific road, and Congress, so stimulated, gave loans and land grants. The Central Pacific, working from Sacramento, and the Union Pacific, starting from Omaha, met near Ogden in Utah in 1869. In 1871 the Southern Pacific and the Texas Pacific were fighting for subsidies, and Jay Cooke was promoting the Northern Pacific. The young Dominion of Canada was Stirred by ambition to emulate its powerful neighbor.

These factors, then, brought the question of a railway to the Pacific on Canadian soil within the range of practical politics. Important questions remained to be settled. During the parliamentary session of 1871 the government of Sir John MacDonald decided that the road should be built by a company, not by the state, that it should be aided by liberal subsidies in cash and in land, and, to meet British Columbia's insistent terms, that it should be begun within two, and completed within ten, years. The opposition protested that this latter provision was uncalled for and would bankrupt the Dominion, but the government carried its point.

The first task was to survey the vast wilderness between the Ottawa Valley and the Pacific, and to find if possible a feasible route. Explorer and engineer Captain Palliser had been appointed by the British government to report upon the country west of the Lakes. He had declared in 1863, after four years of careful labor in the field, that, thanks to the choice of the 49th parallel as Canada's boundary, there was no possibility of ever building a transconinental railway exclusively through British territory. The man chosen for the task of achieving this impossibility was Stanford Fleming. Appointed engineer-in-chief in 1871, he was for nine years in charge of the surveys, though for half that time his duties on the Intercolonial absorbed much of his energy. Fleming possessed an unusual gift of literary style, and his reports upon the work of his staff gave the people of Canada a very clear idea of the difficulties to be encountered.

*Below:* The Canadian Pacific's first locomotive, the 4–4–0 woodburner *Countess of Dufferin*, is shown here on display in the 1950s. The locale of this photo is Winnipeg, Manitoba, but the CP's influence had come to be known from coast to coast. *At right:* The *Countess of Dufferin*, with cars, arrives at Winnipeg on 9 October 1877, via a barge pushed by the sternwheeler *Selkirk*. This loco greatly aided the building of the CP.

Early in the survey a practical route was found throughout. Striking across the wilderness from Lake Nipissing to Lake Superior at the Pic River, the line might skirt the shore of the lake to Fort William, or it might run northerly through what is now known as the clay belt, with Fort William and the lake made accessible by a branch. Continuing westward to the Red River at Selkirk, with Winnipeg on a branch line to the south, the projected line crossed Lake Manitoba at the Narrows, and then struck out northwesterly, through what was then termed the 'Fertile Belt', until the Yellowhead Pass was reached. Here the Rockies could be easily pierced; but once through Fleming was faced by the huge flanking range of the Caribou Mountains, in which repeated explorations failed to find a gap. At the foot of the towering barrier lay a remarkable deep-set valley 400 miles in length, in which northwestward ran the Fraser and southeastward the Canoe and Columbia. By following the Fraser to its great southward bend, and then striking west, a terminus on Bute or Dean Inlet might be reached, while the valley of the Canoe and the Albreda would give access to the North Thompson and lower Fraser to Burrard inlet. The latter route, on the whole, was preferred.

It was estimated that the Canadian road would cost $100 million and it was certain that the engineering difficulties would be staggering. In Canada few roads had paid the shareholders, and though some had profited the contractors, the new enterprise meant such a plunge in the dark that contractors and promoters alike hesitated. In the United States, however, the Pacific roads had proved gold mines for their promoters.

In June 1880, Sir John MacDonald, speaking at Bath, made the announcement that a group of capitalists had offered to build the road, on terms that would ensure that in the end it would not cost Canada a single penny. Four months later a contract was signed in Ottawa by which the Canadian Pacific Syndicate undertook to build and operate the whole road. An entirely new turn had been given to the situation, and the most important chapter in Canada's railway annals, if not in her national life had begun.

In the months and years that followed, no men were so much in the mind and speech of the Canadian public as the members of the new syndicate. The leading members were a remarkable group of men. Probably never in the history of a railway building, not even in the case of the 'Big Four' who built the Central Pacific—Huntington, Stanford, Crocker, and Hopkins—had the call of the railway brought together in a single enterprise men of such outstanding individuality, of such ability and persistence, and destined for success so notable.

They were Norman W Kittson, head of a small transportation company; James J Hill, Donald A Smith and George Stephen, pioneers in the true sense who had come West while young to try their luck, and were at the time employed in various respectable but unnotable occupations; and Richard B Angus, a shrewd financier.

The Canadian Pacific was not their first joint enterprise. It was the direct outcome of a daring venture in connection with a bankrupt Minnesota railway, which had brought them wealth beyond their wildest dreams, and had definitely turned their thoughts to railway work.

These were the men to whom the Canadian government turned when the minister of Railways, Sir Charles

*Opposite:* The first president of the CP, George Stephen, served from 1881–1888. The building of the CP was financially risky, at the least. *Above:* Hudson's Bay chief commissioner Donald A Smith envisioned the railroad's role in building a strong Canadian commerce.

Tupper, urged them to unload upon a private company the burden of completing the road to the Pacific. 'Catch them before they invest their profits,' was the advice of Sir John's most intimate adviser, the shrewd Eastern Townships politician John Henry Pope. Probably they came halfway. They knew the West as well as many men, and with their road built to the Canadian boundary and with a traffic arrangement beyond to Winnipeg, they were already in the field. Of all the group Stephen was most reluctant to undertake the new enterprise, but he was assured by his associates that the burdens of management would be shared by all. The government had also approached Duncan M'Intyre, a Montreal financier who controlled the Canada Central, running from Brockville by way of Ottawa to Pembroke, and under construction from that point to Callender, the eastern end of the Canadian Pacific main line. He was more than willing to link up this railway with the larger project, and the group was formed.

They debated the question with the government early in 1880. It was felt, however, that negotiations could not be concluded in Canada. More capital would be needed than even these new millionaires could furnish, and nowhere was capital so abundant as in London. In July, therefore, Sir John MacDonald, Sir Charles Tupper, and John

Henry Pope sailed for London, accompanied by George Stephen and Duncan M'Intyre. London financiers did not bite as freely as anticipated. Barings and Rothschilds alike were cautious about the enterprise. Sir Henry Tyler, president of the Grand Trunk, was approached and agreed to build if the link north of Lake Superior were omitted in favor of a line through the United States, south of the lake, a condition which Sir John, strongly urged on by Tupper, would not accept.

The group returned to Ottawa on 21 October 1880, the contract was signed by Charles Tupper for the government and by George Stephen, Duncan M'Intyre, James J Hill, John S Kennedy, Morton, Rose & Company of London, and Cohen, Reinach & Company of Paris. Donald A Smith's name was not there. It was only two years since he and Sir John, on the floor of the House of Commons, had called each other 'liar' and 'coward' and it was to be a few years more before the two Highlanders could cover their private feud with a coating of elaborate cordiality. So, to preserve appearances, Smith's interest was kept a secret—but a very open one.

When Parliament met in December 1880 the contact was laid before it. For constructing some 1900 miles the syndicate would be given free the 710 miles already under construction by the government, $25 million in cash, and 25 million acres of selected land in the Fertile Belt. They were promised exemptions from import duties on construction materials, from taxes on land for 20 years after the patents were issued and on stock and other property forever, and exemption from regulation of rates until 10 per cent per annum was earned on the capital. Assurance was given that for 20 years no competitive roads connecting with the western states would be chartered. Ten years were given to complete the task, and a million dollars were deposited as a security. The contract was ratified by Parliament and received the formal royal assent in February 1881.

George Stephen was chosen president, and held the post until 1888. To him more than to any other man the ultimate success of the Canadian Pacific was due. Indomitable persistence, unquenchable faith and unyielding honor stamped his character. He was one of the greatest of empire builders. He never despaired in the tightest corner and never rested while a single expedient remained untried. Duncan M'Intyre became one of the two vice presidents and took an active part in the company's affairs until he dropped out in 1884. Richard B Angus came back from St Paul to become vice president and a member of the executive committee. His long banking experience and his shrewd, straightforward judgement proved a tower of strength in days of trial.

Donald A Smith, while after 1883 a director and a member of the executive committee, took little part in the railway's affairs, though at Stephen's urging he more than once joined in lending security when help was most needed. James J Hill left the directorate and unloaded his stock at the close of 1882. With him retired John S Kennedy. The Baron de Reinach also withdrew at an early stage. The English directors, representing Morton, Rose & Company of London, retired as soon as the road was

*At left:* The Canadian Pacific's original engineering marvel, Mountain Creek Bridge, on the eastern slope of the Selkirks. This structure was 164 feet high, 1086 feet long, and contained more than two million board feet of lumber in its intricate underpinnings.

completed, being replaced by representatives of Morton, Bliss & company of New York. E B Osler came in with the Ontario & Quebec in 1884. The board became more and more distinctively Canadian.

One of the first steps taken by the directors was to open offices in Winnipeg, and put two men with United States experience in charge—A B Stickley, later president of Chicago Great Western, as general superintendent, and General Rosser as chief engineer. The rate of progress was not satisfactory, and early in 1882 a fortunate change was made. William C Van Horne, at that time general superintendent of the Chicago, Milwaukee & St Paul and still under age forty, was appointed general manager with wide powers. Some years earlier, when he was president of the Southern Minnesota, the leading members of the St Paul syndicate had had an opportunity of learning his skill. He had been railroading since he was fourteen, beginning as a telegraph operator on the Illinois Central, and had risen rapidly in the service of one Midwest road after another. His tireless driving force was precisely the asset the company now most needed.

Stephen and Smith and M'Intyre pledged their St Paul or other stock for loans in New York and Montreal, but still the financial gap was unfilled. They turned to the government, requesting a loan of $22.5 million, to be secured by a first charge on the main line. In return, they agreed to complete the road by May 1886, five years earlier than the contract required. The request was at first scouted by Sir John MacDonald. Parliament would not consent, and if Parliament consented the country would

revolt. Bankruptcy stared the company in the face when John Henry Pope came to the rescue. He soon convinced Sir John that if the Canadian Pacific was smashed, the Conservative party would smash the day after, and the aid was promised. The cabinet was won over, and Sir Charles Tupper, hastily summoned by cable from London, stormed it through caucus, and the loan was made.

The men behind the Canadian Pacific proved themselves possessed of courage and honorable determination. At more than one critical stage they staked their all to keep the work going even though the bulk of the resources used in the original building of the road were provided or advanced by the people of Canada. The Canadian Pacific is a monument of public as well as of private faith.

Meanwhile the work of construction had been going ahead. Under William Van Horne's masterful methods the leisurely pace of government construction quickened to the most rapid achievement on record. A time schedule, carefully made out in advance, was adhered to with remarkably little variation.

Work was begun at the east end of the line, from the point of junction with the Canada Central, but at first energy was devoted chiefly to the portion crossing the plains. Important changes in route were made. The main line had already been deflected to pass through Winnipeg. Now a much more southerly line across the plains was adopted, making for Calgary rather than Edmonton. The new route was shorter by 100 miles, and more likely to prevent the construction of a rival road south of it later. For many years it had been assumed that the tillable lands of the West lay in a 'Fertile Belt' or rainbow, following roughly the Saskatchewan Valley and curving round a big wedge of the American desert projecting north. Certainly the short, withered, russet-colored grasslands of the border country looked forbidding beside the green herbage of North Saskatchewan. But new investigations reported in 1879 showed that only a very small section was hopelessly arid. With this objection removed, the only drawback to the southern route was the difficulty of finding as good a route through the mountains as the northerly Yellowhead Pass route, but on this the company decided to take its chances.

Engineering difficulties on the plains were not serious, but the pace of construction which was demanded, and the fact that every stick of timber and every pound of food, as well as every rail and spike, had to be brought a great distance, required remarkable organization. Three hundred subcontractors were employed on the portion of the line crossing the plains. Bridge gangs and track layers followed close on the graders' heels. In 1882 over two-and-a-half miles of track a day were laid. In the following year, for weeks in succession, the average ran three-and-a-half miles a day, and in a record smashing three days 20 miles were covered. By the end of the year the track was within four miles of the summit of the Rockies.

The change of route across the plains had made it essential to pierce the Rockies by a more southerly pass than the Yellowhead. The Kicking Horse or Hector Pass, short but steep, was finally chosen.

It was not until 1884 that the wilderness north of Lake Superior was attacked in strong force. Nine thousand men were employed here alone. Rock and muskeg, hill and hollow, made this section more difficult to face than even the Fraser Canyon. In one muskeg area seven layers of Canadian Pacific rails are buried, one below the other. The stretch along the shore of the lake was particularly difficult. The Laurentian rocks were the oldest known to geologists and, more pertinent, the toughest known to engineers. A dynamite factory was built on the spot and a road blasted through. One mile cost $700,000 to build and several cost half a million. The time required and the total expenditure would have been prohibitive had not the management decided to make extensive use of trestle work. It would have cost over two dollars a cubic yard to cut through the hills and fill up the hollows by team haul; it cost only one tenth of that to build timber trestles, carrying the line high, and to fill up later by train haul.

In 1885, thousands of Chinese laborers working on the difficult Kamloops-Port Moody section finished their task, and the government work was done. The only gap remaining lay in the Gold Range. There, in the Eagle Pass at Craigellachie, on 7 November 1885, the eastward and westward track layers met. It was only a year or so before that the Northern Pacific had celebrated the driving of the last golden spike by an excursion which cost the company a third of a million dollars and heralded the bankruptcy of the road. There was no banquet and no golden spike for the last rail in the Canadian Pacific. William Van Horne had announced that 'the last spike would be just as good an iron spike as any on the road,' and had it not been that Donald A Smith happened along in time to drive the spike home, it would have been hammered in by the

worker on the job. Six months later the first passenger train went through from Montreal to Vancouver. The longest railway in the world was opened from coast to coast, five years before the time required by the original contract.

To realize how great a work had been accomplished requires today some effort of the imagination. The Canada the present generation knows is a united Canada, an optimistic, self-confident Canada, with rapidly rounding-out industries which give scope for the most ambitious of her sons as well as for tens of thousands from overseas. It is a Canada whose provinces and whose railroads stretch from ocean to ocean. But the Canada of 1870 was much different. On the map it covered half a continent, but in reality it stopped at the Great Lakes. There was little national spirit, little diversity of commercial enterprise.

The Canadian Pacific Railway changed the face of Western Canada. Towns had sprung up all along its route. Winnipeg and Vancouver became cities; farms were spread across the prairies; mining and lumber companies were formed in British Columbia.

Certainly not least among the makers of Canada were the men who undertook that doubtful enterprise and carried it through every obstacle to success.

## The Expansion of the Grand Trunk: The Grand Trunk Pacific

In the East, however, many small lines were finding it hard to stay in business. There were nearly 200 of them, most with only a few miles of track, and the population of the young country could not support them all. The Grand trunk bought up many of the lines and by 1900 owned more than 3000 miles of track, mostly in Quebec and Ontario. Among the lines it took over was the Great Western.

The year 1883 saw the high-water mark of prosperity for Grand Trunk. In that year dividends were paid not only on guaranteed but on first, second, and third preference stock.

In 1895 Sir Henry Tyler resigned from the presidency after 23 years of service. His place was taken by Sir Charles Rivers-Wilson, who had a record of efficient service on the borders of politics and finance. The new president and a committee of directors made a thorough investigation of the Grand Trunk and recommended some immediate improvements. Their chief contribution to its success, however, was the discovery of Charles M Hays.

The great rival of the Grand Trunk had pressed forward to prosperity under the driving power of an American general manager. The new administration decided that it, too, would look to the United States for a chief executive of the ruthless efficiency and modern methods which the crisis demanded. They found him in the man who had pulled the Wabash out of a similar predicament. Hays was not quite forty when in 1895 he was appointed general manager. His presence was soon felt.

Equipment was overhauled, larger freight cars were ordered and new terminals acquired. The main bridges on the road—the suspension at Niagara Falls, the International at Fort Erie, and the Victoria at Montreal—were all

*At right:* The party surveying the route for the Grand Trunk Pacific sets out from their camp near Mount Robson, British Columbia in the early 1900s. At the western terminus of the rails through this rugged scenery, the seaport city of Prince Rupert, British Columbia, was born.

rebuilt on a larger scale between 1896 and 1901. The double tracking of the main line from Montreal westward was continued, and many of the sharp curves and heavy grades of the original construction were revised.

The rush to the Klondike in 1897 started a rate war between the Canadian Pacific and the Grand Trunk, with its American connections, which lasted nearly a year. In its course rates were cut in the East as well as in the West and the Canadian Pacific sent its westbound freight from Toronto by Smith's Falls rather than the direct line of the Grand Trunk to North Bay. Peace was patched up, but the Canadian Pacific shortly afterwards set about building a road of its own from Toronto north to its main line, thus threatening the Grand Trunk with permanent loss of western business, and providing it with one incentive toward the great westward expansion it was soon to undertake.

In 1902 Hays announced that the directors were considering building a line from North Bay, through New Ontario westward, to a terminus on the Pacific at Port Simpson or Bute Inlet. It would be a line of the highest standards. Government aid, the announcement continued, would certainly be sought and expected. However, 1903

was not 1873, and Hays had learned on the Wabash and on the Grand Trunk how difficult it was for a second-class road to compete and how costly was the process of rebuilding with the line in operation.

The Grand Trunk Pacific was organized as a subsidiary company of the old Grand Trunk, which secured control of ownership of all but a nominal share of the $25 million common stock, given it in return for guaranteeing part of the Pacific bonds. Only $20 million preference capital stock was provided for, and this was not issued. The interest of the independent shareholder was thus negligible. The money required was secured by the issue of bonds and debenture loans guaranteed by the government or the Grand Trunk.

On the western section a good route through the prairies was decided upon, not without vigorous protest from the Canadian Pacific because of the close paralleling of its line. After repeated surveys of the Peace, Pine, Wapiti, and Yellowhead Passes, the last was chosen, and a line was settled upon down the Fraser and Skeena valleys, passing through two million acres of fertile land.

From Edmonton to Yellowhead Pass in British Columbia the lines of the Canadian Northern and the Grand Trunk Pacific were very close to each other, following the same route through the Rockies. The Grand Trunk Pacific, however, did not go south to Vancouver but in-

stead continued west. Kaien Island, 550 miles north of Vancouver, was chosen as the terminus, rather than Port Simpson as originally designed, and soon on its magnificent harbor and most unpromising site of rock and muskeg the new and scientifically planned seaport city of Prince Rupert began to rise.

As the main line ran far to the north of the St Lawrence lake and river system, the original plan provided for the construction of branch lines to Fort William, North Bay and Montreal. Of these only the first, aided by the Dominion and also by the Ontario government, was built. Later, in 1914, the Dominion government itself decided to build the Montreal branch.

The great Canadian railway companies are much more than railways. The Grand Trunk system, in its new expansion, branched into every neighboring field which could be made to increase the traffic. It (as well as the Canadian Northern) crossed the Prairies roughly 200 miles north of the Canadian Pacific. People were just beginning to settle in these northern parts of Alberta and Saskatchewan so very few towns had as yet been established. To encourage new farming communities, the Grand Trunk Pacific decided to build a railway station every 15 miles along its line, in the hope that new settlements would grow up around them. That particular distance was chosen so that farmers living along the line would have no more than 7-and-a-half miles to travel to deliver their wagonloads of grain.

Stations were given names in alphabetical order from East to West. In many cases, towns did develop around them, taking their names from the railway station. Today, you find names such as Atwater, Bangor and Cana, or Unity, Very, and Winter, all neatly in order along the railway's route.

Many other western towns were named after railway people—conductors, engineers, superintendents, or company directors. One of the more unusual place names in Saskatchewan is Hemaruka. It comes from the first names of the four daughters of a railway vice-president: 'He' is for Helen, 'ma' for Margaret, 'ru' for Ruth, and 'ka' for Kathleen.

This line was very expensive to build. The Grand Trunk had to borrow huge sums of money from England; now it was deep in debt.

The early 20th century also saw a setback for the Grand Trunk. It has been almost 75 years since the 'invincible' Titanic slipped to a watery grave off the coast of Newfoundland on its maiden voyage from Liverpool, England, to New York. Among the 1503 passengers and crew who perished in the 15 April 1912 disaster was Charles Hays. To one extent or another, Hays' death altered the course of railroad history.

Hays had gone to England to discuss construction of the Southern New England Railroad with British financiers, who had underwritten much of the expense for building the Grand Trunk. It was his dream to extend the Grand Trunk-owned trackage from the Central Vermont at Palmer, Massachusetts, to Providence, Rhode Island, (and ultimately to Boston) to provide a deep-water port in the US for the import of Canadian-bound trade and the export of Canadian products.

Governor Aram Pothier of Rhode Island, a native of Woonsocket, was a strong advocate of the SNE and personally took the controls of a massive steam shovel during groundbreaking ceremonies on 11 May 1912, three weeks after Hays died.

However, without Hays' leadership, the project was plagued by one setback and problem after another—not the least of which was the fact that New York financier J P Morgan and New Haven Railroad owner Charles Mellen opposed any intrusion by Grand Trunk into a territory serviced by railroads in which they had substantial financial interests.

War clouds were hovering over Europe and the outbreak of World War I on 28 July 1914 brought to an end the somewhat-tenuous support of the SNE project by British financiers. By 1915, all construction ended and the SNE started fading into history. It took another 16 years to untangle a maze of legal and monetary problems. On 30 January 1931, the receivership of SNE was officially discharged … ending forever the elegant vision of railroad pioneer Charles Hays.

At the same time as the Grand Trunk Pacific was being built, the Canadian Government was laying track for another very long line from Moncton, New Brunswick, to Winnipeg. This was the National Transcontinental, to run far north of Montreal and Toronto, through wilderness filled with lakes and swamps. Finding the best route was extremely difficult.

At the time it was built, there were practically no settlers living that far north of the St Lawrence River and the Great Lakes. Still, the National Transcontinental Railway did establish a short route to the West and, when valuable minerals were found in several areas there, it was used to ship many thousands of ton of ore to ports and smelters in Quebec and Ontario.

The discovery of gold in the Klondike in the 1880s afforded good advertising for Canada. In government, finance, industry, and the railway were men who rose to the opportunity: no longer was Canada's light hid under a bushel of wheat. The most was made of the alluring gifts she had to offer. Men the world over who strove to better themselves began the flood of immigration.

The first result of the swarming of thousands to the West was a demand for new railways, to open up plain and prairie and mineral range, and to make connection between East and West. The building of the railways in its turn gave a stimulus to every industry. As in the early 1850s and early 1880s, this period of rapid railway expansion was an era of optimistic planning and feverish speculation.

First to seize the golden opportunities was the group of men who built the Canadian Northern. Railway history offers no more remarkable record than the achievement of

*At left:* The overstuffed, luxurious interior of a Victorian-era passenger coach.

*These pages:* Providing the power for the plethora of Grand Trunk Western trains in this 1903 photo taken at Durand, Michigan, trusty 4-4-0 American-type locomotives are in much evidence. The GTW was incorporated into the Canadian National system in 1923, following the GTW's reorganization.

The Canadian Pacific couldn't meet the challenge presented by the rapidly growing western territories of the early 1900s. so William Mackenzie *(at top)* and Donald Mann *(above)* seized the opportunity and built the Canadian Northern. *At right:* Grand Trunk locomotive number 2365. in 1889.

these few men. who. beginning in 1895 with a charter for a railway 100 miles long in Manitoba leading nowhere in particular. succeeded in building in 20 years a road from ocean to ocean. and in keeping it in their own hands through all difficulties.

It was in 1895 that William Mackenzie and Donald Mann. along with two fellow contractors. James Ross and H S Holt. decided to buy some of the charters of projected western roads and to build on their own account. They secured the charter of the Lake Manitoba Railroad & Canal Company. carrying a Dominion subsidy of 6000 acres a mile for a line from Portage la Prairie to Lake Manitoba and Lake Winnipegosis. They induced the Manitoba government to add a valuable guarantee of bonds and exemption from taxes. In 1896 running rights were secured over the track of the Manitoba & Northwestern from Portage to Gladstone. and construction was pushed 100 miles northwest from Gladstone to Dauphin. The coming need of the West was an outlet from Winnipeg to Lake Superior. to supplement the Canadian Pacific. Accordingly in 1898. under powers given by Dominion, Ontario, and Minnesota charters, construction was begun both at Winnipeg and near Port Arthur. Three years later the line was completed. Meantime the earlier road had branched westerly at Sifton, and by 1900 had crossed the border into Saskatchewan at Erwood. In 1899. in amalgamation with the Winnipeg Great Northern, chartered and subsidized to Hudson Bay, the name of the combined roads was changed to the Canadian Northern.

Then came the coup which first made the public and rival railways realize the ambitious reach of the plans of the new railway. In 1888. when the ban upon competition southward with the Canadian Pacific had been lifted, the Northern Pacific had entered Manitoba. It had gradually built up a system of three hundred and twenty

miles, but had not given the competition looked for, dividing traffic with the Canadian Pacific rather than cutting rates. Now the parent line was in the receiver's hands, and its straits gave the Manitoba government its opportunity. It leased for 999 years all the Manitoba lines of the Northern Pacific, but decided it could not profitably operate them itself without connection with the lakes. The only question was whether to lease them again to the Canadian Pacific or to the Canadian Northern . After a lively contest the younger road secured the prize. At a stroke it thus obtained extensive terminals in Winnipeg, a line south to the American border, branches westward through fertile territory and a link which practically closed the gap between its eastern and western roads.

The Canadian Northern had now become the third largest system in Canada, stretching from Lake Superior to Saskatchewan, with nearly 1300 miles in operation in 1902. The feeders were extending through the rich farm-

ing lands of the West. The line to Port Arthur supplemented the Canadian Pacific, providing a second spout to the funnel. This merely local success, however, did not long content its promoters. They announced their intention to build from sea to sea. The Grand Trunk, the Trans-Canada and the Great Northern all planned extensive projects.

In 1902 and 1903 a junction of forces between the Grand Trunk and the Canadian Northern was proposed, and would have had much in its favor. The negotiators could not come to terms, however, and each road continued on its independent plan. Undaunted by the Canadian government's decision to recognize and aid the Grand Trunk, the Canadian Northern turned to a policy of piecemeal construction, seeking aid from the provinces as well as from the Canadian government. The Canadian Northern pressed forward extensions, flung out branches, filled in gaps on every side.

By 1905, the year Saskatchewan and Alberta entered Confederation, Canadian Northern lines had crossed the Prairies to Edmonton. Track was laid quickly and perhaps not too well, because MacKenzie and Mann were in a hurry to get things moving. They did, however, keep upgrading it to meet the demands of use as traffic increased.

The Canadian Northern was known as 'the farmers' railway', because it served the often isolated people of the prairies as individuals even while earning money from them. There is a story about one of its trains stopping near a cabin and staying there so long that a passenger asked the conductor about the delay. He explained that the woman who lived in the cabin down the line had to sell two dozen eggs, but she was an egg short so the train had to wait until a hen laid one.

On one occasion a train struck a heifer, breaking its legs. The crew knew from experience that the farmer would make a claim against the railway for the animal without taking into account the additional value of its meat. So a brakeman who had been a butcher quickly killed and dressed it, the carcass and hide were put in the baggage car, sold that same day, and after the farmer's claim was paid in full there were four dollars left for the company.

In Ontario the gap north of Lake Superior was bridged by a line from Port Arthur to Sudbury, not completed until 1914. Toronto and Ottawa were linked with the western lines, and several feeders were acquired which gave connection with Kingston and Brockville.

Having reached Edmonton, Mackenzie and Mann saw the Pacific as their next goal. That, of course, meant building in the mountains, which was much more difficult

*Below:* The Canadian Northern was known as 'the Farmers' Railroad.'

than on the flat central plain. Surveys for a road from Yellowhead Pass to Vancouver by Sandford Fleming's old route were begun in 1908. By the aid of lavish guarantees and subsidies this last link in the transcontinental system was pushed to completion in 1915.

The men behind the Canadian Northern not only planned such a project, but carried it through, displaying at every stage of the project a mastery of political diplomacy, and untiring persistence, and great financial resourcefulness.

Dominion and province vied in aid which took many forms. In 1894 Canada had abandoned its policy of giving land grants, but the original companies which combined to form the Canadian Northern had previously been promised and later received over four million acres. Up to 1914 about $18 million had been realized from the sale of parts of this land, and the grants unsold were worth millions more. In addition, Ontario gave two million acres and Quebec one-third as much. The Liberal government of Sir Wilfrid Laurier voted cash to aid in building the link between Winnipeg and Lake Superior. It declined to recognize or aid the extension to the Pacific coast, but in 1912 the Conservative government of Sir Robert Borden gave over $6 million for this work, and in the following year $15 million more for the Ontario and western Alberta sections of the main line. The provinces were less lavish; Quebec, Ontario, and Manitoba offered a total of six million.

In 1896, the Canadian Northern was a railway 100 miles long, beginning and ending nowhere, and operated by thirteen men and a boy. In 1914, a great transconinental system was practically completed, over ten thousand miles in length, and covering seven of Canada's nine provinces. The impossible had been achieved.

The Grand Trunk, Great Western, and Northern roads owed the old province of Canada on 1 July 1867 $20 million for principal advanced and over $13 million for interest. Other roads were indebted to Canadian municipalities nearly $10 million for principal alone. There had been waste and mismanagement, but the railways had brought indirect gain that more than offset the direct loss. Farming districts were opened up rapidly, freights were reduced in many sections, intercourse was facilitated, and land values were raised.

In the first 30 years of Canadian railway development no question aroused more interest than that of the gauge to be adopted. The width of the carts used in the English coal mines centuries ago determined the gauge of railway track and railway cars over nearly all the world. When the steam locomotive was invented, and used upon the coal-line tramways, it was made of the same four-foot-eight-and-a-half-inch gauge. In England, in spite of the preferences for a seven-foot gauge, the narrower width soon triumphed, though the Great Western did not entirely abandon its wider track until 1892. In Canada the struggle was longer and more complicated.

It was a question on which engineers differed. Speed, steadiness, cost of track construction and cost of maintenance were all to be considered, and all were diversely estimated. In early years, before the need of standardizing equipment was felt, many experiments were made, especially in the United States. In the southern states five feet was the usual width, and the Erie was built on a gauge of six feet, to fit an engine bought at a bargain. But in the United States, as in England, the four-foot-eight-and-a-half-inch width was dominant, and would have been adopted in Canada without question except that local interest, appealing to patriotic prejudice, succeeded in clouding the issue.

But experience proved that it was impossible to maintain different gauges in countries so closely connected as Canada and the United States. As roads became consolidated into larger systems, the inconvenience of different gauges became more intolerable. The expedients of lifting cars bodily to other trucks, of making axles adjustable, and even of laying a third rail, proved unsatisfactory. Late in the 1860s and early in the 1870s the Great Western and the Grand Trunk had to adopt the four-foot-eight-and-a-half-inch gauge only, and other lines gradually followed.

The Canada Southern was built in 1873, running between Fort Erie, opposite Buffalo, and Amherstburg on the Detroit River. It was controlled by the Vanderbilt interests and operated in close cooperation with their other roads, the Michigan Southern, Michigan Central, and New York Central. The Great Western met this attack upon its preserves by building in the same year the Canada Air Line, from Glencoe near St Thomas, to Fort Erie, giving more direct connection with Buffalo. Both roads made use of the magnificent International Bridge, built across the Niagara in 1873 under Grand Trunk control.

An interesting experiment, motivated by the same desire for cheap pioneer construction which in Ontario brought in the narrow gauge, was the wooden railway built in 1870 from Quebec to Gosford. The rails were simply strips of seasoned maple, fourteen feet by seven inches by four inches, notched into the sleepers and wedged in without the use of a single iron spike. The engines and wheels were made wide to fit the rail. In spite of its cheap construction the road did not pay, and the hope of extending it as far as Lake St John was deferred for a generation. A similar wooden railway was built from Drummondville to L`Avenir.

# The St Clair Tunnel

## Bridging the 19th and 20th Centuries

Close to a century ago, in an age of grand engineering projects, a railroad tunnel was completed under the St Clair River linking the United States and Canada—the world's first international submarine railroad tunnel. Employing innovative construction methods, the tunnel was completed in a relatively short time, the two bores from opposite shores meeting only a fraction of an inch off center. First employing steam locomotive power, the tunnel was later wired for electric operation until the diesel retired it in the 1950s, thus making the St Clair one of the few railroad tunnels in the world to use three types of motive power—perhaps the only tunnel with this distinction.

The St Clair Tunnel has many firsts to its credit. When completed in 1891 it was the largest submarine tunnel in North America. It was the first underwater tunnel built using the shield method of construction and, in fact, was such an engineering achievement that it was widely acclaimed throughout the world in scientific journals as well as the press, rivaling in international attention the Eiffel Tower of 1889.

The story of the St Clair Tunnel begins in the cold mists of a prehistoric ice age when a great glacier carved out the Great Lakes, creating those immense bodies of fresh water so vital in a far future to establish a vast inland waterborne transportation system but establishing physical barriers for road and rail.

As commerce gravitated to the waterways, strategically located cities such as Chicago, Detroit, Toronto and Milwaukee grew fueled by the movement of grain, lumber and people. The Port Huron-Sarnia area was tied closely to shipping, the natural result of an advantageous position at the southern end of Lake Huron. The transportation industry, an economic mainstay of the two cities almost from the start, included ship building, repair yards, ferries, tug boats, piloting, chandlers and sail lofts. When steel rails began pushing their way west, it was inevitable that these lake ports would also become railroad terminals. By the 1850s the Great Western Railway of Canada completed a line into Point Edward, Ontario, then a small community at the confluence of Lake Huron, and the St Clair river. On the Michigan shore in 1859 rails were spiked down on a line between Detroit and Fort Gratiot, now a section of Port Huron. This trackage was incorporated as the Chicago, Detroit & Canada Grand Trunk Junction Railroad, and later became a component of the Grand Trunk system.

Even before 1859 there was lively traffic across the river and a fleet of ferries was then in service.

The Grand Trunk devised a solution for moving railroad cars across the swift river when it became apparent that transhipping people and goods from cars to wharves to ferries to wharves to cars was a slow and uneconomical process. It used a swing ferry, that is, a ferry that had no on-board propulsion system but depended on the force of the current to push it back and forth as it swung tethered to an anchor placed a considerable distance upstream. The swing ferry was an environmentalist's dream—no smoke, fumes or noise, and it certainly was easy on fuel and repair bills. But this method must have posed problems in the spring when ice floes choked the river and there surely were problems with other shipping. Nevertheless, the swing ferry remained in service for thirteen years and was retired in 1872.

Her successor, *International II*, was perhaps not quite as unusual, only slightly so. She was a gem of technological innovation, being the first propeller-driver carferry on the Great Lakes and the first carferry to carry three sets of tracks on her decks. *International II* wasn't the complete solution to the physical barrier of the broad St Clair River, however. Limited car-carrying capacity, combined with growing traffic demands and the continuing problem of

*At right:* A 3000hp Grand Trunk Western road switcher emerges from the St Clair Tunnel—which was, when built, the world's first international submarine railroad tunnel, and stretches from Ontario to Michigan.

ice, were creating a backlog of cars on both sides of the river, some of them carrying perishable meat and produce. Another means for crossing the water barrier was needed, and soon. The climate at the time was excellent for a bold scheme to break the barrier at the St Clair River.

The Grand Trunk considered both a bridge and a tunnel. Although a bridge was a logical solution and was given serious consideration, there were problems with the concept.

Both sides of the river are low and flat so a very high bridge with long and expensive approaches would have been required to allow the tall masts of sailing vessels to pass underneath. A draw or lift bridge was ruled out because constant marine traffic would have placed it out of railroad service most of the time, at least during the navigation season. Probably the strongest reasons for abandoning the idea of a bridge were legal and political opposition from shipping interests who not only feared that a bridge would restrict the passage shipping but also because marine operators opposed any construction by transportation rivals threatening to waterborne commerce. So the tunnel option was settled upon, a courageous decision in the face of the failure of an earlier tunnel attempt at Detroit.

The prime mover of the project, Sir Henry Tyler, president of the Grand Trunk, was a business leader who liked to take calculated risks in order to turn a good profit. As an added stimulus, British investors, the majority shareholders in the Grand Trunk, although making a good profit from their shares, desired even larger returns and complained about the slow and conservative pace of the company. Tyler could, therefore, with one move solve both his internal management problem and the challenging river crossing bugbear. And he did, but not without an unsettling beginning. Learning from the Detroit tunnel failure, benefiting from the newest tunneling technology and from the experience provided by the recently-built New York subway system, Tyler engaged an engineer, Walter Shanley, to study the project. Initially, Shanley's charter was to look at both bridge and tunnel concepts and he made test borings in the most obvious place, the narrows at the head of the river where the swing ferry and its successor operated. He found that the subsoil structure was unsuitable for either project and declared that a bridge could never be built on the site. (Sixty years later the Blue Water Bridge opened to motor traffic in that same location). Nevertheless, the tunnel idea persisted and in 1884 the Grand Trunk incorporated a Canadian subsidiary, The St Clair Frontier Tunnel Co, to construct and operate a tunnel, and in 1886 a similar corporation in Michigan, the Port Huron Railroad Tunnel Co. A fifty-year bond in the sum of $2,500,000 was floated (it was then the largest mortgage ever negotiated in Michigan) and the project was under way.

There was little lost time from this point on. There were no environmental impact statements to file in those free-wheeling days and within a few months of incorporation, a new site was selected and new test holes bored. Fortunately, a talented engineer, Joseph Hobson, was put in charge as project engineer. By one account there was reason for haste to complete the tunnel: the Grand Trunk had a lucrative trade carrying meat from the packing house in Chicago to the East, but the shippers were con-

The St Clair Tunnel was completed on 30 August 1890. With both success and tragedy in the tunnel, the Grand Trunk continued briefly to ferry passengers and vehicles across the Saint Clair River with such ferries as the *Grand Haven* (above). Marine transport would come into use again—to compensate for the tunnel's narrow dimensions—in the 1970s.

cerned with delays at Port Huron and were threatening to find another route if shipments could not be expedited.

Construction sites were surveyed on opposite sides of the river and excavation began, but a setback occurred before the drifts progressed far. The problems of quicksand, methane and water seepage proved to be too much and the project was temporarily abandoned. The Canadian cut extended 186 feet, but on the US side where the problem was more severe, the cut reached a length of only 20 feet. Excavations were made with standard techniques of the time but these were not good enough. New technical solutions were essential.

The difficulty was caused in part by the strategy for the tunnel which made good economic sense, but was tricky to execute. The tunnel would be cut through a layer of blue clay and had to be bored with considerable precision since just below the clay was bedrock and not far above it coursed the cold waters of the river. By drilling through the clay, blasting would be unnecessary and forward progress swift. Unfortunately, the clay bed wasn't quite uniform, with water strata and areas of quicksand leading to so much seepage that the pumps were unable to clear water from the bore.

New financing was arranged and a request for bids was issued but there were no takers because of the failure of

the Detroit tunnel and the ill luck of the first attempt at Port Huron-Sarnia. Now Tyler and the tunnel company would have to do it themselves.

Hobson decided to apply three technical innovations in combination, the first company in North America to use this arrangement. It was this technology that brought the tunnel to the attention of scientists and engineers worldwide.

The most important of these innovations was Hobson's use of the Beach hydraulic tunneling shield. Just as a cookie cutter with a sharp edge might be pressed through soft material, the shield method of tunneling would cut through the blue clay under the St Clair River. Two shields were used, each a massive eighty-ton cylinder twenty-one feet seven inches in diameter and sixteen feet long. Built of one-inch thick steel plates, the shield was pushed forward by 24 hydraulic rams spaced around its circumference. A specially-designed circular crane was attached at the rear of the shield to position the half-ton permanent sections of tunnel casing in place after the shield had been pushed forward and the clay removed by hand.

The other solutions for attacking the relatively soft, water-gassy ground were the use of compressed air during construction and a permanent cast iron casing for the tunnel's walls. Conventional wisdom was upset by the use of iron linings instead of traditional bricks and mortar. A more serious drawback, insufficient knowledge of the effects of working under two or three atmospheres of pressure, was limited. The lining performed superbly, but the little-understood problems of working under pressure

resulted in the death of three laborers, several horses and a few mules. The hydraulic shields attracted much popular attention and there were countless lithographs and engravings of them. Few had been built up to this time and then only of very small dimensions. Because engineer Hobson could not obtain drawings of the original shield developed by the British engineer Greathead, he designed his shields on the basis of a few small drawings found in a book. Hobson's shields were almost twice the size of Greathead's. To limit the possibility of a disaster, the vertical shafts were dug at both river banks to start tunneling before digging the expensive approaches. Before reaching the proper depth, fluid clay and silt floated into the diggings faster than it could be removed.

Now a more thorough beginning was made with long and wide approach cuts several thousand feet back from the portals, after which brick bulkheads with air locks were built and the underground construction pushed forward. No underwater tunnel had ever been driven as swiftly. The average monthly headway for both the Canadian and American bores totalled 455 feet and the tunnel was driven through, though not completed, in just one year.

Other new technologies contributed to this unusual and unexpected speed. Electric arc lights were used from the start and telephone communications were also employed. Within the tube, work progressed continuously. Dirt shoveled by hand into small flat cars pulled by mules was removed for two feet ahead of the shield, then the hydraulic jacks pushed the shield forward and the circular

*Above:* This 0–10–0 engine is typical of those Baldwin designed for use in the St Clair Tunnel. These 'steamers' were replaced with Baldwin-designed electrics in 1908, as smoke and gas accumulation in the tunnel resulted in several deaths by asphyxiation, despite the (Grand Trunk subsidiary) St Clair Tunnel Company's careful safety planning.

cast iron casing, each ring consisting of thirteen 1,000-pound pieces, was bolted into place behind it. Each segment was eighteen inches wide and two inches thick and had been made rust resistant by heating to 400 degrees followed by immersion in pitch. As the shields cut their way forward under the river, water leakage increased but the Ingersoll air compressors at each entrance forced the water and quicksand back and work continued.

The restricted area inside the tunnel shafts certainly could have provided a chapter for Dante's *Inferno*. Tunnel crews consisted of 75 men per shift—26 diggers, 15 section or casing workers, and the rest at various jobs such as mule skinning. Men and mules, working shoulder to shoulder in the foul air under the glare of arc lamps, were covered with blue mud under conditions of 100 percent humidity. The noise level must have been deafening and odors formidable. Added to this was the ever-present danger of a blowout, which would lead to flooding the tunnel. There also was the little understood danger of working under pressure. On the positive side, however, was the increased pay of an extra dollar a day for working under pressurized air conditions and the fact that temperatures in the tunnel remained in the fifties no matter how hot it was outside. So close were the tolerances through the blue clay that workers could hear propellers of steamships passing overhead.

It was routinely expected that an engineering project of any magnitude would take its toll of human lives—it was part of project costs and indeed costs of fatalities in those days of no liability and minor insurance coverage was neg-

ligible, except, of course, to the families of the victims. Working conditions on the railroads of the time were no better and probably switchmen and trainmen suffered as many casualties—maiming and fatalities—as did the troops involved in any of the small colonial wars of the period. Although railroading was a hazardous occupation, there was an extra dimension of danger in tunnel work with the threats of cave-ins, flooding and explosive misfires. The St Clair tunnel added the basic dangers of being underwater and of being driven through ground saturated with methane. To protect against methane and to hold back the blue clay and the cold waters of the St Clair River, the tunnel was pressurized from ten to thirty-four pounds per square inch above normal atmospheric pressure. Pressure varied depending on the degree of seepage and consistency of the clay.

In the 1880s pressurized tunnel work was still a new technique and little was known about the physical effects of working under pressure. With reasonable care, laborers were not excessively bothered or harmed, at least in the short term. The pressure was too great for horses, however, which initially were used to haul trains of flats removing the excavated material. Mules mostly survived where horses quickly died. There are no reports on whether or not the mules were given a period of slow decompression—it would be interesting to know if they did—but the men were all instructed on the need for this process, which they apparently did on their own time. Although the tunnelers were instructed about the need for decompression before leaving the tunnel, nevertheless three men died from nitrogen embolism or 'the bends.'

Construction continued to advance at a good rate underground. On 23 August 1890, a hole was punched through the clay between the shields. It was claimed that the first freight through the tunnel was a plug of tobacco passed through this hole on the end of a shovel.

After passing through thousands of feet of clay, the two shields met almost exactly, off only a small fraction of an inch, on August 30th. The interior of the Canadian-built shield was then torn out and the outsides left in position to become tunnel walls where they remain in place to this day. The first man through the tunnel was the Canadian engineer, Sir Joseph Hobson. Freight service started 27 October 1891, and passenger service began on December 7th.

The opening of the St Clair Tunnel was celebrated in a proper style that reflected well on tradition. The first celebration, although not the official one, was touched off at noon on Sunday, 25 August 1891, when Hobson, who clearly had a flair for the dramatic, removed the last shovelful of dirt remaining between the US and Canadian diggers, and stepped through the opening. As he did, shrieking steam whistles on the surface gave the long-awaited signal that the first international underwater connection now existed.

The Port Huron *Daily Times* prepared an extensive edition to mark the opening, banquets were planned, and the entire area geared to the event. On Friday evening, September 18th, Port Huron held its banquet celebration with Canadian guests arriving from Point Edward aboard the steam passenger ferry, *Omar D Conger*. Among these was Sir Henry Tyler, Mayor Watson of Sarnia, and of course, Joseph Hobson. The most notable American present was Governor Vinans of Michigan. The dinner ended at an early hour so that the guests could return to Point Edward in time to prepare the extensive activities scheduled for the next day.

The following day a seven-coach inaugural train left Point Edward at 12:30 pm headed by a tall-stacked 4–4–0 type locomotive with a huge oil lantern atop the smoke box. It carried several flags and bunting and it was said to have been decorated with flowers as well.

At 1:00pm the train started for the tunnel entrance amid the cheers of the crowd, and three-and-a-half minutes after entering the Sarnia portal it emerged from the flag-draped stone portal on the US side as a grand orchestra of steam whistles greeted it, continuing to blow until the train passed through that exuberant archway. Then it rolled on on more decorous quiet to the new 22nd Street depot. A large freight house nearby was decorated with flags, bunting and evergreen boughs with a speaker's platform constructed on the east end and this was the next center of activity. Hobson received a tumultuous ovation which reportedly visibly affected him. The stay in Port Huron could not have lasted too long as tickets for the primary formal celebration showed that it was to begin at two o'clock that afternoon. And a grand affair it was with 350 people attending in the cavernous flag-draped Sarnia freight house.

As construction crews were inching through the heavy blue clay, orders were placed with the Baldwin Locomotive Works of Philadelphia for four of the largest engines yet built. Heavy steam power in the enclosed space of a tunnel posed a difficult problem for locomotive designers as did the steep gradients, but Baldwin's solutions were very logical and resulted in a locomotive dramatic in its appearance.

The major danger after the tunnel became operational was not compressed gases, but flue gases. The tunnel company took what they considered to be exceptional precautions by building a ventilation system with 'extraordinary capacity.' A *Scientific American* article published during the construction of the tunnel declaimed on how the redundant system would ensure that there were no problems with the air in the tunnel. But there were problems, nevertheless. A set of blowers and vents built throughout the tube could circulate 10,000 cubic feet of air a minute, but in practice, more time was needed since the air was removed somewhat irregularly. The first recorded casualty was Thomas Wright, a Port Huron mason who was overcome by smoke on 20 November 1897, but survived his dose of carbon monoxide, nitrous oxide, sulfur dioxide and other gases. Eight days later a coupling gave way on a twenty-car train working up the grade and several cars rolled back to the lowest point in the tunnel. Engineer PO Courtney, probably more concerned about the views of his superiors than his own safety and that of his crew, backed his locomotive down the tunnel to recouple the cars without waiting for the ventilation system to clear the fumes. It was a fatal mistake followed by still another: Courtney and his crew were overcome, and when his engine did not return another was dispatched. The crew of the rescue locomotive also was asphyxiated and both engines were trapped at the center of the tunnel, spewing out deadly gases. Courtney, the conductor and a brakeman died but the fireman recovered.

On 9 October 1904, a similar but even more tragic disaster took place. A livestock train eastbound and on the upgrade at Sarnia lost cars which, as before, rolled back to the lowest part of the tunnel. Tunnel crew engineer Joseph Simpson was in a caboose with the lost cars and was probably the first to die. When the remainder of the train emerged the crew, with vivid memories of the 1897 disaster in mind, had some sharp discussion on what they would do. One brakeman refused to go back, another returned in a later rescue attempt, but the engineer and fireman decided to enter the tunnel at once. The engineer died but the fireman put his head in a partially-filled fresh water tank and breathed the relatively pure air in the tank until rescued. Another rescue engine also went in from the Canadian side, and from the American end tunnel superintendent Alexander S Begg and two others along with a pumpman entered on foot. Begg collapsed and died before he reached the caboose. An engineer, Morden, collapsed as he tried to reach Begg but was later removed and he recovered. Three crewmen on the rescue locomotive also died in the deadly gases. The livestock, sheep and cattle, were all asphyxiated.

The tunnel engines, however, performed as anticipated with a limit of six trains per hour, hauling between twenty-five and thirty-three cars, with a total weight of no more than 760 tons at a speed of three miles per hour. With the opening of the tunnel, travel time to New York was cut by two hours and the Grand Trunk save a then-princely $50,000 a year by elimination of its ferries. Traffic soon exceeded expectations, however, and it became apparent that more frequent and longer trains were urgently needed to cope with the tonnages that had to pass through the single-track tunnel. By 1900 alternative motive power was being considered and by 1904 the Grand Trunk was seriously exploring electrification, a system then still in its infancy for running trains. Motivated by the tragedies in the tunnel, the railroad decided to operate it with electric locomotives.

The General Electric Company had aquired several contracts for DC (direct current) equipment but its competitor, Westinghouse, was anxious to secure a foothold in the railroad electrification field with its AC (alternating current) system. A combination of technical arguments and a favorable price won the day for Westinghouse and once more the tunnel was the site of extensive construction as eight heavy copper power lines were installed the length of the tube. A brick power house was built in Port Huron, furnished with two Westinghouse generators. Boilers, coal bunkers and a coal dock were also built on the river bank. Over nine miles of track were put under wires at a cost, by one estimate, of $500,000. Inside the tunnel, an additional 500 lights were installed, and the soot-begrimed walls were cleaned and painted white. All work was completed in 1908.

Once again, Grand Trunk and St Clair Tunnel Co officials turned to Baldwin for the new locomotives and once more Baldwin turned out sturdy specimens of utilitarian design. Not a trace of decoration appeared on the interior or exterior. These were large, slow three-axle engines that drew 3300 volts and reduced it to 300 volts for use at the motors. They were designed to provide enough power to start a 1000-ton train on the two percent grade. Thus the tunnel, with electrification and in particular AC electrification, a 'big project first' was back in the forefront of scientific and engineering news.

The initial electrified trip through the tunnel took place in February 1908 with a 700-ton train. All steam operations ended in May. On November 12, the Grand Trunk formally accepted the contractors' work and there was another celebration, not of the magnitude of the tunnel opening festivities but still a redoubtable one. A party of railroad officials, electrical engineers and members of the press were carried through the tunnel on a 'special.' They then adjourned to the Hotel Vendome in Sarnia to face the usual formidable dinners of the era and the even more formidable round of speeches by Grand Trunk officials, Westinghouse executives, other railroad men and doubtless, several local politicians.

Running time was reduced for the three-mile trip from 15 minutes for steam to 10 minutes while the tunnel's capacity was increased by about one-third. The St Clair Tunnel was the heaviest railroad service powered by electricity in the world.

More changes were in store and in 1917 the Detroit Edison Company was awarded a contract to supply electrical power and a new substation was built to furnish 50,000 watts to the locomotives and for the lights, ventilation system and drainage pumps. Boilers, generators and other equipment were torn out of the old generating plant. The coal bunkers were converted to storage bunkers. The nine electric locomotives were maintained in exceptional condition and served very well even though they accumulated enough years of service to have retired other locomotive types. When Westinghouse discontinued manufacturing replacement parts, the railroad acquired all of the jigs, mandrels and related equipment and in a Canadian shop were able to make any required replacement items.

The electrics were still functioning smoothly and effectively when they were finally retired in favor of diesels.

The beginning of the end came in the spring of 1957 when diesels were coupled at the head of passenger trains, although freights were still pulled by the electrics. Extensive tests indicated that the old problem of exhaust gas was too much to handle, although lighter passenger trains were able to drift well past the tunnel's mid-point, thus limiting the fumes. However, reviving the old ventilation system from steam days and augmenting it with new fans at the portals largely solved the problem. On 28 September 1958, the electrics were withdrawn ending the last electric main line railroad operation in Michigan and the last 'tunnel only' railroad electrification in the United States.

Today the colorful diesel locomotives of the Grand Trunk Western, Canadian National, Amtrak and VIA Rail move across the border through the tunnel and it seems quite possible that diesel motive power will be pulling trains under the river for the foreseeable future.

Because of its vital international importance as a transportation link, the St Clair Tunnel has been the target of two ill-fated sabotage attempts. As World War I began, an extraordinarily successful German sabotage ring operating out of the Imperial German Embassy in Washington, DC, was activated, headed by some daring naval attaches and diplomats amply supplied with cash, and said to be responsible for the great Black Tom explosion which destroyed a huge New Jersey powder factory.

Shortly after the main German thrust into France was halted, the attention of the saboteurs turned to the main communications arteries between Canada, which was in the war, and the United States, still neutral but selling war material to Canada. Several bridges were targeted as was the Port Huron-Sarnia tunnel and the Detroit River railroad tunnel. One operation involving local people was identified: Altert Kaltshmidt of Detroit, president of the Marine City Salt Company, was said to have been in charge of sabotage operations for the German government over most of the northern United States and central Canada. Kaltschmidt hired four agents, presumably familiar with explosives, and sent them to blow up a bridge in western Canada. They abandoned this project and he next assigned them to the St Clair Tunnel. They checked and reported back that the tunnel couldn't be easily wrecked, and that the scheme should be forgotten. Kaltschmidt told them to proceed anyhow.

Working in Kaltshmidt's home was a young girl who could understand German. She overheard the plotters, gained some knowledge of what they were planning and reported these plans to nearby authorities who told her to stay on the job and learn whatever else she could. She subsequently heard that the plotters had decided to send a carload of dynamite through the tunnel with a timer set to explode when the car reached center. The authorities moved in and some 50 people were detained and arrested. The tunnel was heavily guarded for the rest of the war.

In 1940 another attempt to sabotage the tunnel was made. In June of that year a fire was discovered in a freight car headed from Port Huron to Sarnia. Holes had been bored in the car's floor, oil-soaked rags inserted and ignited. The fire was extinguished with only modest damage. Railroad detectives, the Royal Canadian Mounted Police, the St Clair County sheriff's office and

Above: A Grand Trunk Western doubleheader emerges from beneath the St Clair River; electricity eventually gave way to diesel, and nearly 100 years after its opening, the St Clair Tunnel continues to serve international rail traffic. The tunnel's smallness, however, is a problem.

the Michigan State Police mounted a massive investigation which turned up no culprits but arrived at an interesting conclusion: they believed the arsonists intended to hit a carload of munitions that had, fortunately, been moved across the previous day. Had an explosion occurred it could have closed the tunnel and possibly severely damaged the large Imperial Oil refinery located near the Canadian entrance.

The whole tunnel system was carefully guarded thereafter with round-the-clock squads of home guards at strategic places. In spite of German agents and human fallibility, the 1904 tragedy was the last involving life and limb and, with a few short closures, the tunnel has been available for service almost continuously ever since.

Today, the 96 year-old tunnel has settled into a respectable and serviceable old age. At this time it looks as though the St Clair Tunnel will make its centennial anniversary still useful and an important part of North American rail transportation. The main threat now come from its size, a problem that has plagued it for almost fifty years. In the 1930s and 1940s freight cars were getting larger and some cars could not be sent through the tube although when the tunnel was built planners allowed good margins for growth. In 1946, a low roadbed was laid dropping the

rail seven inches. It was announced that year that all equipment could now be routed through, but that seven inches was not enough as cars were built with ever increasing dimensions, particularly automobile carriers.

In 1971, the Canadian National system returned car ferries to the St Clair River to handle the auto carriers and other oversize cars. If freight cars continue to expand in size and as older cars are retired, the historic tube may become obsolete. On the other hand, it is possible that new and changing traffic patterns could produce a trend toward more compact cars, particularly given the recent enormous growth of small high-tech industries with small tonnage shipping requirements. Moreover, pressures for coal and ore slurry pipelines may mean that railroads will again have to compete for the smaller shipper, with lesser volume needs per car. If so, the tunnel could be a commercial success for the foreseeable future.

Since the opening days, international passenger trains running from Toronto to Chicago have been an integral part of tunnel operations. In 1971, the service through the tunnel ended. Amtrak re-established international service on 31 October 1982, running a train daily each way between Chicago and Toronto via Port Huron. Despite limited promotion, reports are that patronage is reasonably good.

There are some 'ifs' in the picture but from a current perspective it looks as though this engineering marvel will serve for many years to come.

# Canada's Railways Enter the 20th Century

### The Turn of the Century and World War I

**A**t the turn of our century, Canadians were very optimistic about the future. Many people believed this would soon become one the greatest nations in the world. Prime Minister Sir Wilfrid Laurier said, 'The 20th century belongs to Canada.'

But the young land needed more people, to open up the wilderness and establish industries. The government began advertising to attract immigrants, with huge posters displayed all over England and in Europe's major cities. They described the rich farmlands and wonderful opportunities to be found in Canada. The campaign worked; thousands upon thousands of immigrants began pouring into Canada, many of them heading for the West. More and still more new rail lines were needed in the West. Canadian Pacific could not keep up with the demand.

'Railway mania' held Canadians in thrall for decades. Railways and their progress were a constant major topic of conversation across the country; newspapers were full of stories about them. The government led by Sir Wilfrid Laurier in 1903 began generously handing out loans or guaranteeing bonds to build, build, build! Money also poured in from investors in Britain.

Between 1870 and 1900, rail travel became much more comfortable. In fact, some of the passenger trains became quite elegant. On the outside, coaches were beautifully painted in bright colours. Inside, first-class parlour cars had wood carvings on the ceilings, and paintings displayed on mahogany-panelled walls. Plush carpets were laid, and at windows hung draperies of rich fabrics. By 1888, certain trains had coaches lighted by electricity and heated by steam. Some cars even boasted a primitive form of air-conditioning: fans blowing across blocks of ice. Dining cars offered six-course meals, served in the style of fine hotels.

*At right and above right:* These 4–6–0s provided northern rail speed at the turn of the century. At that time, some railroads 'farther south' were doing well with 4–4–2 Atlantics and, eventually, 4–6–2 Pacifics.

The railways made many other, practical improvements, too. Iron rails were replaced by steel which took much longer to wear out, and major wooden bridges were replaced with iron. As wood-burning locomotives were replaced with by ones using coal, trains could travel longer distances without stopping to refuel.

In just 50 years, Canada's railways had made amazing progress—from 80 miles of trackage in 1850 to 16,950 in 1900—and the country grew along with them.

When the pace of construction slackened in 1914, Canada had achieved a remarkable position in the railway world. Only five other countries—the United States, Russia, Germany, India and France—possessed a greater mileage, and relative to population none came anywhere near her. Three great systems stretched from coast to coast. Need still existed for local extensions, but by great effort the main trunk lines had been built. Not only in mileage were the railways of Canada notable. In the degree to which the minor roads had been swallowed up by a few dominating systems, in the wide sweep of their outside operations, in their extension beyond the borders of Canada itself, and in the degree to which they had been built by public aid, they challenged attention.

While there were nearly 90 railway companies in Canada in 1914, the three trancontinental systems—the Canadian Northern, the Canadian Pacific and the Grand Trunk—controlled more than 80 percent of the total mileage and also owned a variety of subsidiary undertakings such as steamships, hotels, express service, irrigation and land development and grain elevators. The control by Canadian railways of seven or eight thousand miles of lines in the United States, with corresponding extensions into Canada by American lines, was an outcome of geographic conditions, intimate social and trade connections, and a civilized view of international relations which no other countries could match.

However, since the companies doing the building were privately owned, they owed it to their shareholders to follow the shortest routes to major ports and centres of population, because that was how profits would be made. This didn't always serve the nation's future interests. Geography, climate, and patterns of settlement in Canada and the United States favoured north-south traffic, and the Grand Trunk, for example, preferred the year-round harbor at Portland, Maine, to any port in Atlantic Canada.

Opposition Leader Robert L Borden began arguing for a Canadian line, owned by the Canadian people, through Canadian people, through Canadian territory, to Canadian ports.

In 1915, the CPR already had a system running from Saint John, New Brunswick, to the West Coast. Now the National Transcontinental, the Canadian Northern, and the Grand Trunk Pacific began cross-country operations. The nation had a fantastic 34,915 miles of trackage.

When the First World War began in 1914, British money was needed at home to train and equip an army, and there was none to spare for loans to Canada's railways. The flow of immigrants to Canada from Europe also stopped, but industrial and commercial development flourished across the land.

Locomotives and facilities were very important as the 20th century dawned—high hopes for Canada's future made the railroading picture doubly bright. Such facilities as this roundhouse, shown *at right* during its construction at Durand, Michigan in 1912, made yard work easier.

*Left:* This Canadian National 4–6–0 was built at Montreal in 1913, and is shown here at the Vancouver, BC Steam Expo on 22 May 1986. This loco is almost as tall as a two-story house, and its high, narrow stack identifies it as a coal burner. *Above:* A period photo of CN Chairman DB Hanna.

It was the patriotic duty of Canada's railways to carry men and matériel from as far as the West coast to eastern ports, where ships waited to take them to England. However, the government paid unremunerative rates for their efforts. Within a couple of years all the companies except Canadian Pacific were deep in debt.

## The Creation of Canadian National

Sir Robert Borden, who had become prime minister in 1911, kept arguing for public ownership of a nationwide railway system. He pointed out that 90 percent of the Grand Trunk's transcontinental ambitions were already publicly funded by government loans, and for only 10 percent more the country could own and control the system. Faced by the urgent demands of the war, Parliament decided to act on his suggestion.

It began in 1917 by obtaining the Canadian Northern and appointing a board of directors chaired by DB Hanna. The following year, the board's jurisdiction was extended over the Canadian Government Railways, 15 lines in all, the main ones being the Intercolonial, the National Transcontinental, the Hudson Bay Railway, and the Prince Edward Island Railway.

Then, on 6 June 1919, Parliament passed an Act incorporating the Canadian National Railway Company and appointed Hanna as president. The first major acquisition made by the new corporation was of the Grand Trunk Pacific the following year.

The first annual report issued by the board of directors was for 1921, the third year in the life of the National System.' They gave details of the assets and liabilities of the component companies as well as those of Canadian National. They reported net earnings in 1921 of

$47,321.44, compared with a 1920 deficit of $4 million. Then they went on with their work of assembly. By 1923, with the takeover of the Grand Trunk Railway, they had laid a solid foundation.

When the Government of Canada incorporated Canadian National, it created one of the largest railways in the world, with various railway-related services operated for the benefit of its sole shareholder, the people of Canada. It had 105,905 employees and 2078 pensioners. From the many companies assembled in it came 3268 locomotives pulling 138,925 cars of various types along more than 21,700 miles of track, and also telegraph lines, hotels, steamships, car ferries, barges and tugs.

Canadian National Telegraphs had 3852 employees serving the railway and the public by sending messages along 113,105 miles of wire. The Express Department had 3255 employees, as well as '628 horses, 111 motor trucks, 1095 waggons and sleighs, 2959 platform trucks and sleighs, and 584 safes.' Among the business handled during the year were 47 million pounds of fish, 3500 live foxes and 4400 'Horses, principally race horses.'

Eight major hotels, built by some of the companies which made up 'the CNR' to provide their passengers with first-class places to stay as they travelled, were not operated by a separate department but rather entrusted to a 'General Manager, Hotels and Sleeping and Dining Cars.'

*Above:* An early 20th century CN 4–6–4 Hudson passenger loco. *At right:* A somewhat later CN 4–8–4 Northern freight loco. Note these locomotives' short stacks and heavy tank tenders. *Below:* This coal burning 2–8–2 CN Mikado class loco is similar to the larger 2–10–2 'Santa Fe' class locomotives.

*Above:* These hopeful-looking folks were part of the huge Hungarian immigrant influx of 1926. *Below left:* An elegant, powerful CN passenger engine leads its train at Shawinigan. Quebec. This photo was taken in 1970, during an exhibition run. Regular Canadian steam service ended years earlier. *Above left:* The CN's Saskatoon freight yard in the 1930s.

Although the basic groundwork of consolidation had been completed by 1923, a great deal of fine tuning remained to be done, and it took many more years. The timetables, work rules, salaries and services originated by different companies had to be adjusted to conform across the country. Many of the lines assembled in the CNR had been built close together to compete for traffic in the same areas, and much of the track belonging to smaller and poorer railways was in sorry condition. Decisions had to be made regarding which lines were worth repairing and which should be kept. Many of the lines had been built close together to compete for traffic in the same area. These extra lines were no longer needed. Much of the track belonging to the smaller and poorer railways was in bad shape. Men who had worked in fierce competition with one another now had to learn to work together. At first, it was hard for them to forget their loyalty to the old companies.

The CNR's first president, DB Hanna had been a vice-president of the Canadian Northern. When the Canadian Government gave him the huge job of pulling the new company together it made an excellent choice.

The next president, Sir Henry Thornton, appointed in 1922, was an American businessman known on two continents.

In 1923, Sir Henry established the first radio network in Canada, to entertain the CNR's passengers. Special railway cars were equipped with receivers, and headsets through which travellers could hear programs broadcast by the station in the vicinity of the train. There were stations in eight cities, their call letters all beginning with 'CNR', for example CNRM in Montreal and CNRE in Edmonton. In the 1930s, this network became a separate company, the forerunner of today's Canadian Broadcasting Corporation.

To attract new immigrants to settle near the railway's lines, Sir Henry created a special service which helped them find jobs and adjust to their new environment.

In addition to helping grain farmers by shipping their wheat to market, the railway each fall ran special 'harvest trains' that carried hundreds of young men from Eastern Canada out to the West to help bring in the crops. At each stop on the Prairies, farmers waited to pick out strong-looking workers and offer them jobs.

Perhaps the most unusual special trains of the 1920s were those that carried raw silk. It was shipped in huge quantities from Japan to New York City to be processed and woven into beautiful, expensive cloth. Because the raw silk rotted very quickly if it was not processed within a few days, speed was essential in its transportation. Some

of the fastest ships in the world were used to carry it from Japan to Vancouver, where it was loaded into trains in less than 30 minutes, and then, as the trains sped across the country, all other traffic halted to give them the right of way. With essential stops for fuel and water lasting only 10 minutes each, the entire journey across North America took only 80 hours.

After the Canada-West Indies Trade Agreement was signed in the mid-1920s, the government asked the CNR to establish a fleet of passenger ships. Seven luxury liners flew the company's marine pennant for the next few decades, from Montreal, Halifax, and Saint John to the Caribbean, until competition from airlines became too great.

One of the railway's most important tasks during the 1920s was moving Canadian grain from the Prairies to seaports on both coasts. In 1929, a new direction was inaugurated, to Churchill on Hudson Bay. However, although it took less time for ships to reach Europe from Churchill, the port at what is now called Thunder Bay (known then as the twin cities of Fort William and Port

Arthur) remained the major grain-handling position of central Canada because it had more ice-free weeks each year.

## Troubles: The Great Depression and World War II

The Great Depression of the 1930s meant hard times around the world. Industries, struggling to survive, produced fewer goods for railways to ship. And then came long years of drought on Canada's prairies, during which grain traffic fell off drastically.

Few people earned enough to be able to pay for train tickets, but thousands began to travel about the country in search of jobs. Always hoping to find work, spurred on by countless rumours as to where it might be found, scores of wandering men hid in empty box cars to ride to yet another city. Or, when the weather was good, they simply lay on the roofs of cars, risking their lives out of sheer desperation.

Although it touched every aspect of Canadian life, in many cases hindering or even obliterating the natural course of development, the Depression did not stop progress in technology.

During the 1930s, aircraft—not only planes but hydrogen-filled dirigibles—became sophisticated enough to carry passengers, mail and cargo on regular schedules. The Canadian Government decided a national airline was needed, and in 1937 Trans-Canada Air Lines was incorporated, but as part of the CNR because its officers had the transportation experience required to get the new venture started. The then president of the railway, SJ Hungerford, was appointed as first president of TCA. Thus in its formative years the airline known as Air Canada was, like the CBC, guided by the Canadian National.

Just as the Depression ended, much of the world went to war again and from 1939 to 1945 Canada's railways were involved in an all-out effort. Tanks, guns, planes, ammunition, supplies, food, and men all had to be

*Below:* These unfortunates were photographed in the midst of a Depression-era resettlement from Montreal to Lois, Quebec. Folks with money enough for tickets travelled far for work; others 'hopped freights.'

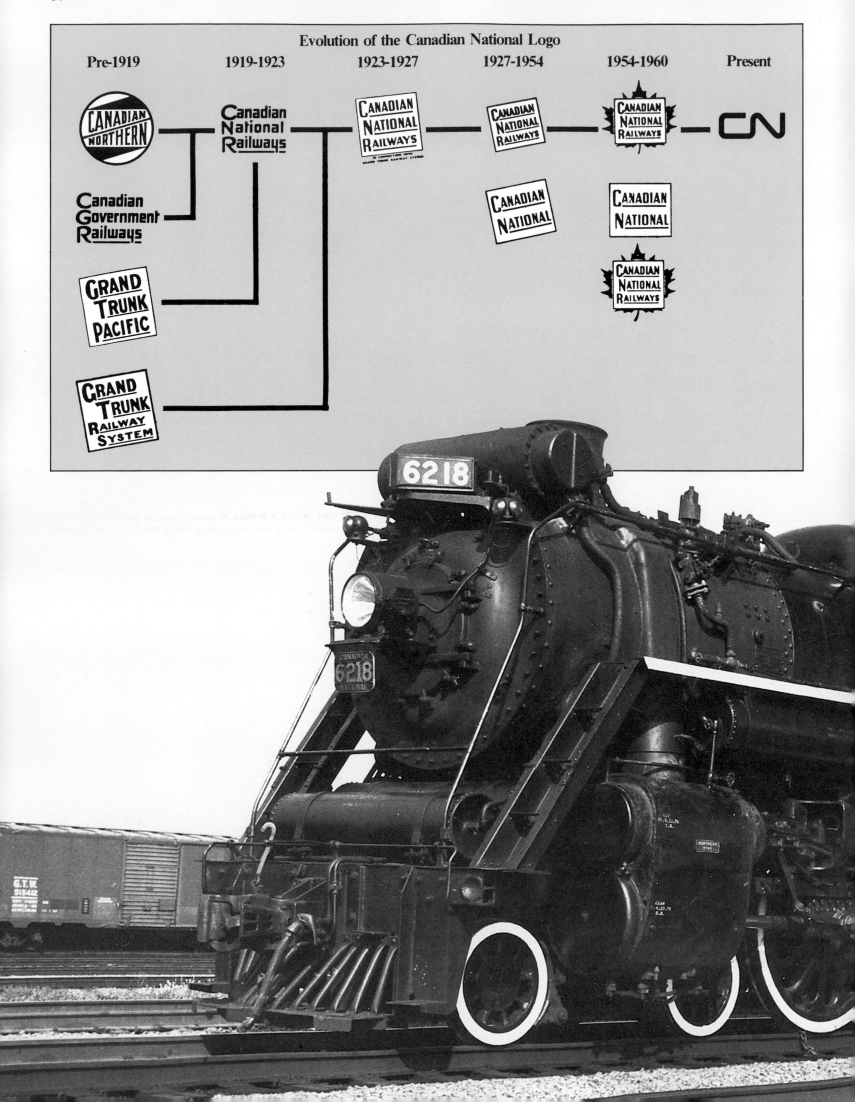

Evolution of the Canadian National Logo

| Pre-1919 | 1919-1923 | 1923-1927 | 1927-1954 | 1954-1960 | Present |

The last Canadian National steam locomotive in regular service was CN loco number 6218, a 4–8–4 Northern class oil burner, which is shown *below* on a siding in a CN yard, where it is kept in good condition for exhibition runs. *Above:* Number 6400 was a very hot-looking 4-8-4 streamliner of the early 1940s, complete with ride-smoothing 12-wheel tender.

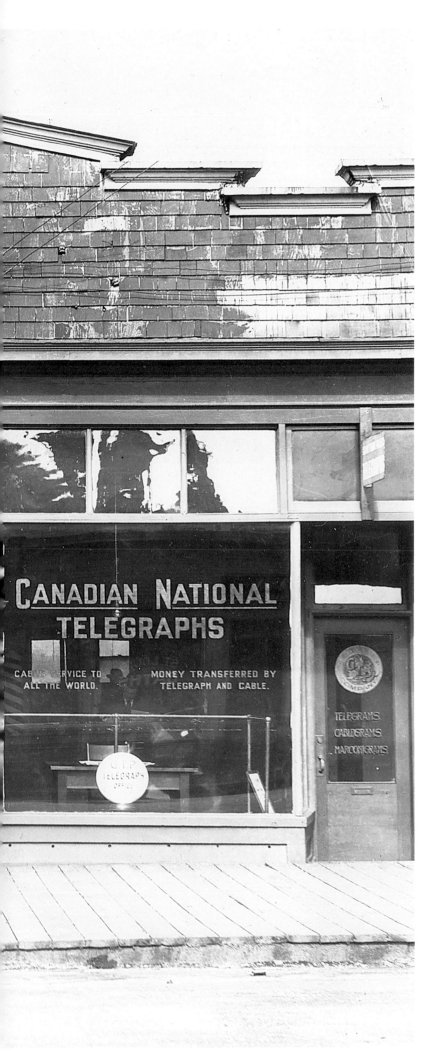

transported to the East Coast, where ships waited to take them to Europe. Because troops and matériel took precedence over passengers, schedules for the travelling public became chaotic.

Canadian National's traffic doubled so quickly that the company did not have enough equipment to handle it. Old box cars and passenger cars were taken out of retirement and rebuilt. Some of the company's work shops, normally used to repair cars and locomotives, also served as munitions factories. Because more than 20,000 men of the CNR served in the war, much of the hard work that kept the railway going was done by women.

Wars, inevitably, are the pivotal experiences for the nations involved in them. While a war is in progress, nothing can possibly be normal; when it ends 'normal' means completely different things than it did before. After a war, one can truly say that 'Nothing is the way it used to be.'

During the Second World War, Canadian National was unable to buy new rolling stock because none was being built (steel went into war-related products), so the cars it did have were used to their limits. When the war ended, the company needed a great deal of money to replace worn-out equipment.

There was also a new challenge railways had never encountered before: good highways had been built right across the country, and people had acquired the habit of using other vehicles instead of trains. Driving a car meant having the freedom to travel when and where you pleased. Trucks offered door-to-door freight services, taking a lot of business away from railways. And airplanes were becoming popular with travellers in a hurry.

Some people said railways weren't needed any more because the world had encountered a new age in which they would be replaced forever by other modes of transportation. Stiff competition for traffic was the toughest challenge railways had ever had to face, and if they could not find ways to compete, it really would mean the end.

The man asked by the Canadian government in 1950 to take up this challenge at the CNR was Donald Gordon, a strong, able leader who had chaired the Wartime Prices and Trade Board. He, along with many other people, believed railways were still very important and would continue to be so.

As president, Mr Gordon immediately set about pulling the company back into shape. To replace the old, worn-out cars, he ordered new specialized ones which shippers liked because they were easier to load and unload, and could carry more freight. Also, over a period of some ten years, he brought an entire fleet of new diesel-electric locomotives which were much less expensive to operate and maintain than steam locomotives.

Along with new equipment and improved methods of operating came a new way of thinking. Before this, trains were the only choice passengers and shippers had; railways could offer the kind of service they chose to provide because traffic had to come to them anyway. Faced by competition from other modes, Canadian National realized it would have to offer its customers the service that best suited *them*. Only be serving people's needs better than other modes of transport would the company pay its way.

*At left:* The CN's Prince Rupert, BC Ticket Office in the mid-1930s.

*These pages:* Hauling a train of grain cars, vintage CN locomotive number 6060 arrives at Boston Bar en route to Vancouver for the Steam Expo there in 1986. Note the unusual use of two 12-wheel tenders coupled to this semi-streamlined 2–8–2 Mikado class engine. The age of diesels made engines such as this classic locomotive obsolete.

# CN Today

## A New Era

Canadian National is today a public utility whose activities, in one way or another, touch regularly the day-to-day lives of most Canadians. In addition to the movement of people and products by rail, it operates trucking lines, a coast-to-coast chain of hotels, an extensive telecommunications network, a fleet of coastal ships, and a variety of related services in such fields as industrial location, customer research, physical distribution, real estate and urban renewal. Through its wholly owned United States subsidiaries, most notably the Grand Trunk Western Railroad, CN's operations reach into 12 of the American states. CN had always had links with Europe, but today it also has offices or agents in Australia, China, Hong Kong, Japan, Korea, Malaysia and Taiwan. The development of CN into the advanced system we know today took some time and hard work.

Most of the track built before the 1920s ran across Canada from east to west to bind the nation together. Now, to find new traffic, the CNR began building lines to the north, to transport ore from areas where minerals had been discovered. Hauling many tons of raw materials over long distances is a job railways do best, and most of the new lines were very profitable. The longest one, the Great Slave Lake Railway, stretches from northern Alberta into the Northwest Territories.

To compete with airlines and trucking companies, new technology and equipment and working methods were introduced on the railway to make service faster and less expensive.

As the railway was modernized, so too were the services which had grown up around it. During the 1970s, departments such as hotels and telecommunications became separate profit centers, and the pattern of a diver-

*At right:* Two SD40-2 road switchers sandwich an Alco C-630 in a 9000hp freight train crossing Montreal's Victoria Bridge. *Above right:* A Canadian National passenger train speeds along a causeway through beautiful countryside. in CN's passenger train days—before VIA Rail.

*Above:* Here represented sequentially, from right to left, is the history—from steam to diesel—of CN locomotives. *Left:* Five 3000-horsepower EMD SD40–2s haul a CN iron ore train through wintertime Ontario. *Above right:* This CN Electro Motive F7 diesel developed 1500hp, and was but a harbinger of more sophisticated diesel locomotives to come.

sified corporation with interactive, mutually supportive parts emerged.

One can scarcely imagine a business more sensitive to change than a railway. Its fortunes can be suddenly and adversely affected by anything from the spring flooding of an obscure river to a shift in political alliances among nations or a drop in the world price of potash. And all the activities surrounding a railway are exceptionally vulnerable as well, to external forces ranging from new technology to public taste.

The way Canadians use their railways never stops changing. In 1977, the passenger services of both CN and Canadian Pacific were entrusted to a new Crown corporation, VIA Rail. Since the Second World War, many freight customers relocated from the center of cities, railway lands were freed for new uses and urban renewal blossomed.

CN Real Estate was set up to develop the railway's lands in the hearts of Canada's major cities by building major office complexes and underground shopping malls. Other railway lands, in the West, were found to be rich in oil and gas, and CN Exploration Inc has many wells in production.

CNR Telegraphs grew into a subsidiary company, CN Communications, which operates NorthWesTel in the

Yukon and northern British Columbia, and Terra Nova Tel in Newfoundland, and, in partnership with Canadian Pacific, runs the giant CNCP Telecommunications system and Telecommunications Terminal Systems. CN Communications leases space in The CN Tower to CNCP Telecommunications and other companies which provide the Metro Toronto area with 'ghost-free' television, radio, and mobile radio systems.

## The Business End

CN today is one of the largest Canadian corporations, with most of its $5 billion in assets devoted to transportation.

Private companies have shareholders who elect a board of directors. In CN's case, the shareholders are the people of Canada and the federal government appoints CN's board of directors. This means that each Canadian owns a part of CN.

Each year, a portion of the profit made by CN is paid to the federal treasury, as a dividend for the people of Canada.

As in most corporations, CN is organized into divisions which carry on the various activities in the railway, trucking, hotels, telecommunications and other fields. The main divisions are CN Rail, Grand Trunk Corporation, CN Communications, CN Trucking, CN Express, CN Hotels and Tower, CN Marine and Terra Transport.Not surprisingly, CN's broad-ranging experience in transportation, communications, and related fields resulted in the establishment of Canac International Inc, the domestic and international consulting arm of Canadian National. This business unit assembles teams of specialists, as required, from other parts of CN to work on contract for private enterprises or governments in Canada and around the world.

## The Railway

The railway arm of Canadian National is called CN Rail and its performance as a freight-hauling railway is very good. The rail operation of today is not the same as it was years ago. For example, productivity gains obtained through computerization and modernization have enabled CN Rail to double the traffic carried while cutting the work force in half.

To get an idea of the size of the railway, we need only consider the earnings of $6 million a day from hauling such items as resource products, manufactured goods and processed foods.

This requires a fleet of 2200 diesel-electric locomotives and about 92,000 railway cars of all types. There are 24,950 miles of main railway line operated by CN Rail, making it one of the longest railways in the world.

CN Rail's status as one of the largest and most successful railways in North America came about in part because of its efforts to introduce and follow through on innovations. In one of its boldest moves, it enlarged upon a new way of handling cargo, called the intermodal concept. Each type of transportation, whether truck, train or ship, is called a mode. When two or more modes are used together it is referred to as intermodal.

Freight is the modern CN's mainstay, and improvements in this area of burdenage include the use of laser beams *(upper left)* in freight yards to identify cars and cargo for more efficient car placement and routing; specialized carriers such as the high-capacity grain cars at *lower left*; and cargo specialty diversification, as is evidenced by the long sulfur 'unit' train shown *above*. Unit trains are comprised of semi-permanently coupled cars.

This can take the form of containers, huge metal or plywood boxes which carry most types of merchandise, loaded on a ship overseas. On arrival in Canada, the containers are later taken off the ships and placed on railway flat cars which are then hauled in special trains to their final destination. In those cities, the containers are taken off the flat cars and placed on small flat-bed trucks and driven to factories or business locations.

Other forms of intermodal travel include piggybacking of highway trailers on railway flat cars, to reduce truck miles and fuel consumption, and Cargo-Flo, in which liquid and liquidized forms of a wide variety of raw materials can be pumped from a railway tank car to a tanker truck for local hauling purposes.

CN Rail also works with water transportation in other ways. Coal, potash, grain and a multitude of other bulk products can be carried by train to bulk storage facilities on the Great Lakes and on either coast of Canada. The bulk storage bins can then be emptied into ocean-going vessels and lake carriers for transportation to user industries in North America or around the world.

On the west coast, east coast and St Lawrence River, another system enables railway cars to be carried on ferry boats and barges. The vessels have actual railway tracks fastened to the deck and the railway cars roll on those tracks.

Symbolic of CN vitality is this freight train, shown *above*, coming head-on over the rails near Snider, Ontario. *Right*: Another CN freight 'makes book' amid the sunset wilds of Fraser Canyon, British Columbia.

The most unusual application is on the east coast where rail ferries operate between North Sydney, Nova Scotia, and Port aux Basques, Newfoundland. The railway line operated by Terra Transport, the division which controls CN's transportation activities in Newfoundland, is a narrow-gauge line. This means that the distance between the two rails is narrower than on CN Rail lines.

To accommodate this change in track width, a special shop in Port aux Basques lifts the box cars, removes the mainland-width wheel assemblies and installs Newfoundland-width wheel assemblies.

The emphasis on maintenance pervades CN Rail's operating philosophy. Money spent permits continuing and efficient use of existing rolling stock and rail facilities. That is why the basic tools of the system—roadbed, rails and rolling stock—are constantly being upgraded and maintained.

CN Rail's main line across Canada has been dramatically improved with continuously welded rail, upgraded roadbed, extended sidings and new automatic central traffic control equipment. Some of the latest mechanized equipment is being used to carry out this work.

Maintenance of the rolling stock and locomotives is carried out on a regular basis to avoid premature wear and failures in service. To increase the car life of its existing fleet, CN Rail conducts an ongoing repair program which results in the overhaul of some 6000 freight cars annually.

*These pages*: Two heavy road switchers pull a Canadian National grain and freight train along and over the Thompson River in British Columbia. The long train is indicative of the health of the CN's freight business, as is the well-kept rolling stock of which this train is comprised.

The purchase of new rolling stock is still made on a regular basis. However, the demand for new cars is actually decreasing because computer technology and better car management have resulted in faster turnaround of railway cars. This means the same number of cars can now handle more traffic. Improvements in locomotive traction have also meant that fewer locomotoves are needed to have the same number of cars.

Where maintenance alone is not sufficient, CN Rail does not hesitate to adopt or develop new technology to meet its needs. Many of the innovations that have produced savings or efficiencies have been developed at CN Rail's own technical research center. Some examples: a CN Rail locomotive mini-computer that detects wheel slippage and automatically reduces power to the traction motors; self-steering freight cars which significantly reduce friction of car wheels against rail on curved sections of track; and the world's most advanced locomotive simulator, developed by CN Rail engineers. Used for training locomotive engineers, it is a full-size cab that does everything an operating locomotive does—except ride the rails.

*Above:* This 'Draper taper' locomotive has a cutaway behind the cab to give the engineer a view to the rear. The broad front of the loco *(at right)* is due to its 'safety cab' and 'cowl'. *At top:* A CN boxcar train.

A source of special pride to CN is the development of a new type of locomotive, the Draper Taper, with many advantages in safety and design. The new locomotive, given its name by Bombadier Inc, builders of the first production run, is in large measure the brainchild of W L 'Bill' Draper, assistant chief of motive power for the railway's operations department.

The locomotive, a mainline freight-haul unit, is of a wide car-body design, but features a revolutionary cutaway behind the cab. It is the cutaway which gives rise to the 'Draper Taper' nickname. It permits the engineer exceptional rear visibility for a wide car-body, and allows full-view inspection of the train, even on a very slight curve. The new locomotive also incorporates a number of other design features which should improve reliability of train operations, particularly in cold weather and heavy snow conditions. The combination of features built into 'Draper Taper' locomotives have become standard for all CN mainline freight-haul locomotives.

*Above:* A 1750hp EMD FP9 diesel hauls yet another VIA Rail train through the beauteous Canadian countryside. *Above left,* vacationers make their plans comfortably in a regular coach car; *at lower left,* mom and pop relax in their VIA sleeper; and *at right,* fun with mommy in a warmly-colored 'Daynighter' car. VIA Rail provides a full range of excellent passenger services, and runs schedules using such classic rail service as the *Canadian.*

## VIA Rail Just for Passengers

CN has been a staunch supporter of passenger train travel and has introduced many on-train features that were copied elsewhere in North America.

By the time Canadian National was created there were two main routes—the traditional CP one and the new CN one—the Continental Ltd: Montréal to Vancouver via North Bay and Cochrane. The National, the Toronto section, joined the Continental at Winnepeg for the trip to the Pacific coast.

Various trains operated over these routes—names such as the Trans Canada Ltd, the Vancouver Express, The Dominion and the Coast Express come to mind. Some featured a choice of accommodations, ranging from deluxe bedrooms and dining cars to coaches and special 'Colonist' cars for immigrants heading west to homestead. Some were sleeping-car-only limited expresses.

In the 1950s, both CN and CP launched their ultra-modern transcontinental services, the Canadian and the Super Continental. Both these services were launched the same day, 24 April 1955. Both offered passengers the latest in travel comfort.

Both railways had just taken delivery of large orders of new cars. However, CP's train captured the limelight with its stainless-steel cars and sleek looks. The Canadian fea-

VIA's revolutionary Light. Rapid. Comfortable (LRC) service began in the early 1980s. Cars *(above)* and locos *(at top)* were designed for high speed operation—up to 125 mph—but haven't yet got all the bugs worked out. *At right:* VIA Rail's luxurious passenger train. the *Canadian.* tours the beautiful Rockies with its cars full of delighted passengers.

tured our country's fauna and flora in its decoration, hence its name. CN's Super Continental was pulled by twin gold and green diesels and featured pastel colours in its day coaches and parlour cars. It took its name from the Continental Ltd, which continued to run until 1964 when it was replaced by the Panorama.

But continuing losses made the passenger operation a financial drain on the railway. To remove this burden, the federal government created VIA Rail Canada, a separate Crown corporation. VIA entered into contracts with CN Rail and CP Rail for the use of rail lines and operating personnel for intercity trains across Canada. CN Rail is continuing to contribute to passenger train comfort because it has major contracts for repairing and maintaining VIA's passenger car fleet and also makes roadbed improvements.

The Super Continental. discontinued in 1981, resumed service 18 June 1985. It offered passengers the latest in travel comforts and its attractiveness provided a spur to tourism in Canada as it aroused a great deal of interest in trancontinental travel, both at home and abroad. The equipment ordered for this train is still being operated by VIA Rail Canada Inc 30 years later.

### Lines in the US

CN Rail has direct ties with the United States through the Grand Trunk Western which connects with CN Rail at

Sarnia and Detroit, through the Duluth, Winnepeg and Pacific Railway which connects to the Winnipeg-Thunder Bay railway line, through Central Vermont which meets CN Rail at St Alban's, Vermont, and the Grand Trunk New England line which connects at Island Pond, Vermont. All of these subsidiaries are part of Grand Trunk Corporation, a holding company established by CN in 1971.

Grand Trunk Western is by far the largest and most important American railroad owned by Canadian National. Its 1311 miles of trackage connect Canada with some of the major industrial centres in the United States—Detroit, Toledo, Chicago, and Cincinnati. The history of the company began in the 1850s, when the Grand Trunk Railway of Canada decided to expand into the rich and growing Midwest of the United States. The first step was the construction in 1858 of a short railway with a very long name: the Chicago, Detroit and Canada Grand Trunk Junction Railway.

Others followed, and by the 1870s the Grand Trunk's directors realized they needed a line of their own to Chicago.

*Above:* This modern Grand Trunk Western freight seems to issue forth from the gleaming modernity of Detroit's Renaissance Center, towering in the background. The Central Vermont train shown *above right* is passing the CV's historic headquarters in St Albans, Vermont.

Two events in June 1878 convinced British managers of the Grand Trunk they would have to fight to survive in the American marketplace. Need for their own line to Chicago became a critical issue on 21 June 1878. On that date, William H Vanderbilt, son of Commodore Cornelius Vanderbilt and heir to the Commodore's $100 million New York Central empire, seized control of the Michigan Central Railroad in a Detroit stock vote. This action exposed Grand Trunk traffic moving between Detroit and Chicago to exorbitant rates imposed by Michigan Central.

Three days later, Vanderbilt unveiled another surprise. He sent a locomotive to blockade the Chicago and Lake Huron connection at Flint to deny Grand Trunk use of that line to Chicago. In dramatic fashion, Vanderbilt let the world know that he was the true owner of the Lansing-Flint 49-mile Chicago and North Eastern virtually in the middle of Chicago and Lake Huron trackage. Un-

known to the Chicago and Lake Huron owners, Vanderbilt had earlier bought $1.2 million of Chicago and North Eastern bonds in a secret deal with James M Turner, the C&NE president. Believing they controlled the Lansing-Flint connection, the surprised Chicago and Lake Huron owners discovered too late that the little Chicago and North Eastern in their midst had suddenly become a Vanderbilt viper and nearly as deadly.

Grand Trunk had little choice but to meet the rail rates imposed by Vanderbilt on the movement of its traffic. But, Grand Trunk's President Sir Henry Tyler and General Manager Joseph Hickson prepared counter-action to break the strangle-hold.

Six month after the uneasy truce set in between Grand Trunk and Vanderbilt, Hickson met secretly in Montreal with disgruntled Chicago and Lake Huron bondholders. He agreed to purchase their line. In May 1879, Sir Henry Tyler arrived in the United Sates from London and joined Hickson for a round of meetings with railroad executives and financiers.

Although Grand Trunk's interest in the Chicago and Lake Huron was rumored, Tyler and Hickson talked

about various Chicago routes and met with so many different railroad people that no one was sure of their plans.

During their whirlwind inspection tour, they rode a special Chicago and Lake Huron train from Wellsboro, Indiana to Lansing, Michigan on 5 June. Despite lengthy stops at South Bend, Cassopolis, and Battle Creek, and 12 stops for grade crossings and orders, they completed the 115-mile trip to Lansing averaging better than 40 mph. They were greeted by the mayor of Lansing and Michigan Governor Charles M Croswell before traveling to Port Huron.

On 21 June 1879, Hickson's secret December negotiations with Chicago and Lake Huron bondholders brought results. At a Detroit auction, in which Grand Trunk was the only bidder, the Port Huron-Flint section of the Chicago and Lake Huron was purchased for $300,000. A few weeks later, Grand Trunk announced bids to build its own line between Lansing and Flint by way of Corunna and Owosso.

Realizing he had been outmaneuvered, William Vanderbilt offered to sell his Lansing-Flint (Chicago and North Eastern Railroad) property to Grand Trunk. He wanted

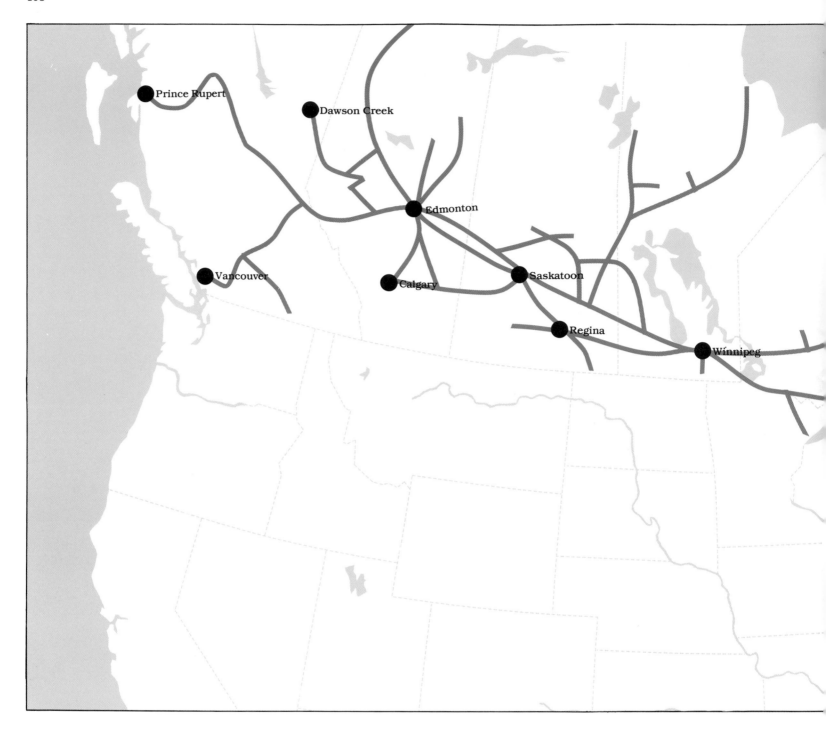

$600,000 or half the price he had paid in his secret deal to gain control. By 25 August Grand Trunk's Hickson had purchased the western section of the Chicago and Lake Huron (from Lansing to the Indiana boundary; 108 miles). This move totally isolated Vanderbilt's Lansing-Flint line. On September 3, he capitulated and sold the line to Grand Trunk for $540,000.

In London, England at the October 30 meeting of Grand Trunk Shareholder, Sir Henry Tyler said, 'The acquisition of this line to Chicago is, perhaps the most important event that has happened in the history of Grand Trunk.'

Twenty years after its formation, the Chicago and Grand Trunk Railway suffered financial difficulties and was reorganized on 22 November 1900 as Grand Trunk Western Railway.

In Canada, government officials and politicians viewed the activities and operations of railroads more closely than ever before. Railroad financial problems and overbuilding of lines demanded attention. Then, came World War I, the government's emergency use of railroads, the rise of nationalism, and serious talk of nationalizing Canadian railroads. Because of its size, the Grand Trunk Railway Company of Canada became a prime target.

Despite a desperate and bitter fight by Grand Trunk shareholders, the proud company was nationalized with other Canadian roads by passage of the Canadian National Railways Act of 1919. In 1923, Grand Trunk was consolidated into the Canadian National Railway.

Ten short-line Grand Trunk railroads, mainly in Michigan, were consolidated by Canadian National into one US railroad, Grand Trunk Western Railroad, 9 May 1928.

Although the railroad today handles many different types of goods—grain, chemicals, lumber, paper—its most important customers are automobile manufacturers.

# The Canadian National and Grand Trunk Western Routes

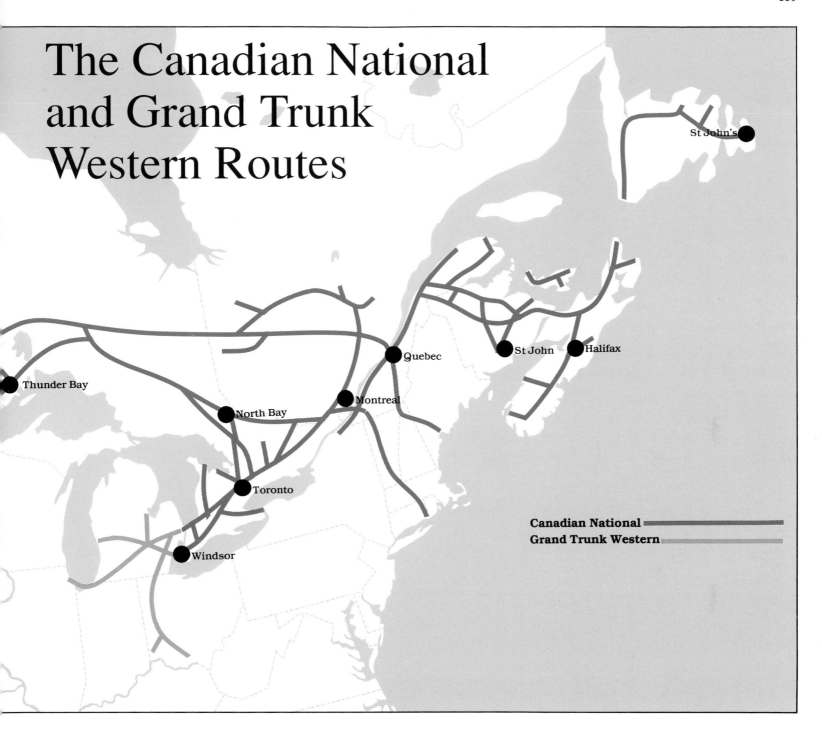

**Canadian National** ════════
**Grand Trunk Western** ════════

Thunder Bay

North Bay

Toronto

Windsor

Montreal

Quebec

St John

Halifax

St John's

Many thousands of tons of steel, plastics, and other raw materials travel to their huge plants each year. New cars and car parts are shipped by rail to car dealers all over North America and abroad. The railway's motto is 'Grand Trunk—the Good Track road.'

The Central Vermont Railway operates 375 miles of rail in the states of New York, New Hampshire, Massachusetts, Connecticut and the province of Quebec. In addition to serving shippers in its New England territory, it handles US—bound Canadian traffic from CN's eastern lines to the US rail system south of New England. It is headquartered in St Albans, Vermont.

The story of the CV goes back a long way. It was started by Vermont businessmen who needed a rail line to ship their goods to the rich markets of Montreal and New York City. The first few miles were built in 1848, only 12 years after Canada's first railway, the Champlain and St Lawrence, was opened to traffic.

*Above:* The Canadian/US trackage of the Canadian National and Grand Trunk Western rail systems. The CN operates some 22.520 miles of tracks with approximately 1830 locomotives of varying configurations. and approximately 80.690 various freight cars.

Canadian railwaymen first became involved in the CV in 1898, when the company needed more money and decided to allow the Grand Trunk to buy some of its shares. When Canadian National took over in 1923, it inherited that heavy interest in the CV. Nevertheless, the CV continued to operate officially as a separate company under its American owners.

Then, in 1927, disaster struck. Four days and nights of heavy rains and flooding wiped out almost one quarter of CV trackage. Bridges were washed away, ties and rails were twisted, broken, and scattered all over the countryside. Since the CV did not have enough money to make repairs, it looked as if the company would have to close down.

Compare the photo. *at left*. of a freight crossing the new International Railway Bridge near Niagra Falls with the vintage depiction on pages 24–25 of this text. Grand Trunk intermodal freight is shown here in some of its diversity—*at top:* piggyback truck trailers; *above:* tri-level enclosed auto trains, which, with tri-level auto parts trains, implement an important GT freight service.

It went into bankruptcy shortly afterwards, and Canadian National bought it at the subsequent auction.

Today, the CV provides CN with an important connection between Montreal and New York City. As well, it serves to link the New England towns along its route with major Canadian and American centers.

The Duluth, Winnepeg and Pacific Railway, headquartered in Wisconsin, has over 165 miles of track and handles US–bound Canadian traffic from CN's western lines to the US rail system south and east of Duluth and Superior.

Duluth, Winnipeg and Pacific is a rather strange name for this railroad. Although it originates in Duluth, Minnesota, and runs north to the Canadian border, it stops far short of Winnepeg, and never reaches the Pacific.

The original line was built in 1908 by local businessmen who wanted a fast, efficient way to ship lumber to the Great Lakes and the big cities in the midwestern states.

In 1902, William Mackenzie and Donald Mann of the Canadian Northern Railway completed their line from Lake Superior to Winnepeg. Because it ran very close to the Canada-United States border and a rail line between the two countries made good sense, Mackenzie and Mann decided to buy the DW&P and extend it south from Virginia to Duluth, and north to Fort Frances, Ontario, where it would link up with Canadian Northern.

Although the land was very rugged, the line was finished in 1912. The Canadian Northern now had access to two major ports on Lake Superior: what is now known as Thunder Bay, and Duluth.

When Canadian National took over the Canadian Northern, the Duluth, Winnipeg and Pacific came with it. Although it is not long, it is still an important railroad, providing a main link between Canada and the States.

It also has an impressive safety record. In 1986, SW&P employees achieved another outstanding year for work safety, with job-related accidents reduced by 30 percent from 1985. This qualified the railroad for the EH Harriman Memorial Silver Award for second place among Class II railroads, marking the third time in four years that DW&P earned the Silver Award, and following a Bronze Award in 1985.

CN's American railroads are important to both countries. Goods made in this country travel over their lines to reach the rich markets south of the border. And, too, their northbound trains carry many products needed by Canadians. It is a profitable exchange between good neighbours.

*At right:* A Central Vermont five-header freight passes through St Albans. *Above:* A Duluth, Winnipeg and Pacific Railway freight in Pokegama, Wisconsin. *Above right:* A train comprised, by mutual operating agreement, of CN, BN, GTW and DW&P rolling stock elements.

## The People

CN is one of the largest employers in Canada. Special training is needed to do most jobs there. Many courses and apprentice programs are offered to help employees learn new skills. However, nearly all jobs require high school education, and quite a few are open only to university graduates.

Track is built and maintained by gangs of workers. The number of people in each gang can vary depending on the size and type of job to be done. Many of the workers in each gang are skilled in operating heavy machinery. Cranes, bulldozers, graders and a variety of special types of railway equipment must be handled safely and efficiently.

The engineering department is in charge of track work. This group also builds and looks after all railway bridges, tunnels and overpasses. Experienced professional engineers are needed to design and supervise the work.

*Above:* Grand Trunk yard workers fuel one of the line's 3000hp 16-cylinder diesels—it sure ain't the family van. *At left:* Cleanliness is part of most railroads' maintenance program—if they've taken time to clean it, they've probably taken time to fix it—and the engineers like to see the world outside. *Facing page:* This loco is taking on sand, to be released on the tracks ahead of its wheels for better traction if needed.

A freight train crew is usually made up of a conductor, an engineer and a brakeman. The conductor is a bit like the captain of a ship. He has to make sure that the train is on schedule and operates safely. The conductor knows the contents, weight and destination of all the cars on the train. If any cars or packages must be left at sidings or stations along the route, he supervises their delivery.

Before each trip, the conductor is given written train orders. These orders provide special instructions on train speeds and routes. The conductor must make sure that all members of his crew know what the train orders say and obey them.

The engineer drives the locomotive. He controls the train's speed using levers, air brakes and a throttle. The engineer must obey all train order instructions. On heavy traffic lines, signal lights along the track warn the engineer if another train is approaching. Sometimes he will have to pull the train into a siding to let a faster one pass. Before starting up again, the engineer waits for a signal from the conductor.

The engineer must be very alert at all times. If the train starts or stops too quickly, the contents of the cars could be damaged.

Many railroaders start their careers as brakemen. The brakeman does many different jobs, including uncoupling and coupling cars to make up a train, setting the brakes by turning the brake wheel on each car to make sure it does not move when it is stopped, and throwing switches so that the train takes the right track.

CN Rail moves passengers trains under contract with VIA Rail Canada and provides a conductor, a locomotive engineer and as many trainmen as are needed for the size of the train. On passenger trains, the brakemen are called trainmen and wear the same style of uniforms worn by the conductor. All other employees on the train, such as porters, in dayniters or sleeping cars, and stewards and waiters, in club cars, lounges and dining cars, work for VIA Rail Canada.

One of the most important and difficult jobs on the railway is that of train dispatcher. Although the dispatcher is not on board a freight train, the train cannot run without him. The dispatcher's job is almost like an air controller's job at an airport, except that it involves controlling train movements over railway lines rather than aircraft over flight paths.

There are two different types of track on the railway. Main line routes handle many trains each day. These lines are electronically wired so that signal lights and switches can be changed automatically. Dispatchers in charge of these main lines work from a large control board. The board shows where the trains are located as they pass through the dispatcher's territory. The dispatcher can change the signal lights and switches by remote control to guide the train on its route. As well, the dispatcher can talk by radio to the engineer.

Rail lines that handle less traffic do not have the costly electronic signal and switch systems. For trains running on these tracks, the dispatcher must make out detailed written train orders which the conductor and engineer follow very carefully. If the orders need to be changed, the dispatcher contacts the engineer by radio or sends a new set of train orders to the next station along the route. As the train passes the station, the station agent hands the orders to the locomotive engineer.

Night and day the railroad yards hum with activity; trains arrive and depart and thousands of cars are sorted onto the right tracks for the next leg of their journey.

Rather than working on trains, some locomotive engineers are assigned to operate yard switching engines. This work takes skill and experience. The engineer must back his locomotive gently up to a line of cars until the lead car couples with the locomotive. The cars are then hauled away onto another track where a train is being assembled for departure.

The locomotive engineer is helped in his job by yardmen. They stand by the cars as the locomotive backs up and guide the engineer with hand signals. Each time cars are move, the yardmen must release the hand brakes. When the cars arrive at their new location, the brakes are tightened again so that the car will not start rolling on its own. As well, the yardmen change the

switches so that the locomotive can move from one track to another.

From their control towers, yardmasters oversee all activity in the yard. They know where each car should be placed and help to direct the work of the switch crews. In some larger yards, the yardmaster electronically controls the switches so that each car rolls down a hump into the right track. As well, the yardmaster has remote control over special retarder brakes on the tracks. These brakes slow the cars down so that they roll at just the right speed to couple gently with the other cars on the track.

CN Rail's training programs and facilities are among the best in North America. And the locomotive and train simulator, located at CN Rail's transportation training center in western Canada, is symbolic of the railway's sophisticated, serious approach to training. Each year, about 1000 locomotive engineers, dispatchers, mechanics and supervisors complete courses under the guidance of a full-time staff of instructors.

For maintenance-of-way crews, CN Rail has established residential training centers where employees learn how to operate mechanized equipment safely and effectively. The equipment department also conducts a training program

The single line flowing motion of Canadian National's present logo *(above opposite)* reflects the efficient operations with which the line was and is kept vital, and replaced the old CN logo *(above)* in 1961. The CN's new 100-ton pressure tank hopper car design *(below)* and 100-ton box car *(below right)* design symbolize the CN's modernity.

for apprentices in those trades related to the maintenance, repair and manufacturing of railway rolling stock.

For managerial staff, CN Rail offers a wide range of courses conducted by a cadre of specialists skilled in training techniques.

## A New Image

There came a day when the CNR was moving into the future so quickly that it felt it needed to streamline its corporate logo. The now familiar 'CN ' has been appearing in red, white, or blue since 1961, not only in Canada but around the world.

In April of 1959, Canadian National received the results of a comprehensive public attitude study based of field interviews with 4000 adult Canadians. This survey indicated that the public had a rather poor impression of CN and of the railway industry in general. Specifically, railways were regarded as being rather old-fashioned, slow to experiment with new ways of doing things and relatively unconcerned about improving their services to the public.

This study clearly showed that Canadian National was getting little public credit for its extensive modernization program. Why did the public still persist in looking upon the railway as unprogressive?

The company's public relations department decided that a large part of the answer could be summed up in the adage, 'Seeing is believing.' Canadian National had done a great deal to improve its plant, but most of the improvements were behind the scenes, largely hidden from public view. Little or nothing had been done to improve the package in which the product was sold. In its outward appearances—offices, equipment, signs, uniforms and graphics—the railway presented a drab Victorian façade, composed of countless unrelated and uncoordinated designs. What Canadian National needed was a fresh modern package to suit and do justice to its product.

There was little difficulty in deciding that what Canadian National needed was a comprehensive design program embracing every aspect of the face the company presented to the public. The objective was to develop a unified design approach aimed at giving CN a distinctive, easily recognizable identity and making it a stand-out in an increasingly complex and competitive business environment.

For these reasons, and taking into account the sort of image problem it faced, Canadian National ruled out the idea of a gradual transition and decided upon a bold and abrupt break with the past.

The Public Relations department engaged Jamas Valkus Inc of New York as a consultant to help CN organize a broad program of visual redesign, including a new corporate symbol. The task of creating the symbol itself was assigned to one of Canada's outstanding graphic designers, Allan Fleming of Toronto.

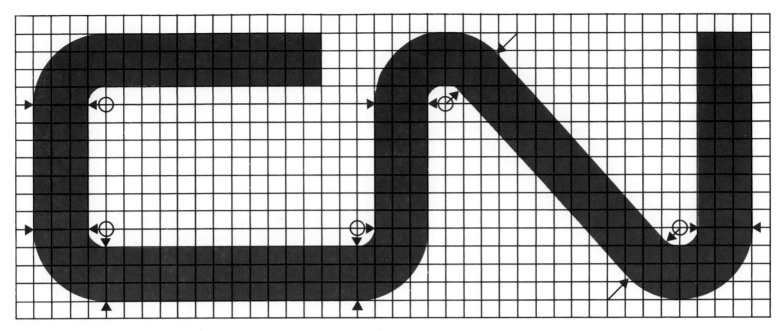

Early in 1960, the director of public relations presented the redesign proposals to the company's board of directors. The directors were unanimous and enthusiastic in their approval of the program. Then began the painstaking task of transforming the designs from a set of attractive and imaginative concepts into practical and economical realities.

The result was the now familiar symbol which spells out CN in one simple flowing line. It symbolized the one thing common to all of CN's principal activities: motion—the movement of men, materials and messages from one place to another.

Other elements in the massive face-lifting operation were to include standardized type styles, the systematic application of bright primary colours, careful attention to form and format; in short, a concern for excellence in design of everything that was to come before the public eye.

But by November it was becoming increasingly difficult to keep the lid on the story. About three weeks before the

publication date of the magazines, the Director of Public Relations received an urgent phone call from the Chief of Motive Power and Car Equipment. The latter explained that some 400 boxcars were almost ready to roll off the assembly line and that the manufacturer was asking for instructions as to how they should be painted. The cars were due to go into circulation as soon as the paint was dry.

To apply the newly approved boxcar design to this equipment order would mean that the new symbol would roll into public view—and perhaps be spotted by a newspaper photographer—in advance of the official announcement. Harris decided to take the risk, rather than have the old insignia applied to several hundred brand new cars.

It wasn't long before the lid was off. A few days before the internal publications were in the hands of employees, a photograph of one of the new boxcars appeared in a Montreal newspaper. The caption suggested that this was probably the first public glimpse of Canadian National's

*Above:* The tail end of this freight sports a caboose in a scene emblematic of the CN's industriousness amid the abundant beauty of its parent nation, Canada. *Right:* Another beauty shot—in this instance, a triple header boiling through the Redpass, Alberta area.

new trademark. It was. The press kit that was being held for later distribution was released immediately.

In other fields the design approach has had to be more durable. In working out exterior color schemes for passenger and freight trains, for example, the objective was to develop, document and distribute to all concerned a consistent design pattern that would be carefully followed for years to come.

The new paint schemes were applied on all rolling stock in accordance with normal maintenance schedules, as the locomotives and cars were shopped for their regular overhauls. New interior schemes for passenger cars have been worked out with the aim of creating a pleasant contemporary atmosphere while keeping the materials practical and durable. The old uniforms of the passenger train crews with their heavy navy-blue material and brass buttons are being replaced with lighter-weight cloth fashionably tailored in charcoal greys, bright blues and reds.

Certainly the redesign program has served to draw attention to the company in a dramatic way. Not everyone liked the new symbol when it first appeared, but at least a lot of people talked about it. Some described it as a bent paper clip, a tapeworm rampant, printed radio circuit, tortured snake and so on.

Happily, however, in this case familiarity didn't breed contempt. Acceptance of the new symbol, and some of the uses to which it began to be put, grew steadily from the outset.

The program has won a variety of major international awards for design excellence. A number of large companies, both in Canada and the United States, have come to CN for information and advice in the course of developing their own corporate identity programs.

With respect to the general public, a comprehensive study of attitudes conducted for CN by ORC International Ltd in 1966 confirmed that Canadian National had (since the 1959 findings) substantially improved its corporate image. Specifically, it had enhanced its reputation in terms of being 'progressive, efficiently run, trying to serve

*Above left:* This is the electronic train control console at Kamloops, BC, which directs freight movements between there and Jasper, Alberta. *Left:* A technician checks complex circuits at the CN Communications center in Toronto. *At top:* This Battle Creek area traffic control console serves the GTW's Chicago Division. *Above:* A technician attends a CN Communications microwave telephone service antenna.

the public well, providing job security and having good morale.'

In the seven years between the two surveys, the company had done many things to improve its plant and equipment, operating and sales methods and organizational structure. But certainly redesign was one of the key tools used in reflecting and communicating these other changes to the public.

It is the CN's belief that the new symbol stands as a visible mark of progress to remind people of the real and continuing improvements that are taking place behind the scenes in Canadian National, and that the whole visual redesign program is in fact helping to build and extend the company's reputation for providing good service and merchandising it with modern marketing methods.

## Computers and Telecommunications

Railways and computers were meant for each other. Since the CNR began using them in 1958, the company has adapted or developed specific systems to keep track of every piece of rolling stock, to operate switches and signals, and to test tracks and roadbeds. All these uses and many others were adopted in addition to normal business computerization of payroll, inventory control, customer records, and inter-office communication.

The use of modern-day electronics helps CN Rail achieve more efficiency in its operations and today the railway is one of the largest business users of computers in North America.

CN Rail's computer-based information system is one of the most advanced of any railway in the world. Called TRACS, for Traffic Reporting And Control System, it feeds information to central data banks over 299,460 miles of communications circuits.

To complement the TRACS system, CN Rail developed the Yard Inventory System. This computerized system provides yard personnel with the information they need to quickly sort incoming traffic and reassign it according to destination.

Of course, computer applications go beyond actual train movements and CN Rail today relies on computers in just about every branch of service from purchasing to employee record keeping.

Every time a Canadian makes a train or airline reservation, reads an out-of-town story in a local newspaper, listens to a weather forecast or transfers money through a bank, the information he received probably travelled over the CNCP network. CNCP was established as an independent and equal partnership between two owners—CN and Canadian Pacific Ltd.

CNCP introduced the first network designed especially for computers in 1967. It was an analog service called Broadband Exchange Service, and could also handle voice. With the development of more efficient digital technology, CNCP introduced its Infodat service for private dedicated lines in 1974.

Two years later with the development of packet switching—a method by which traffic is broken into small 'packages' for transmission across a network—CNCP introduced its Infoswitch network.

Now CNCP is preparing for the office of the future with Infotex, a new service introduced in 1981.

With the increasing use of personal computers, much of the information now handled in the form of words or figures on paper in offices will instead be generated, edited, transmitted, stored and recalled in the form of electronic signals. Infotex will make possible such services as communicating word processors, electronic mail, electronic filing systems and 'in' baskets from which executives will be able to retrieve their messages on TV-like screens at their desks, at home or with portable units while travelling.

CNCP is also involved in satellite communications and is developing, with the department of communications, new techniques for moving voice, data and video signals via Canada's Anik satellites. Trials have been carried out with fiber optics—glass fibers which can transmit signals

*At right:* A junior computer operator in Quebec retrieves computer program tapes from CN's vast computer library. *At left:* The CN Tower in Toronto, the 'World's Tallest Freestanding Structure,' is 1815 feet, five inches tall. The tower houses multimedia communications, nightclub, dining and tourist facilities whcih include various fascinating scientific and technical exhibits.

as a beam of light—to test their capabilities when laid along railway rights-of-way.

Canadian National, like several other railways, has been involved in telecommunications since its earliest days.

As railways were built across Canada, telegraph lines were strung along poles placed on the right-of-way. Primarily used to endure safe and efficient train operation, the lines also carried inter-office messages for the company. Service to the public took two forms—people could send messages in the form of telegrams and large companies could lease lines exclusively for their messages.

CN Communications today includes NorthwesTel, Terra Nova Telecommunications, CNCP Telecommunications and Telecommunications Terminal Systems. Besides being part of an integrated national network, each division has its separate use.

Through NortwesTel and Terra Nova Tel, CN provides telephone services in two of the remotest parts of Canada, the northwest including Yukon, the western Northwest Territories and northern British Columbia and rural Newfoundland, an area which includes isolated fishing communities around the coast and on off-shore islands.

In northwestern Canada, CN was given the responsibility of operating, on a commercial basis, telephone facilities which had previously been provided directly by government or military authorities.

CN took over limited facilities and invested in modern equipment to provide the latest in telephone service to such places as Inuvik, Tuktoyaktuk and Old Crow, as well as the two territorial capitals, Whitehorse and Yellowknife.

NorthwesTel, CN's northern operation has one of the most challenging jobs of any telephone company, serving an area of 14,570,000 square miles with a population of less than 70,000. Yet its digital switching equipment is among the most up-to-date in the world.

NorthwesTel is now a CN Communications arm in British Columbia, the Yukon, and the Northwest Territories. It has been expanding into the more remote reaches of these areas, and in 1985 it installed satellite communication ground stations to improve service to five communities—Pelly Bay, Spence Bay, Gjoa Haven, Fort Franklin and Telegraph Creek.

In Newfoundland, CN was made responsible for the telephone and telegraph services of the former department of posts and telegraphs following that province's entry into Confederation in 1949. Terra Nova Tel, as CN's Newfoundland telephone company is called, provides telephone service to the entire island of Newfoundland with the exception of the urbanized areas in the Avalon and Burin peninsulas, and around Corner Brook and Grand Falls. It provides telegraph and other specialized telecommunications services for the entire province.

Terra Nova Tel is the local telephone company in such coastal outports as Joe Batt's Arm and St Anthony, as well as to many of the off-shore islands. Its headquarters are in Gander, the largest urban community served.

Terra Nova Tel built the first microwave link across the island, and has an extensive network of submarine cables

to serve outports and off-shore islands. Maintaining telephone service in these rugged conditions is a challenge, and again CN has turned to solid-state and digital technology to provide reliable services.

CNCP Telecommunications is the only coast-to-coast telecommunications carrier in Canada operated under a unified management structure. Backbone of CNCP services is a coast-to-coast microwave network which carries voice, data, facsimile, broadcasting and other electronic signals.

CNCP introduced Telex service into North America in 1956, but the first recorded long-distance transmission of computer data took place over the CNCP network between Saskatoon and Toronto in 1955. Since that time CNCP has move ahead to adapt new telecommunications technology to the task of providing up-to-date service for business, industry and government departments.

Telecommunications Terminal Systems was launched in 1982 as a partnership with Canadian Pacific Limited. It deals with communications equipment. A recent venture was the launching of TTS into the large office automation equipment market during 1984.

With all its emphasis on computers and telecommunications, it is interesting that CN Communications was not

the CN division to build a structure that has been a great help to communications. It was the CN Hotels that built the CN Tower in Toronto.

## The CN Tower

When the CN Tower project was first announced, it seemed almost impossible. At the time, Toronto was reeling from the effects of a major building boom, which had dotted its skyline with monolith buildings. The highest soared a staggering 750 feet. Now CN boasted that it would build a structure more than twice that height—possibly as high as the world-leading Ostankino Tower in Moscow, maybe even higher. Toronto's ascending skyline had introduced a problem for existing communications systems. Pre-skyscraper transmission towers were simply not high enough to broadcast over the new obstacles. As a result, signal-bounce, or ghosting, was becoming increasingly severe.

Fortunately, the Tower designers had the foresight to realize that the new buildings were only the beginning. In the future, they predicted downtown buildings would grow to 1000 feet and more. As a result, the proportions for the Tower were set, with its microwave receivers at 1100 feet and its antenna topping off at the 1815 feet mark.

*Above:* Inside the CN Tower's 'Sparkles' nightclub. *At right:* The CN Tower is the apex, so to speak, of a downtown Toronto CN complex. At the base of the Tower can be seen the CN Convention Center, and CN Hotels' semi-circular L'Hôtel. The Tower's microwave equipment is housed in the 'doughnut' collar under its rotunda, which is below the Tower's long needle antenna.

Its location, at the front door of the city, also determined the need for the Tower to be more than a communications structure. It would have to be attractive. In addition, as an integral part of the populated downtown landscape, the incorporation of public facilities was assumed from the onset.

While several individuals figured prominently, no one person can be given the credit for the total design and construction of the Tower. From the initial proposal in 1968, to the final model in 1972 and eventually the Tower itself, which was completed in 1976, the project involved a consortium of experts from around the world. Initially, the plan called for three towers linked with structural bridges. Prohibited by construction and financial limitations, the design gradually evolved into a single Tower.

Because it is the first of its size and type, the CN Tower broke new ground in many of its answers to engineering challenges. No one had ever built a structure which would rise as high off the ground. Consequently, never had a foundation been devised which would bore so deeply into the ground. This in itself represented many engineering breakthroughs. First, beginning in 1972, an elaborate soil testing operation was put into effect to assess the condition of the bedrock and its reaction to changes in hydrostatic pressure. Equipped with this information, the designers developed foundation specifics which would assure the Tower's stability. On 6 February 1973, construction crews moved in. Over 62,000 tons of earth and shale were removed by giant backhoes, digging 50 feet into the ground. Next, the 22-foot thick concrete and steel foundation was erected on a base of hand- and machine-smoothed shale. When finished, the Y-shaped foundation contained 9200 cubic yards of concrete, 500 tons of reinforcing steel and 40 tons of thick, tensioning cable.

Barely four months after construction began, all was in readiness for the above-ground operation. First, 12 steel and wood brackets, weighing 350 tons had to be systematically lifted, inch by inch, up the sides of the Tower. The task required 45 hydraulic jacks and miles of steel cable. Once in place, one-fifth of a mile above the ground, workmen bolted the brackets to tensioned steel bars and placed concrete in the wooden frames. Next, a three-foot high concrete compression ring was placed around the outside edge of the brackets to make one strong unit.

Twenty-four hours a day, five days a week, concrete was poured into a massive mold or 'slipform.' As the concrete hardened, the 'slipform,' supported by a ring of climbing jacks that were powered by hydraulic pressure, moved upwards, gradually decreasing in size to produce the gracefully tapered contour. To assure its strength and quality, the concrete was mixed on the site, continuously checked and tested, then reinforced with a unique system of post-tensioning which produced a strength of 6000 pounds per square inch. The legs of the Tower are hollow, as is its hexagonal core which houses all of the electrical cables and water piping. The concrete portion of the Tower was completed in February 1974. Situated at the top of the concrete is the 'World's Highest Public Observation Gallery,' the Space Deck. All that extends above it is the 335 foot steel antenna. A two-story structure, the Space Deck was created by cantilevering a concrete platform around the top edge of the Tower. Next, from the overhang of its roof, a glass wall was suspended, banking inwards at the bottom and completely enclosing the upper story in glass. An enclosed elevator transports visitors to the glass-surrounded viewing balcony. In August 1974, work began on the seven-story Skypod which would ultimately house two observation decks.

Intrinsic to the construction of the CN Tower was the mighty crane, which over its four years of round-the-clock service lifted some 50,000 tons of material and machinery. With the completion of the Skypod, however, its usefulness also ended. Fortunately, the answer to dismantling the crane and erecting the enormous antenna came in one solution—'Olga', a giant Sikorsky helicopter. Reduced to eight sections, the crane was brought swiftly down to earth and the 39 pieces of the antenna (the heaviest weighing eight tons) were lifted into place with remarkable precision.

For many, the purpose behind the familiar donut-shaped collar at the base of the Skypod is a mystery. Technically, it is known as a radome and without its protection, the sensitive microwave dishes which receive the transmissions would be ravaged by the elements. Made of teflon-coated, fiberglass-rayon fabric, it is strong enough to hold the weight of an average adult male, yet measures a mere one-thirty-second of an inch thick. Its balloon-like shape is the result of inflating the skin to five times its normal size then maintaining constant air pressure. A second radome protects the full length of the antenna. Designed to prevent ice buildup, it's made of 11/2-inch thick glass-reinforced plastic.

In September 1973, the Tower became the tallest structure in Toronto and by January 1974, it was unrivalled in Canada. The top of the 'slipform' concrete, 1464 feet, was reached on 22 February 1974 and to that was added a special 16-foot concrete extension which would serve as a base for the transmission mast. With the placing of the 36th piece of the antenna mast, at 9:52 am on 31 March 1975, the CN Tower surpassed Moscow's Ostankino Tower to become the 'World's Tallest Freestanding Structure.' On hand to record the milestone was Ross McWhirter, then editor of the *Guinness Book of World Records*, of London, England.

During the Dedication Ceremony on 1 October 1976, presided over by Prime Minister Pierre E Trudeau, a time capsule was placed in the wall on the Indoor Observation Deck. It will be opened on 1 October 2076. Only 17

other self-supporting structures in world history have held the title tallest. At 1815 feet 5 inches, the CN Tower brought the title to Canada for the first time.

The tower has been the site of many height-related records. As a promotion for the Egg Marketing Board, Patrick Ballie, 17, of Toronto, beat the *Guinness Book* record for egg dropping by over 500 feet. He dropped a Grade A egg, unscathed, from 1120 feet into a specially-designed net, on 27 July 1979. The first person to parachute off the Tower was a member of the construction crew, Bill Eustace, aka 'Sweet William', on 9 November 1975: for his daring, he was discharged. Hollywood stuntman, Dar Robinson, made two jumps from the Level 5 of the Skypod. The first was made with a parachute on 21 September 1979, while shooting a scene for the movie 'Highpoint.' The second, which was conducted for the television show 'That's Incredible,' involved only wire cables to break the fall. To mark the Tower's fourth birthday, two mountain climbers, David Smart, 17, and Gerald Banting, 30, attempted an unauthorized climb up the outside of the Tower on 23 June 1980. They made it halfway before backing down. Once a year, the Tower's staircase are opened to the public, to raise funds for the United Way. As a rule, this is an autumn event, with climbers starting their ascent just above the main lobby and concluding at the Skypod. Many records have been set and broken at this event.

Not only is the CN Tower the tallest freestanding structure in the world but it is also probably the safest. Everything from the forces of nature to man-made disasters were considered in the formulation of its design.

The upper reaches of the Tower are continually bombarded by turbulent winds. To test the Tower's design against this and other extreme wind forces, a special 'wind tunnel,' the first of its kind in North America, was created at the University of Western Ontario. Within the tunnel, construction models of the Tower were tested under conditions which simulated the maximum wind strength based on the analysis of a 1000-year time frame. The wind speed reached in the tunnel measured 130 mph.

When plans for the Tower were concluded, their wind resistance factor was established at 260 mph. In addition to the structure, the windows of the Tower, which are armor-plated, were carefully designed for extreme wind tolerance. The outside panes are three-eighths of an inch thick and the inside panes are one fourth of an inch thick. They can withstand internal or external pressure in excess of 120 pounds per square inch. The ability of the CN Tower to wobble under extreme wind conditions was not overlooked either. Two 10-ton swinging counterweights, mounted on the antenna, ensure that the intentional sway of the Tower never exceeds acceptable levels. There's certainly not a more exceptional or perhaps safer place in the city from which to view the awesome spectacle of a raging thunderstorm.

Though the tower is struck by lightning about 60 times a year, there is never any danger. Every surface which could possibly attract lightning is attached to three copper

Despite the Tower's extreme height *(at left),* it is within 1.1 inches of absolute plumb—ie, perfectly vertical. One danger designed against in the Tower's construction was 'torsional oscillation'—the tendency of tall structures to twist with the rotational motion of the Earth, just as water twists down a sink drain. Such 'twisting,' if unprepared for, would no doubt cause a catastrophe.

*Below right:* A view of the Tower from behind L'Hôtel. in downtown Toronto. *Opposite:* CN Hotels' period-style Hotel Vancouver offers its 500 luxurious rooms amid the exquisite natural splendor of British Columbia's queen city. Complete facilities include meeting and board rooms. sumptuous restaurants and bars, and complete health and fitness facilities. *Above:* CN's elegant Château Laurier. which overlooks the Ottawa River. in Ottawa.

strips running down the Tower, connected to 42 22-foot grounding rods buried 20 feet below the surface.

To ensure against the possibility of ice or snow building up and falling to earth, every place where ice is likely to collect (such as changes in the roof contour) is ice-proofed, either with de-icing tracers or sheathed with a cling-proof plaster surface.

Fire prevention has always been a Tower priority. Smoking is not permitted on most of the public areas. All of the construction materials used were either fire-proof or fire resistant. Even the interior furnishings selected are as fireproof as possible. In the unlikely event of fire, emergency generators. located in the basement, are capable of supplying power for the elevators and other systems, including the emergency fire pumps which can pump water to the top of the Tower at a rate of 500 gallons a minute. A reservoir of water is also maintained in the Skypod itself.

Since its opening. the Tower has boasted a perfect record thanks to its carefully conceived design, interior monitoring system, and diligent security force.

Next to the Tower itself, the 'Universal Man,' a 10-foot high by 18-foot wide bronze sculpture, is one of the popular CN Tower subjects for photographers. Created by Canadian artist Gerald Gladstone, it is one of the

*Above:* The impeccable elegance of Zoé's Cafe—part of the luxurious ac-comodations of CN Hotels' Château Laurier. Château Laurier has served kings, queens and heads of state from all over the world since 1912. The elegance which is also evident in Château Laurier's French baroque Grand Ballroom *(above right)* and classically-appointed Reading Room *(lower right)* continues a tradition that began when the CN determined to build not merely adequate, but some of the finest, passenger accomodations in the world. Equally elegant, but in a different style, is the CNH Hotel Newfoundland's Cabot Club Restaurant *(below)*, in St John's. CN Hotels comprises 10 excellently-appointed hotels nationwide, with full service at each.

largest bronze castings ever made and was air-freighted from the Singer Foundry in England in nine sections.

In addition to this impressive artwork (which signifies earthbound human energies reaching towards a higher knowledge through communications), the outdoor plaza also features a mounted 1000-pound piece of the great Matterhorn mountain, which was presented to the Tower in April 1981 in conjunction with the Salute to Switzerland exhibition.

Today, both public and experts from the field of construction come to marvel at the Tower which stands as a testament to human ingenuity and achievement.

Its official owner is CN Tower Limited, a subsidiary of Canadian National and part of the CN Hotels, but few will argue when one says it really belongs to Canada. While some day, some place, someone might build a Tower higher, the significance of the CN structure and its tremendous contributions will never be diminished.

## CN Hotels

It may seem a little odd today that a transportation company should own a chain of hotels and the world's tallest self-supporting structure. Years ago, when all railways operated passenger trains, they needed to set up lodgings for travellers.

Thus railway companies such as Grand Trunk, Grand Trunk Pacific, Canadian Northern and Intercolonial, built large, elegant hotels in cities across Canada.

When CN was formed to take over these early railway companies, it naturally inherited their hotels. Many of them remain impressive landmarks, such as the Chateau Laurier in Ottawa, or beautiful, rustic Jasper Park Lodge.

# Looking Ahead

Growth can only occur where there is a willingness to change. For a company, that means adapting to the reality of the needs of its customers and owners, and of the business environment in which it operates.

When a few Montrealers established British North America's first railway a century and a half ago, they could not possibly have imagined that their efforts would lead to the remarkable company Canadians own today.

The future of CN is not entirely certain—many of its divisions are Crown corporations, of which some are cur-rently being sold off. However, in one form or another, CN and its many services can look forward to being around for a good long time.

Canadian National and Canada have come a long way together.

*Below:* CN Rail freight traffic on the move in Saint John, New Brunswick. With such special services as Dimensional Load Shipment for extra large loads (see the cylindrical items that the train on photo right, here, is carrying), and with such powerful, mechanically sophisticated modern road switchers as those in the yard shown *at right*, CN Rail is indeed ready for the future. Changes are in store, however—as always, in the history of a great railroad.

# Part Three:
# Canadian Pacific

# The CPR – A Peculiarly Canadian Institution

'Institutions, like technology, are materializations of the
fantasies of a past generation, inflicted on the present.'
Philip Slater, *The Pursuit of Loneliness*

The Canadian Pacific Railway turned Canada from a
notion into a nation.

When the last spike of the railway was driven at
Craigellachie, about 30 miles west of Revelstoke, British
Columbia, on 7 November, 1885, Canada gained a new
sense of identity and new world image.

The railway began with the vision of a politician who was
blissfully unaware of the enormous financial, physical and
political difficulties involved in tying together the scattered bits
of Canada. The terms of agreement under which Sir John A
Macdonald brought British Columbia into Confederation in
1871-72 specified:

The Government of the Dominion undertake to secure the
commencement simultaneously, within two years from the
date of union, of the construction of a railway from the
Pacific towards the Rocky Mountains, and from such point
as may be selected east of the Rocky Mountains towards
the Pacific, to connect the seaboard of British Columbia
with the railway system of Canada; and further, to secure
completion of such railway within ten years from the date
of union.

It's hard now to appreciate the sense of achievement and
pride that marked the completion of the Canadian Pacific
Railway. The railway has been called 'a national necessity,'
'the national dream,' 'the wedding band of Confederation,'
Canadian capitalism's 'proudest product' and 'The Domination of Canada on wheels.' It became a clue in a Sherlock
Holmes story, and Baroness Orczy dedicated a romantic
novel to: 'The President, Directors and all connected with that
magnificent organization . . .' E J Pratt wrote a poem entitled
*Towards the Last Spike* which had the line: 'A western
version of the Arctic daring/Romance and realism, double
dose.' Frank Underhill, a pioneer socialist, once suggested

that Canada's greatest need was for 'a moral equivalent of the
CPR.'

The railway has always had about it a touch of magnifi-
cence and majesty, a blend of rightness and righteousness.
The modest last spike ceremony ended a great endeavour on
a low key. But the plaque that marks the site of the ceremony
reads like poetry:

A nebulous dream was a reality: an iron ribbon crossed
Canada from sea to sea. Often following the footsteps of
early explorers, nearly 3000 miles of steel rail pushed
across vast prairies, cleft lofty mountain passes, twisted
through canyons, and bridged a thousand streams.

Here on Nov. 7, 1885, a plain iron spike welded East to
West.

Myth and legend cling to the railway. Walter Moberly,
searching for a pass through the mountains in 1865, shot at
an eagle's nest, and watched the birds fly into a river valley.
Eagle Pass carries the railway line through the mountains,
following the route of these birds. The Connaught Tunnel,
which carries the line through Rogers Pass, is reported to be
the home of sightless mice which live on grain spilled from the
passing hopper cars.

The railway linked the cities of eastern Canada and the
empty lands of the west in the 19th century. Then, during the
20th century, the line took people away from these lands, to
war and the cities of the east. The CPR soon became the one
Canadian institution that non-Canadians had heard about –
apart from the Mounties. Both quickly gained a reputation for
excellence, reliability and dedication to service.

To eastern Canadians, the CPR represented progress and
civilization penetrating an empty wilderness. But to
westerners, the railway soon became visible evidence of
eastern domination and exploitation. When the CPR built its

Windsor Station, Montreal, Québec 6 November 1960. The last remaining CPR steam train completes its last run. An era has ended.

line through the Crowsnest Pass into southern British Columbia at the end of the last century, it received government grants. In return, it agreed to keep the freight charges on western grain at a low rate. This 'Crow Rate' became a symbol of regional relationship, a topic of conversation on the prairies, and a fundamental element in the culture of western families. A joke tells of a prairie farmer arriving home to find his crop flattened by hail, his barn on fire, and his wife running away with the hired hand. He looks up to Heaven, and shouts; 'Goddam the CPR!'

Thus the great national venture aimed at uniting Canada soon began to divide it. As the Canadian Pacific became larger, its very success and bigness was seen as a threat by Canadians. A journalist writing a book on the Company was asked by a former mayor of Vancouver – a city created by the Canadian Pacific – whether she was going to call it *CP: Good Guys or Bad Guys?* A radical writer called his book *The CPR: A Century of Corporate Welfare.* Like many other left-wingers, he believed that the CPR should be nationalized. But he reserved his harshest criticism for officials of the government of Canada, presumably for helping the CPR to become so successful and profitable, not for the Company's officers.

The railway was built through the sort of partnership and compromise between government and the private sector that is peculiarly Canadian. Macdonald knew that the government could not build the railway to the Pacific. It had tried and failed. And the members of the Syndicate who came together to bid for the contract for the line knew that they could not carry it off alone. The CPR had to please the politicians and the public – and make a profit. So a private/government partnership developed – as did a love/hate relationship between the two parties.

Railways are more than steam and steel and balance sheets. They arouse deep emotions in people. The CPR locomotives, concrete embodiments of progress, hauling luxurious passenger trains and heavy freight trains, became a fixed feature in the lives of westerners until other transcontinental lines were completed. Then these lines went broke, and the government took them over and ran them at a loss. But the CPR steamed on.

It's still possible to catch something of what the railways meant in the past as you travel by train across the prairies. Golden and green in summer, black and white in winter, the land stretches to the endless horizon. At night, pinpoints of light mark the small communities, and a sudden flash of neon the larger ones along the railway. The grain elevators loom along the line like giant elephants asleep. On the sidings, the blue hopper cars are labelled 'Heritage Fund,' for they have been paid for by the Conservative government of Alberta. The red ones, paid for by a Liberal federal government, carry the words 'Government of Canada.' The trains bring a flash of moving light and colour into an ageless land tamed now for agriculture.

The steam train, once welcomed or feared as a harbinger of a new industrial order and way of life, has now become an object of romantic nostalgia, a reminder of the good old days.

I came from a railwayman's family, and have no nostalgia for the days of steam. My father worked as a baggage attendant at a station in Britain. He did three eight-hour shifts, on a rotating basis, so that the baggage room could be open round the clock. He had one Sunday off every three weeks. During the Second World War, he cycled to work through the air raids on Liverpool, shaking with malaria picked up during the First World War. He did not do so for love of the railway

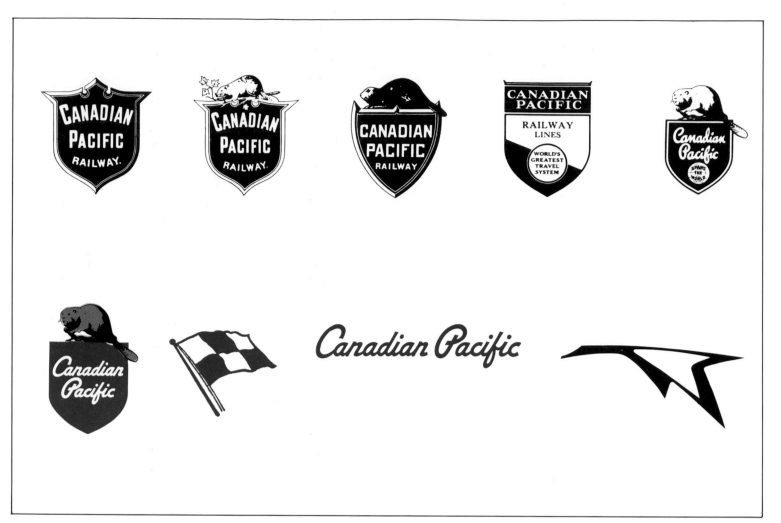

company, or for the convenience of its passengers. He did so from a sense of loyalty to his fellow-workers. He remained in the same job until he retired, never earning much money, but knowing he had a steady job and a steady wage that would support his family.

And that was the attraction for many railway workers in Canada, especially those employed by the CPR. They earned a decent wage – and enjoyed the status that came with working for a large, powerful and successful company.

Over the last two decades, the Canadian Pacific has become concerned about its image. An academic who wrote a commissioned book on the Company in 1968 stated: 'A great many attitudes towards the Company were built up in those early years of strain and difficulty which took on a life of their own and created unnecessary difficulties in later years.'

The concept of corporate culture offers a way of understanding and appreciating the story of the CPR. Those who work for a large company, like members of an isolated tribe, develop a set of attitudes, values, beliefs and expectations. The CPR began with an enormous burst of energy and idealism, fuelled by the desire to serve the national interest in Canada – and to make a profit. The Company kept growing, but as it had to run more and more transportation systems, it had to regulate its affairs to ensure that trains and ships left on time. Thus bureaucratization slowed down the initial energetic thrust. The Company had a series of strong-minded presidents who combined innovative thrusts with the ability to delegate responsibility so that things kept moving.

Like an isolated tribe, the Company has erected its monuments, created its folk heroes and spawned myths and legends. One of its viaducts near Lethbridge, Alberta, a high level steel bridge, 'straight dark line of metal drawn against the prairie sky,' has been elevated to an art object by a writer in a national newspaper. He describes the towers 'which shoulder their burden with the perfect simplicity and athletic grace characteristic of all great twentieth-century engineering.' And so they do.

This Canadian corporation came into being through the efforts of thrifty Scottish entrepreneurs and American railway builders. The labour force came from the farms of the Dakotas and Manitoba, the cities of the east – and the fields of China. Men like George Stephen, Donald Smith, William Van Horne, Sandford Fleming and others have passed into Canadian history books as prime examples of 19th century capitalists and engineers. Others who worked for the CPR remain in the shadow. Kate Reed decorated the Company's hotels with quiet elegance and good taste. Tom Wilson, a western guide, helped the early explorers, surveyors and railway builders. John Murray Gibbon did much to preserve and encourage the culture of Canada before government discovered it. And there are countless others who worked on the railway and have stories to tell.

The Company had to balance two sets of forces – those pushing it towards innovation and expansion, and those pulling it towards contraction so that its resources were not over-extended. To balance these tensions, the CPR established standards of excellence and adopted the newest technology. When it realized that big was no longer beautiful, it broke up into scores of small profit centres. It weathered the depression of the early 1980s, although some of its operations proved to be 'loss centres.' The railway continued to turn a profit when the ships and planes lost money. In the first six months of 1984, CP rail freight tonnage rose by 11.7 percent over the previous year. The profits of Canadian

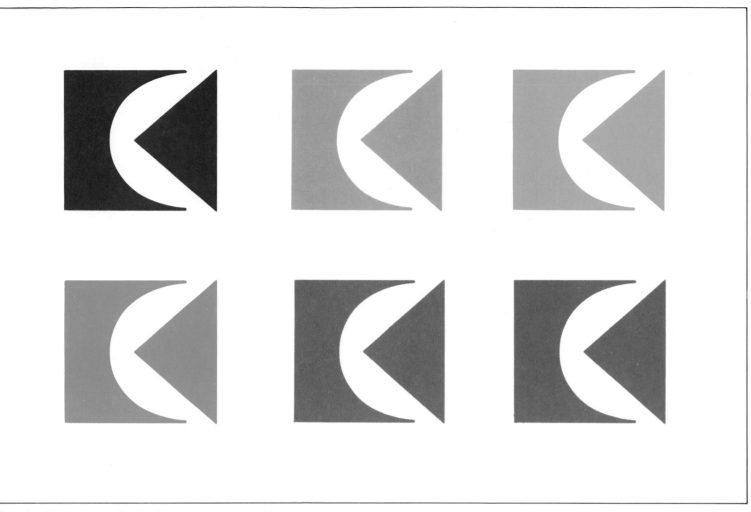

Pacific Enterprises Ltd, the organization that operates the non-transportation sections of Canadian Pacific, increased from $10.8 million in the first six months of 1983 to $125.4 million for the same period in 1984. The size of the Company's operations remains awesome. It plans to spend $7.6 billion in the 1980s.

As the government begins to see private enterprise as the saviour of Canada, the Canadian Pacific has bounced back from the recession in fighting shape. In 1983, the Company hired Donald Colussy, former president of Pan-American Airways, to run CP Air. In June 1984, the airline issued a special four-page advertising supplement headed 'Customer Service is CP Air's Ace.' Colussy was quoted as saying: 'We're looking at increased competition as an opportunity' as the government talked about deregulating the airline industry.

In the same month, Frederick Burbidge, president of the Canadian Pacific, told shareholders at the Company's annual meeting: 'Business should rely on its own initiative and stop crying for government help whenever it gets into trouble of its own making.' The Company had tried to put down a code of ethics on paper, he told another audience, and ended up with a 19 page document. Burbidge cited the head of another international company who had advised him: 'My code of conduct is very simple. Don't do anything you can't explain on television.'

Men like Stephen and Van Horne were never concerned about their image. They knew that the secret of success for any business lay in pleasing the customer.

The company they created remains a great Canadian achievement – and ranks with the world's best run and most successful businesses.

*Facing page:* The original CPR logo, adopted in July 1886, simply carried the company's name on an ornate shield. In December of the same year, the shield was simplified and the beaver was added at the top. When the logo was being developed, the Company's founders felt that the industrious beaver was symbolic of their image of Canadian Pacific.

Over the years the shield went through several permutations and ultimately became a good deal more simplified. The slogans 'World's Greatest Travel System' and 'Spans The World' were put into use during the early years of the century and were used in the Company's advertising. In both cases the slogans reflected the Company's activities in shipping and eventually aviation, as well as in railroading.

By World War II, script lettering came into use. In 1946, after World War II, the shield was further simplified to the simple red form at lower left. The red and white checked flag (originally designed by Van Horne) was adopted for the Company's steamships and the Canada Goose for Canadian Pacific Airlines (established in 1942). The Company name in script lettering was used on the sides of the Company's vehicles, from locomotives to airplanes. Several examples of this usage are seen at various places in this book.

*Above:* The Company's present, severely stylized logos were adopted amid a good deal of fanfare in 1968. They are used along with the names of the Company's six components which are set in the typeface known as Helvetica Bold Italic.

The names of the Company's various components were also shortened and stylized. The logos in the top row are red for CP Rail (formerly Canadian Pacific Railway), orange for CP Air (formerly Canadian Pacific Airlines) and green for CP Ships. The bottom row features blue for CP Transport, gray for CP Hotels and brown for the CP Telecommunications component.

This color coding carries over into the color scheme of the Company's vehicles. For example, CP Rail locomotives are usually red, CP Air airliners are usually orange and CP Transport's trucks are predominantly blue. In use on company vehicles, the triangle is usually in black within a white half-circle, with the rest of the vehicle painted the appropriate color.

(See page 89.)

# A Vision of Unity

'Many in this room will live to hear the whistle of the steam-engine in the passes of the Rocky Mountains and to make the journey from Halifax to the Pacific in five or six days.'

Joseph Howe, 1851

On 10 May 1869, a railway president swung a hammer to drive in the last spike on a railway line linking the Atlantic and Pacific Oceans – and missed. Then Leland Stanford tried again, tapping home the gold spike that linked the Union Pacific and the Central Pacific railways at Promontory Point in Utah. This small noise in the wilderness echoed through the corridors of power in London and Ottawa, making politicians there nervous about the expansion of the United States. The restless Americans, who had ceased to expend their energies in a civil war, were now heading west to open up the frontier beyond the Mississippi. British and Canadian politicians worried that the Americans, fired by their belief in 'manifest destiny,' might move north, settle the prairies and demand annexation by their government.

Canada had come into being in 1867 as a Confederation of Ontario, Quebec, New Brunswick and Nova Scotia; British Columbia remained a colonial province. Between it and Canada lay two large chunks of territory – Rupert's Land, the domain of the Hudson's Bay Company, and the North-Western Territory, a British possession. 'Canada would break off in the middle unless we linked it up with a steel rail' was how one westerner put the new nation's problem. In 1871, Canada had only 23,000 of its population of 3½ million living west of Lake Superior; wandering Indians following the buffalo, Métis creating a new society on the Red River, fur traders, gold miners, and a few restless souls occupied the empty land between the Great Lakes and the mountains. The United States had bought Alaska from Russia in 1867. If it acquired British Columbia, it would have a land link to the new territory and cut Canada off from access to the Pacific coast. If Americans also took over the prairies, the new nation would lose its hinterland.

Internal revolt as well as external domination threatened the backyard of the four provinces. In 1870, Canada acquired Rupert's Land and the North-Western Territory. In the previous year, the Métis, threatened by the expansion of settlers into their lands, had risen under Louis Riel. Sir John A Macdonald, the Prime Minister, sent the Red River Expedition under a British soldier to suppress the rebellion. But he also negotiated with the westerners, and on 15 July 1870, the province of Manitoba came into being. In the following year,

CPR conquered Canada's mountains and exposed their scenic beauty for all to see. Mt Cathedral looms over Cathedral Station in 1949.

Sir John lured British Columbia into Confederation with the promise of a railway to the Pacific.

On the same day that the sixth province joined Canada, a survey party set out from Victoria, its capital, to locate a route for the railway line. The first railway surveyors from the east had left Ottawa about five weeks earlier. In the 1850s 'Railway mania' had swept Canada, and a rash of lines had been constructed to serve local needs. In 1861, the Grand Trunk Railway, built to channel the American western trade into the St Lawrence, went bankrupt with debts of $13 million. After Confederation, Macdonald committed the federal government to completing an Intercolonial Railway to link the networks of Ontario and Quebec with those of New Brunswick and Nova Scotia. That railway opened on 15 July 1876, having cost almost twice the estimated amount.

The gold spike that completed the American interocean line bore a prayer: 'May God continue the unity of our country as this Railroad unites the two great Oceans of the World.' Macdonald knew that he could not rely on the Almighty, nor on unbridled capitalism, to build a railway to the Pacific. The construction of railway lines in the United States had been marked by graft and corruption, haste and waste. Dummy companies built the lines, and entrepreneurs skimmed off millions in government money provided for their construction. They had little interest in operating the railways. Passengers had to change trains to cross the continent, and suffered many other discomforts. When Leland Stanford drove home his last spike, three companies of infantry stood by with fixed bayonets. The Indians had resisted the railway and been subdued by force. When the trains began to run, they attacked them and attempted to lasso the iron horse.

Macdonald wanted more than just two ribbons of steel across the empty west and through the mountains. He wanted an instrument of national unity, and an opportunity to serve the needs of the British Empire.

A road from Halifax to the Fraser River had been proposed by a British writer in 1849 '. . . to link up the whole English race, and to furnish Great Britain a soil for her population and a market for her labour.' The road could be built for £150 million by convicts and Indians, with the help of local labour. In 1850, A B Richards, another British visionary, promoted the same idea in *British Redeemed and Canada Preserved*.

The arrival of Joseph Whitehead's first locomotive at Winnipeg on 9 October 1877 was a cause for celebration. The presence of a locomotive, the first one on the Canadian prairies, enabled tracklaying to begin on the Pembina Branch. The sternwheeler *Selkirk* pushed a barge laden with the locomotive, conductor's van and six flatcars. The barge is grounded against the muddy riverbank. Flags flap in the fall river breezes as the sternwheeler's crew and deckhands pose for their picture on the third flatcar, to the left of the tender. Note that the name Canadian Pacific appears on the equipment, though the CPR company was still three-and-a-half years in the future. The locomotive, the *Countess of Dufferin,* is now on display in Winnipeg.

His scheme involved using 20,000 convicts, guarded by 5000 men and aided by 6000 able-bodied paupers. Joseph Howe had visited Britain in 1850 to seek funding for a railway to link the Maritimes with Upper Canada, and come back with visions of steam whistles blowing in the Rockies and of a journey from Halifax to the Pacific of only five or six days. In 1857, an Imperial Commission inquired into the 'suitability of the colony of Canada for settlement and the advisability of constructing a transcontinental line of railway.'

The North West Transportation, Navigation and Railway Company, established in 1858, proposed to connect points in the interior with the rest of Canada, but little came of its dreams and schemes. Three years later, E W Watkins of the Grand Trunk Railway tried to secure the co-operation of the Hudson's Bay Company in building a telegraph line and a common highway between Canada and the Pacific. The idea sent one governor of the Company into hysterics; 'What! Sequester our very tap roots! Take away the fertile lands where our buffalo feed! Let in all kinds of people to squat and settle and frighten away the fur-bearing animals they don't kill and hunt. Impossible!'

By 1870, the only land link between Canada and the West was the Dawson Route, a rough wagon road built in 1870 from the head of Lake Superior to the Red River settlement to speed up the passage of troops to suppress the first Riel uprising. A few hundred settlers trickled into Manitoba along this route. But most people went west by first going south, using the American railways, and then heading north up the Red River Valley to Winnipeg.

In 1870, Macdonald wrote to T C Brydges, manager of the Grand Trunk Railway: 'It is quite evident to me from advices from Washington, that the United States Government are

142

resolved to do all they can, short of war, to get possession of the western territory, and we must take immediate and vigorous steps to counteract them. One of the first things to be done is to show unmistakeably our resolve to build the Pacific Railway.'

Macdonald had never visited the west. His promise to link British Columbia with the rest of Canada had been made in blithe ignorance of the financial and physical difficulties involved. Gold created British Columbia – and an impatient people who wanted quick action on Macdonald's promise of a railway. In other places, the transcontinental railway was being dismissed as an impossible dream. One old judge snorted that Macdonald had 'gone clean crazy . . . the next thing he will be talking about a railway to the moon . . .'

The politicians in Ottawa had received widely differing reports on the west. The British officer who led the Palliser Expedition in the late 1850s reported that the west was a desert and the Rockies impassable: 'The knowledge of the country, on the whole, would never lead me to advocate a line of communication from Canada across the continent to the Pacific, exclusively through British territory. The time has now forever gone by for effecting such an object.' Two Canadian travellers, Simon J Dawson and Henry Youle Hinds, reported more favorably about the potential of the land between the American border and the boreal forests. But the west's first truly enthusiastic supporter was John Macoun.

Macoun, a self-taught naturalist, joined Sandford Fleming's exploring party in 1872. Fleming, who had completed the survey of the Intercolonial Railway in 1869, had overall direction of the transcontinental one. Macoun applied his boundless enthusiasm and energy to its cause. He reported that Palliser's 'conclusions regarding the passes through the mountains were as accurate as his conclusions regarding the lands.' Fleming's survey located the line to the north of Lake Superior, across the northern prairies and through the Yellowhead Pass down to tidewater on the Pacific. Since most Canadian voters in British Columbia lived in and around Victoria, one route included a bridge over the Seymour Narrows to Vancouver Island, and thence to that city. Fleming estimated the cost of the railway at around $100 million.

Macdonald granted federal charters to two private companies in 1872. The Canadian Pacific Railway Company, headed by Sir Hugh Allan, a shipowner and one of the wealthiest men in Canada, consisted mainly of Montreal interests. A competing group, the Inter-Ocean Railway Company, headed by D L MacPherson and associated with the Grand Trunk Railway, also received a charter. Macdonald tried to merge the two groups, but the Toronto company objected because Allan's backers included Americans.

After the election in August 1872, from which Macdonald emerged victorious, Allan agreed to exclude the American interests. The Prime Minister promised his company a new charter, a subsidy of $30 million and 50 million acres of land. Someone then leaked correspondence revealing that Allan had given Macdonald $300,000 to help him to win the 1872 election. The 'Pacific Scandal' erupted, some of his party

abandoned Macdonald and he was forced to call another election, which he lost.

The Liberals under Alexander Mackenzie, a dour stonemason, took office in 1874. The new Prime Minister decided to build the transcontinental line in bits and pieces, linking up waterways in the west with short pieces of track. Money was short, but time was not. Mackenzie dismissed the 1881 deadline for the completion of the line to British Columbia, claiming in 1875 that '. . . all the power of men and all the money in Europe could not likely complete the Pacific railway in ten years.'

*Right:* The locomotive which started it all, CPR No 1, is lovingly maintained and displayed in Winnipeg, Manitoba. It is named *Countess of Dufferin* after the wife of the then Governor-General who was in Winnipeg on the day the locomotive arrived. In the inset, the famous locomotive is commemorated by a Canadian 32 cent stamp.

During Mackenzie's administration, work on the line continued in a desultory manner, with the government hiring contractors to build sections of track. An attempt was made to turn the Dawson route into a railway, the first sod on this part of the line being turned on 1 June 1875, near what is now the city of Thunder Bay. Rock, forest and muskeg severely hampered the railway builders as the line slowly advanced.

The first locomotive in the Canadian west arrived by barge in Winnipeg on 9 October 1877. Its owner, Joseph Whitehead, named it *Countess of Dufferin,* in honour of the wife of the Governor-General who was in the city when the barge arrived. It carried on its side the proud designation 'CPR No. 1' and the tender and the rolling stock bore the words 'Canadian Pacific.'

The vision of a transcontinental railway remained alive.

Monsignor Taché, the Catholic Archbishop of Winnipeg, wrote early in 1878 that rails had been laid 25 miles to the north and east, and an embankment completed south to Pembina. Next fall, he had been told, it would be possible to take a train from a mile from the Cathedral and reach Montreal in a few days, changing only at Chicago: 'O tempora! . . . Would you have believed it?'

Countess of Dufferin 4-4-0 type / Countess of Dufferin type 4-4-0

# The Team

'Nothing is too small to know, and nothing too big to attempt.'
William Cornelius Van Horne's maxim

In October, 1878, Macdonald and his Conservatives swept back into power.

The Prime Minister made the completion of a transcontinental railway part of his National Policy. Much more was now known about the west as a result of the railway surveys. Passes had been found through the Rockies, and red fife wheat was yielding 25 bushels an acre in Manitoba. In 1877, the irrepressible John Macoun, 'cautioned, in plain words, not to draw upon my imagination,' had written a report for the government identifying 80 million acres of arable land and 120 million acres of pasture, swamp and lakes in the west.

When Macdonald introduced his Railway Bill into Parliament in 1879, the Liberal Opposition attacked the 'road from Ocean to Ocean.' Manitoba was dismissed as 'little more than a bog or marsh.' At one point, Macoun joined in the debate from the gallery, suggesting that Opposition leader Mackenzie read his report. A royal commission on the government's attempts to build a transcontinental line reported in 1880 that the 'construction of the Canadian Pacific Railway was carried on as a Public Work at a sacrifice of money, time and efficiency.'

Macdonald, a tired man, had seen his vision of national unity divide the country and his dream of a transcontinental railway become a nightmare. He tried to interest British investors in his scheme, with no success. Then, in the spring of 1880, he received an offer from a group of Montreal entrepreneurs. It included George Stephen, president of the Bank of Montreal, R B Angus, its former general manager, Donald Smith, chief commissioner of the Hudson's Bay Company, James J Hill, a railway builder and Duncan McIntyre, who controlled the Canada Central Railway.

George Stephen, son of a carpenter, was born in north-eastern Scotland in 1829. Early in life he had been told by his mother 'that I must aim at being a thorough master of the work by which I had to get my living, and to be that I must concentrate . . . my whole energies on my work . . . to the exclusion of every other thing.' Leaving school at 14, Stephen had been apprenticed to a draper and silk mercer in Aberdeen before moving to Canada in 1850. There he became a successful entrepreneur in the dry goods, wool and cotton industries and a member of Montreal's commercial and social four hundred.

His cousin, Donald Smith, had served the Hudson's Bay Company on the coast of Labrador. In this tough training ground for traders, he had not been blinded by the Bay's traditional view of the west as a pristine wilderness for fur-bearers and Indians. He knew that the prosperity of his company and of Canada lay in peopling the prairies with settlers.

Stephen and Smith had seen how railways had opened up the American West. In the early 1870s, they had applied to build railway lines from the American border to Fort Garry, and from Prince Arthur's Landing on Lake Superior to Fort Garry.

As the Canadian economy stagnated through the 1870s, the idea of a transcontinental railway as a catalyst for development became attractive to Canadian capitalists. The *Montreal Journal of Commerce* of 19 October 1877 lamented: 'Money, floating capital, unused funds, are more abundant than ever; the cash-boxes overflow; the large banks literally sweat with gold; and this excess, this plethora of unemployed capital, causes the public funds to advance and the price of money to decrease. It is business that is wanting; it is the employment of capital that is in default . . .'

George Stephen believed that a railway would bring western wheat to the world through the ports of the St Lawrence, and take manufactured goods to the prairies to supply the settlers who would pour into this empty land. His business vision complemented the political one of Macdonald, and Stephen played the leading role in moving the Canadian Pacific Railway from an idea and a few stretches of track towards a reality.

The group (or Syndicate as it became known) had recently rescued the St Paul and Pacific Railway, which speculators, grasshoppers, unfriendly Indians and a lack of traffic had forced into receivership in the 1870s. In 1879, Stephen recalled the misery he had suffered during the ten years he had worked to secure control of the line (renamed the St Paul, Minneapolis and Manitoba Railway) and turn it into a profitable venture. But, he added, 'what maun [must] be maun be.'

*Right:* Cornelius Van Horne, a large man of large appetites, a nineteenth century capitalist of mythic proportions, was general manager of the CPR. His drive and organizing skills took CPR across the continent.

Donald Smith, who represented a Manitoba riding in Parliament, had earned Macdonald's mistrust by bolting Conservative ranks during the Pacific Scandal. Stephen bore the main burden of dealing with the Prime Minister and finding the funds to build the railway.

As negotiations over the building of the line proceeded, Stephen wrote to Macdonald that 'my friends and my enemies agree that the venture will be the ruin of us all.'

The Prime Minister needed a group of people who could operate a transcontinental line as well as building it.

The Syndicate, now enjoying profits from the St Paul, Minneapolis and Manitoba Railway, drove a hard bargain with the government, requesting a subsidy of $26.5 million and 35 acres of land. The contract with the government gave the Canadian Pacific Railway Company $25 million in cash and 25 million acres of land ('fairly fit for settlement'), exemption from taxes, and the promise that no other railway would be built south of the main line west of Lake Superior for 20 years. Introduced into Parliament on 9 December 1880, the Railway Bill became law on 15 February 1881, and the Canadian Pacific Railway charter was issued on the following day. The Syndicate put down a $1 million cheque as security, and the new company held its first meeting on 17 February 1881.

The new railway also received over 710 miles of line already contracted for or completed, including the section between Port Arthur and Selkirk, near Winnipeg; a link between Selkirk and Emerson on the American border and the section from Kamloops to Port Moody in British Columbia.

The seemingly endless prairie stretching west from Winnipeg to the foothills of the Rockies was patrolled by the North West Mounted Police. Created in 1873, this force had moved into the vacuum left when the Hudson's Bay Company gave up its lands to Canada. The Mounties brought peace to the west, evicted American whiskey traders, and made contact with the Indians. But the vanishing buffalo and the starvation years that followed made the Indians restive. No one knew how they would react to the coming of the powerful symbols of central Canadian domination. In the United States, 5000 troops had protected the first transcontinental line.

A competent American engineer, Andrew Onderdonk, had a $9.1 million contract to build 127 miles of track between Yale and Kamloops. From there the line would head northeast through the Yellowhead Pass and slice across the prairies along the route surveyed by Sandford Fleming. In all, the transcontinental line would stretch for 2600 miles between Callander and Port Moody on the Pacific, and the new company would have to build 1900 miles of this.

James Hill, short, bandy-legged, barrel-chested and one-eyed, took charge of the construction. He appointed Alpheus Stickney of the St Paul, Minneapolis and Manitoba Railway as superintendent of construction, and made Thomas A Rosser, a former Confederate general, chief engineer. He also sent Major A B Rogers to find a route through the Rockies south of the Yellowhead.

Accompanied by his brother and ten Indian packers carrying 100 pounds each, the peppery 'master of picturesque profanity' plunged into the mountains in 1881. The Company had promised that they would name the pass he found after him, and pay him a $5000 bonus. In 1882 he discovered a route through the Selkirks. When first he saw Rogers Pass, he exclaimed: 'Hell's bells, ain't that a pretty sight!'

*Facing page:* George Stephen was the first president of CPR, 1881-1888. *Above:* Donald A Smith was Stephen's cousin, a former Hudson's Bay Company trader who envisioned CPR's role in the future commerce of Canada.

In negotiations with Macdonald, the Company had stated that it 'should expect to be allowed to locate the line as we would think proper.' Hill hoped the transcontinental line would bypass the rough terrain north of Lake Superior and connect with the St Paul, Minneapolis and Manitoba Railway and a line that he controlled between St Paul and the Sault. This idea proved unpalatable to Stephen and Macdonald who wanted an all-Canadian route. Hill left the Syndicate in May 1883, swearing to build his own railway to the Pacific. He completed the Great Northern Railway, the fifth American transcontinental line, on 3 January 1893 – without a grant of land or government loan. Hill became a thorn in the Company's side, continually trying to divert traffic south of the border.

The railway generated a land boom in Winnipeg in the early 1880s, as speculators poured into town, and local people expected instant wealth from the sale of land to settlers.

Stickney and Rosser became more interested in making money from speculation than in pushing ahead with the railway. Hill invited 38-year-old William Cornelius Van Horne, General Superintendent of the Chicago, Milwaukee and St Paul Railway, to visit Winnipeg in 1881 to examine the progress of the line. When this remarkable man returned to town on Christmas Day of that year, and took over as general manager of the CPR on 2 January 1882, things began moving.

Born in 1843, Van Horne left school at 14, and became a telegraph operator. Railways, the high technology of their time, offered ambitious young men a way to the top. Railways had made Van Horne – and he made the CPR. While George Stephen retained absolute control of the Company, Van Horne took all the power he could to build the line. When completed, it was known for years as 'Van Horne's Line.'

The *Winnipeg Sun* claimed that 'Van Horne is calm and harmless-looking. So is a she-mule; and so is a buzz-saw.' David Hanna, first president of Canadian National Railways, wrote in 1926 that 'Among the Grand Trunk wise men, the enterprise that was poking its nose into the barbarian wilderness was looked upon with an almost amused toleration . . . The CPR was very much a colonial affair, don't you know – indeed with a general manager from Milwaukee, rather too Yankee an affair . . .'

But Hanna described Van Horne's approach to railway building as 'the most remarkable innovation that has happened in the business life of the Dominion . . . His vocabulary had all the certainty that belonged to the Presbyterian conception of everlasting retribution, without its restraints. He laughed at other men's impossibilities, and ordered them to be done – a dynamo run by dynamite.'

Van Horne himself dismissed sleep as merely a habit, and said: 'I eat all I can, I drink all I can, I smoke all I can, and I don't give a damn for anything.' When an engineer refused to take a locomotive across a difficult place, Van Horne ordered him out of the cab, and prepared to take the train across. The engine driver said; 'If you're not scared I guess I ain't.' Van Horne liked 'fat and bulgy' things like himself. He designed the sleeping car berths to match his girth. But he had a gentler side, collecting Japanese porcelain and French Impressionists, and played his violin in the stillness of the Rockies.

*Above:* Construction workers of the St Paul, Minneapolis & Manitoba Railway stand atop their dormitory cars. The military escort was to guard against hostile Indians.
*Right:* This historic SPM&M locomotive arrived by river barge in 1861 to run between St Paul and St Anthony.

# Across the Prairies

'The so-called Prairie Section is not prairie at all in the sense
that the Red River Valley is a prairie. The country west of
Portage la Prairie is a broken rolling country . . . it is costing us
a great deal more than the subsidy and a great deal more than
we expected.'

George Stephen to Sir John A Macdonald, 1882

George Stephen remains a shadowy figure in Canadian
history, especially in contrast to the flamboyant Van
Horne. But they got on well together, and the
American once said, 'Stephen did more work and harder
work than I did . . . I only had to spend the money, but
Stephen had to find it when nobody in the world believed [in
the railway] but ourselves.'

The political hurdles had been overcome, although British,
American and Canadian newspapers continued to snipe at
the enterprise. On 1 September 1881, the British periodical
*Truth* noted that the CPR had launched its bonds. The railway, it claimed, 'will run, if it is ever finished, through a
country frost-bound for seven or eight months of the year . . .'
British Columbia, dismissed as a 'barren, cold mountain
country that is not worth keeping,' could not be 'galvanized
into prosperity by fifty railroads.' *Truth* did not think that even
New Yorkers were 'such fools as to put their money into this
mad project.' Two years later, on 17 November 1883, the
*Wall Street Daily News* called the railway a 'Northwest
wildcat,' and its stock a 'dead skin.'

Stephen estimated the cost of the road at $45 million. To
avoid fixed charges he refused to issue mortgage bonds. To
the $25 million from the government, the Syndicate added
$6.1 million from the sale of shares to directors and others.
Stephen resigned from the Bank of Montreal in June 1881 to
devote his full time to the CPR, and to avoid any conflict of
interest, since the bank handled the land grant bonds. He
held back on a public offering of shares until the CPR had
some cash flow from sales of land, and from freight and
passengers on the completed sections of the line. The more
successful Van Horne was in laying track, the more money
Stephen had to raise. Both knew that transcontinental – not
local – traffic would generate the revenue they needed.

Van Horne promised to complete 500 miles of main line
across the prairies by the end of 1882. He almost made it. In
the spring the Red River flooded, cutting off the supply route

between Winnipeg and the United States. Railway construction had created a corps of trained men who went home each winter. Van Horne drew them into his scheme, and hired men who had come west in search of new opportunities.

The track-laying, done entirely by hand, required an efficient supply system. Van Horne hired Thomas Shaughnessy, general storekeeper of his former company, in November 1882. Aged 29, Shaughnessy arrived in Winnipeg dressed like a dandy in black felt hat, black tie, morning coat and light striped trousers – and went immediately to work. The previous government attempts at railroad building had suffered because the friends of politicians quickly stuck their noses in the trough, demanding jobs and special deals in supplying the project. Shaughnessy, as general purchasing agent, soon showed that only 'price, quality and rapidity of delivery' mattered to him. No one, not even friends of directors, received special consideration. Shaughnessy also showed great skill in keeping creditors at bay when the line ran out of money.

In February 1882 a contract for the 675 miles from Oak Lake in western Manitoba to the end of the prairie section at the Bow River near Calgary was awarded to Shepard and Company of St Paul.

The work went astonishingly well. The railway route was located and staked by CPR surveyors and engineers. Then construction crews graded the line, prepared the roadbed, laid the ties and hammered home the spikes that held the rails

*Above:* The famed 'tracklaying machine' is shown in use, possibly on the Algoma Branch. Later it was used on the main line west of Sudbury.
*Below:* Flimsy, non-standard construction marked this timber trestle near the Lake of the Woods. When CPR took over the Lakehead-Winnipeg section in 1881-83, these were replaced with earth fills.

The way of life of the Plains tribes was altered forever by the building of the transcontinental railroads. The bones of buffalo (an animal once a major part of the Indian lifestyle) were used by white men as fertilizer. The bones are being loaded into a CPR boxcar near Moose Jaw, Saskatchewan, in the late 1880s.

in place. The grade stayed above ground level to keep it snow free. Construction depots at 100-mile intervals held material and supplies to be sorted and forwarded in train lots. Steel rails came from the Krupp works in Germany and from England, tamarack ties from the forests of the Lake of the Woods. Crews erected stations at eight-mile intervals. One group would frame the building, the next enclose it, and the third plaster and paint it. Four or five identical stations were built at one time, and no community could boast that it had a better one than its neighbour. Telegraph lines paralleled the railway, and soon the chatter of the Morse key joined the other prairie noises. Division points at 125-mile intervals allowed for crew and locomotive changes, and for refuelling.

Every town wanted a water tank – 'to make the place look busier,' one westerner claimed. The CPR's 'Flying Wing' followed the contractor's crews, to ensure that everything was up to the standards set by Van Horne.

Grading ended on 13 November when the frost came, but track-laying went on until the end of the year. By that time, the crews had built 419.86 miles of main line, 28 miles of sidings, and a 100-mile branch line in Manitoba. By early October, trains were running to Pile of Bones, on Wascana Creek, later to be known as Regina, capital of the Northwest Territories. Van Horne, an avid gardener, realized the value

of the buffalo bones that strewed the prairies. They had been left by the Indians to ensure the return of the great beasts. Van Horne paid the Indians, Métis and settlers $4.50 to $5 a ton to collect them and sold them in the east as fertilizer.

Early in 1883, Langdon and Shepherd, railway contractors, ran advertisements offering wages of $1.50 a day with board at $4.50 a week for 'good, able-bodied, steady men' to build the railway. They were asked to 'apply on the work at end of track, now near Cypress Hills, about 600 miles west of Winnipeg.' Track-laying began on 18 April 1883. On 48 consecutive working days – Sunday was the only day of rest – crews laid an average of 3.46 miles of track a day. On two days, they laid over six miles.

The railway brought in settlers who sought to buy land

On a perfect summer day Locomotive No 14 puffs across the vast prairie. This still is from the CBC documentary drama 'National Dream.'

cheaply. In Winnipeg, citizens held 'indignation meetings' to protest the high price for lots being charged by the Canada North West Land Company, the selling agent for government and CPR land. As the track approached Moose Jaw, James H Ross and three others homesteaded on a nearby bluff in January 1882. The others soon sold out, but Ross remained to become the largest landlord in the new community created by the railway. In the summer of 1882, the Company raised money by selling five million acres of its land in 47 townsites to the Canada North West land company at $2.70 an acre, for a total of $13.5 million. Controlling interest in the land company belonged to Donald Smith, British aristocrats, and eastern Canadian capitalists. They resold the land at $6 an acre, payable over six years at 6 percent interest. Land in the

Moose Jaw townsite went for $30 an acre – half the profits went to the CPR. At that time, the community consisted of frame buildings and tents. The wind blew through cracks in the walls of the first church, the post office was a packing crate near the station, and the stench from dead horses worked to death by contractors pervaded the town when the wind blew in the wrong direction.

Whores and gamblers flocked to the construction camps to alleviate the monotony of life there. The sale of liquor was forbidden in the Northwest Territories, and the Mounties strove valiantly to stamp out bootleggers, hampered by their number and ingenuity and their own need for strong drink to relieve the monotony of policing the plains. On 1 January 1883, Van Horne wrote to NWMP Commissioner Irvine: 'On no great work within my knowledge where so many men have been employed has such perfect order prevailed.'

The Indians gave little trouble, although they unnerved the crews by silently watching them at work. When the Cree chief Piapot and his people pitched their tents on the right of way in 1882, a Mountie pulled out his watch and gave them 15 minutes to move. When they refused, he kicked down the center pole of Piapot's tent, then did the same to the other lodges. Father Albert Lacombe, an Oblate missionary whom the Indians trusted, averted trouble when the track encroached on the Blackfoot reservation at Gleichen in July 1883. Later Van Horne entertained the chief and the priest in his private railway car, giving each a lifetime pass on the railway. One story claims that he also made Father Lacombe president of the line for an hour for his services. Like other CPR legends, this one grew with the telling. One version claims that the priest promptly ordered that all materials for his mission henceforth be carried free, and also issued himself two lifetime passes. Even if this incident did not happen, it illustrates how the CPR was viewed as it moved into the west. If it threatened traditional ways of life, it could also be the source of riches for those who knew how to manipulate it.

Turner Bone, a Scottish CPR engineer, recalled in later life how he travelled west on a freight train in 1883, on a car loaded with telegraph poles: 'I quite enjoyed the novelty of the ride.' He stumbled off the train at night to be met by a CPR night watchman who took him to the Royal Hotel, 'a large marquee tent.' At that time, the construction crews were 12 miles beyond Medicine Hat. In his eighties, Bone could 'still picture the busy scene, and . . . hear the clang of the rails as they were dropped on the ties.' End of track 'was something more than the point to which the track had been laid. It was a real live community, a hive of industry' in an empty land. In late June, the temperature soared to 107°F, then plunged to 58°F as a storm swept through the camp on 2 July. Everything blew down. Dry sand from the sidings filled the air, and ripped the tracings of plans from the work tables.

The rails reached Calgary on 13 August 1883.

By the time the Indians had ceased to be a menace and had become tourist attractions. Every visitor wanted to photograph them, but they would cover up their faces or demand money. Commissioner Irvine reported in 1883 that 'the Indians were so kept in subjection that no opposition of any moment [to the railway] was encountered from them.' Piapot had styled himself 'Lord of Heaven and Earth.' A photograph of him later in life shows him dressed in a blanket coat, cradling a rifle, baring his teeth in a half-grin, half-snarl. This picture was sold to tourists who had come to see the wonders of the railway and of the west. On the stock of the rifle appear the words: 'Pi-a-Pot copyrighted J A Brock, Brandon.'

# Along Lake Superior

'Two hundred miles of engineering impossibility.'
William Cornelius Van Horne

Van Horne had no illusions about the difficulties of building the 650-mile line across the Laurentian Shield between Callander and Port Arthur. Hard old rocks thrust south to meet the waters of Lake Superior, offering no hope of settlement or of local traffic. This land, untraveled by whites, offered little to sustain life. Twisted rocks, numerous lakes, short, fast streams and thick forests strewn with windfalls made passage on foot difficult. Bitterly cold in winter, the land turned into a morass of swamp and muskeg in summer when the heat and the mosquitoes, no-see-ums and other pests tormented men and beasts.

The only advantage the stretch along Lake Superior offered was the possibility of supply by water. In 1883 the CPR bought the *Champion No. 2* – its first shipping venture.

Turner Bone noted that this wilderness did not deter George Middleton who surveyed the Lake Superior section for the CPR. He took only a brush and comb and an extra pair of socks in his pocket when he traveled: 'He told me that he made no written report on that survey, but had just gone to Van Horne and told him all about it.'

The line between Winnipeg and Port Arthur, built under government contract, had been completed on 17 June 1882. Poorly sited and badly ballasted, the tracks had begun to show wear and tear in the following year, with rails becoming bent and worn. Sidings, stations, freight sheds, yards and engine facilities had not been built. The Company took over the line in May 1883, and received just under $1 million from the government to bring it up to standard. The first scheduled passenger train between Port Arthur and Winnipeg ran on 10 June, and Van Horne began to negotiate for the construction of elevators at the head of the lake.

The shoddy work slowed down traffic, as the CPR upgraded the line. In September the track near Oxdrift sank into the ground, requiring piles to be driven 135 feet into the muck to support it. In November, a trestle collapsed under an eastbound grain train. Then an iron bridge failed. Forest fires burned down telegraph poles and consumed ties during that hot summer.

Van Horne marshalled 12,000 men, 5000 horses and 300 dog teams in 1883-1884 to build the section round Lake Superior. He tried to ensure that the men were well fed, but encountered problems in keeping the demon drink out of the

*Above:* A curving section of fill crosses Jack Fish Bay. This particularly difficult section of track, including a tunnel, cost $700,000 to build.

*Below:* A construction camp on Lake Superior's north shore lies just to the left of the route. The hard-working navvies have already cut down trees and cleared brush.

*Above:* Five navvies pose in front of their tents in a construction camp north of Lake Superior. The man seated has a mournful expression, no doubt, because the bottle he holds is empty.

*Opposite:* The navvies at the left are actors in the CBC epic 'National Dream.'

camps. The Ontario government, eager to cash in on the construction boom, issued liquor licenses to traders – but did not set up any system of controlling the resulting excesses.

John Macoun visited the north shore of Lake Superior with his son in the summer of 1884. 'Tormented by flies,' he walked towards a cutting just as the workmen set off an explosion. They retreated to a shanty, which Macoun did not reach in time. But 'no stones came near me,' he reported. Macoun found that the 'whisky pedlars were so bad that they had disorganized the whole work on the line.' At one camp, a half-drunken teamster objected to young Macoun's appearance. When Macoun reproved him, the man 'immediately pulled out a pistol and swore he would blow my brains out.' The naturalist had been appointed magistrate for the County of Hastings, but had no jurisdiction on the north shore. But 'being a good temperance advocate, I was easily pressed and swore in two special constables who immediately went to work and confiscated all the whisky in the camp and around it, and took the owners prisoners.'

It's easy to understand why men sought escape in drink. Railway construction created a new Canadian class, the 'bunkhouse men,' who lived in dank dwellings, slept on straw mattresses and ate salt pork, beans, molasses, potatoes, oatmeal, tea and bread. At times even these ran short because of poor organization and careless contractors. In May 1884, 300 men at one camp had only three-quarters of a barrel of flour, a week's supply of pork, and no sugar, beans or other foodstuffs.

Work proceeded slowly in 1883. By the end of the year, the end of track lay ten miles west of Sudbury.

In mid-March, 1884, Van Horne received a 'special informal report' from an inspecting engineer. 'Men are plentiful, but the supply of horses and plant is utterly inadequate to the work or "portaging" and grading,' it said. Nor were there enough dump cars, wheelbarrows, drills, picks and shovels. Van Horne induced James Worthington, who had built only 130 miles of new railway during the three years he had supervised construction, to retire. On 1 May 1884, Harry Abbott took charge of building the line west of Sudbury. After his first inspection trip, Abbott reported that he had found everything 'in worse condition than I had anticipated.' It took his train 4½ hours to cover 22 miles. Abbott increased the maintenance crews, doubled the work force building a trestle and checked the food supplies. He also found that 'liquor sellers are becoming troublesome.'

*Left:* CPR workers overlook their handiwork, Morrison's Cut, in 1884. This area was built as part of Ogilvie's Jack Fish Contract.
*Right:* The excavation of the Mink Tunnel was serviced by three narrow-gauge tracks for quarry cars hauled by draft animals.

The navvies began to encounter rock where soil had been expected as the line moved towards the Pic River where it drained into Lake Superior. In places, seemingly solid sections of the line collapsed under trains, and had to be rerouted. Elsewhere, these sink holes had to be filled with rock.

Money began to run short. John Ross, building the section east of Nipigon, used masonry where Van Horne believed that timber and fill would serve just as well. Trains could travel at slow speeds for two or three years until more solid structures could be built to replace any temporary works, he argued. Storm waters on Lake Superior licked away the rock banks constructed to support the line and other works. Tunnels had to be hacked through the granite where it lined the lakeshore. Dynamite cost $7.5 million, and three miles of track near Jack Fish, $1.2 million.

By mid-March 1885, only five gaps totalling 98 miles remained between Port Arthur and Sudbury.

But the cost of this 'national link' had strained the Company's resources, and almost pushed it into receivership. The CPR had spent $56,695,377 up to 31 December 1883, of which it had raised $37,377,151, the rest coming from government subsidies and land sales. The line generated some revenue, but its most costly sections along Lake Superior and through the western mountains drained its cash resources.

This steam shovel was built by the Bucyrus Steam Shovel Manufacturing Company of Bucyrus, Ohio. It is shown here working in a ballast pit.

CP in the building

164

The western land boom collapsed in 1883, and a severe frost ravaged the prairie crops in September. Manitobans hated the CPR for its high freight rates and its monopoly. The market for railway securities had been damaged when the Northern Pacific went into receivership, and an economic depression still gripped Canada. Stephen needed hard cash to keep construction moving. Macdonald hoped that a government dividend guarantee for CPR stock would rescue the company.

Rather unwisely, Van Horne had told the *Montreal Star:* 'The CPR has never estimated the cost of any work. It has not had time for that . . . If we haven't got enough, we will get more, that's all about it.'

Liberal leader Edward Blake quoted these words in the House of Commons in February 1884 as the financial plight of the railway worsened. Macdonald introduced a railway relief bill that provided a $22.5 million loan to the railway, and it became law on 6 March. But Stephen had mortgaged the line to secure this money. On 19 July the Prime Minister informed him that he 'must not look for any more legislative assistance for the CPR', but rather 'work out your own salvation.' According to one story, John Henry Pope, acting Minister of Railways, told Macdonald: 'The day after the Canadian Pacific busts, the Conservative party busts the day after,' and this thought must have tortured the aging prime minister as the costs of the line escalated through 1884.

On 9 February 1885 Stephen wrote to Macdonald, pointing out that he and Donald Smith had endorsed a five months' note for $1 million to keep the Company operating, adding: 'I venture to say that what Smith and I have done and are doing individually, is simply absurd on any kind of business grounds. I venture to say that there is not a business man in all of Canada, knowing the facts, but would say we were a couple of fools for our pains.' Treasury officials had even made an inventory of Stephen's assets – including the china and household linen in his Montreal mansion – and Van Horne and senior staff took a 20 percent pay cut.

Macdonald, tired and beset by provinces demanding help for their railways, did not dare to try to convince his cabinet that just one more infusion of cash would save the CPR. In mid-March, Stephen proposed to the government that it turn

*Above:* A view of the newly-laid main line at Jack Fish Tunnel in the spring of 1885. The new tracks were unballasted, but troop trains, moving at 5 mph, passed here moving troops to suppress the Northwest Rebellion.
*Above left:* A newly-excavated rock cut north of Lake Superior.

its $35 million in unissued CPR shares into first mortgage bonds – and let the Company have $5 million immediately. The cabinet rejected the plan, and Stephen sent a sad little note to Macdonald lamenting the demise of their dream. On 17 March 1885, Sir John wrote to Charles Tupper: 'How it will end God knows – but I wish I were well out of it.'

But when Senator Frank Smith, an influential Conservative, championed Stephen's cause, the cabinet agreed to give the funding idea further consideration.

Then a western radical saved the capitalists.

On the day that Stephen wrote his note, the second Riel rebellion erupted – sparked in part by the arrival of the railway in the west and its impact on the lives of the Métis. Many of these people had moved west from Manitoba into

the Northwest Territories, settling on the North Saskatchewan River. The CPR destroyed their transportation system, the hated surveyors moved over the land, and a remote and incompetent bureaucracy delayed their acquisition of land.

This time, Riel had with him Gabriel Dumont, an able guerrilla leader. In March 1885 the rebels cut the telegraph wires at Batoche, their headquarters south of Prince Albert. A force of Mounties and militia sent to put down the rebellion suffered a defeat by Dumont at Duck Lake. The Indians attacked a mission and forced the Mounties to abandon Fort Pitt.

The federal government did not have enough troops in the west to suppress the rebellion. The Mounties formed a thin red line across the prairies, and a handful of them had to contain a strike in the Rockies on 1 April.

But Canada did have a railway line to the west.

Van Horne promised to move troops to Qu'appelle, the station nearest the uprising, in 11 days. He bent his organizing genius and the resources of the railway to this task. Troops marched or sleighed over the 89 mile gap in the line, travelling on flatcars where no coaches were available before speeding across the prairies.

The CPR saved itself by saving the west.

Even before the Riel Rebellion collapsed at the Battle of Batoche on 9 May, Macdonald had announced a bill to assist the CPR. The last of the missing links in the Lake Superior section was closed. Van Horne even organized a last spike ceremony on the shore of Jack Fish Bay on 16 May for Lieutenant Colonel Oswald, one of the commanders of the troops. The victorious soldiers returned home all the way by rail, singing the praises of the CPR.

The bill to aid the CPR cleared the House on 10 July.

On 16 November 1885, nine days after the final last spike was driven in the Rockies, Louis Riel died on the gallows in Regina. Van Horne claimed that 'in simple gratitude, the Company ought to erect a monument to Riel as its greatest benefactor.'

# Through the Rockies

'Have no means of paying wages, pay car can't be sent out, and unless we get immediate relief we must stop. Please inform Premier and Finance Minister. Do not blame me if an immediate and most serious catastrophe happens.'
Van Horne to Donald Smith, 15 April 1885

Van Horne's wire to Smith indicates how taut nerves had become in the spring of 1885. Crews were working from west and east to complete the line through the western mountains. Andrew Onderdonk and his men drove in from Yale, the head of navigation of the Fraser River. The mountain section started at Calgary. From here James Ross, the CPR's manager of construction, pushed the track through the mountains towards the line moving from the coast.

A blast of dynamite at Yale on 14 May 1980 had made known the start of construction of the western part of the line.

Three mountain chains lie between tidewater and Calgary. A profile of the line drawn by the CPR in 1886 shows the long slope from the prairies into the Rockies, reaching a summit at 5296 feet. Then the profile plunges sharply below the Kicking Horse Pass to the valley of the Columbia River. The Selkirk Mountains, pierced by Rogers Pass at 4300 feet, appear as a single pyramid, and then the line drops steeply again to the Columbia Range and Eagle Pass at just under 2000 feet.

Sandford Fleming and his party barely averaged three miles a day on the survey through these mountains. Dripping rain from bushes and branches soaked them, devil's club clawed at them, fallen trees tripped them, and they had to cross patches of skunk cabbage – 'acres of stinking perfection.' And all around loomed the mountains, magnificent and menacing, cutting off the sun as the men stumbled through the valleys.

Fleming had selected the Yellowhead Pass through the Selkirks. But 'Hell's Bells' Rogers had located the more southerly pass named for him. It looked like a good idea at the time to take the line through Rogers Pass. A Scottish elder once remarked, 'The fact is that if the good Lord had not bored through the mountains with rivers, there is not enough money in the Empire to build to the coast.' This pious sense of certainty about the divine order kept men like Stephen and Van Horne going when the money ran out and the physical obstacles seemed unsurmountable.

The track followed some of the river valleys the Good Lord had provided. But the line had to be notched into the sheer face of canyon walls, pushed through rock, and carried on spider's web trestles across rivers. The grade had to be kept at 2.2 percent, a drop or rise of 116 feet in a mile.

Andrew Onderdonk, under the government contract, used a mixed force of Chinese, Americans and Canadians to carve the line through the coastal mountains. From Yale the line followed the west bank of the Fraser River, crossed it, then headed inland along the Thompson. Onderdonk used the Caribou Road to supply the line, and took his sternwheeler *Skuzzy* through Hell Gate for use on the Upper Fraser and Thompson. One hundred and fifty of 'Onderdonk's Lambs' – the Chinese workers – hauled the vessel upriver against the current. The Chinese had been employed in railroad construction in the United States, and came to Canada from there and in batches from China as contract labourers. Earning a pittance, living on rice and salmon, meticulously clean, they dreamed of a return home or of a new life in the 'gold mountain.' The Chinese did most of the heavy rock work, while the whites did the easier timber work, cutting trees and building trestles. The workers carved fifteen tunnels along the lower Fraser. In February 1882 Onderdonk turned his crews around and began the line between Yale and Port Moody at tidewater. The last spike on this section was driven on 22 January 1884.

The local press blew hot and cold about the new railroad – an indicator of the ambivalence that Canadians would develop towards this new national institution. While complaining that the $5.50 fare between Port Moody and Yale was thrice that for the same distance in England, the *Port Moody Gazette* also wrote about the 'iron horse' bounding over the Fraser and taking Lytton by storm.

By the end of 1884, Onderdonk's men had pushed the line to Savona, heading towards the old Hudson's Bay Company post at Kamloops, and the lakes in the shadow of the Selkirks. The government-built section of the line had a rickety look to it. A tunnel through a mud cliff collapsed, so the line was run around it on trestles. The *Port Moody Gazette* complained on

*Right:* Onderdonk's crews work in the forested lower Fraser Valley in 1883. The railroad ties, piled on flatcars, are being unloaded and carried forward on the shoulders of the tracklayers.

*Above:* On the original transcontinental railway there was no structure which surpassed the Mountain Creek Bridge in the Selkirks. Constructed of more than two million board feet of timber, it was 164 feet high and 1086 feet long. In its own way it was a thing of beauty.
Left I Another view of the towering bridge; Locomotive No 132 pauses with its cars extending back past mid-span. Another locomotive can be seen to the right at the far end of the bridge.

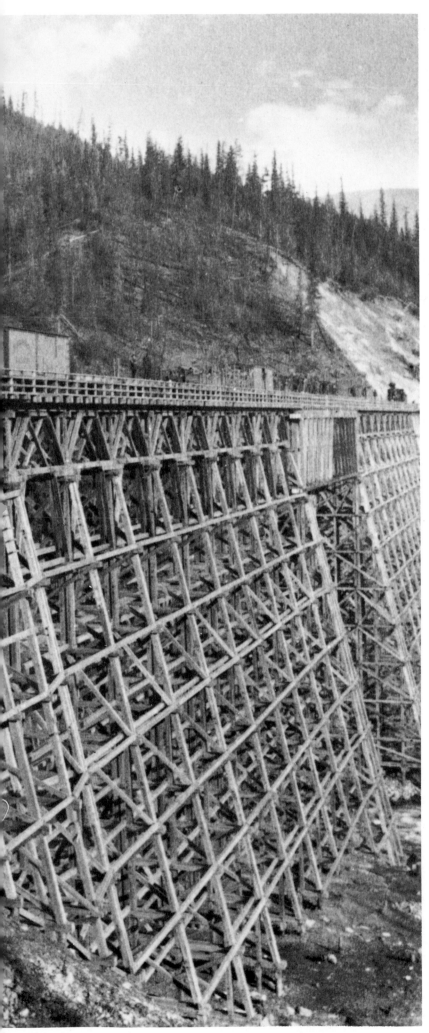

6 September that 'along the line you will see signs of the stupidity and want of engineering skill that are always visible on railroads where death comes without warning.' Van Horne, himself bent on cutting every corner to conserve the CPR's scarce funds, described the truss bridges on this section as the 'worst I ever saw in a railway.'

The CPR crews building the line from Calgary through the Rockies had a sense of high adventure about the project. Turner Bone had travelled to the tent town of Calgary in 1883 on a train which had 'rolled and pitched like a ship in a choppy sea.' He laid out and superintended the construction of a round house and a turntable, then encountered the power of the conductor and the emerging bureaucratization of the CPR. He'd put his stuff on a flatcar, but the train did not move. The conductor was 'waiting for orders,' the usual answer 'given by the conductor of a construction train which might be waiting – for no apparent reason – at a siding when anyone ventured the remark: "What are we waiting for?" '

The Indians thought the 'crazy white men' were driving stakes in the ground to find their way back – and played a trick on them by pulling them up.

One of these crazy white men in Bone's crew started to drag a survey chain across a frozen lake. The ice gave way, but he ploughed on and smashed his way to the opposite shore. The five men engineering crews received 125 pounds of bacon, 65 pounds of ham and 30 pounds of oatmeal and other food to last them a month. Itinerant photographers wandered along the line, and two clergymen ministered to the spiritual needs of the men. Bone mentions a contractor named Isaacs, a hotel owner from Niagara Falls with no experience in railway building. He ran a popular camp – 'everything had to be neat and tidy. No rubbish lying around.'

Men constantly arrived to work on the road. Bob Woods, known as Dago Driver, 'marshalled them at HQ' and took them out to the camps. He was 'like a general in command of an army, riding along the tote road with his company.' Bone relished the life in the mountains. He missed the 'rhythmic sound of the tumbling waters of the Kicking Horse River' when his camp moved to Golden, and had difficulty sleeping

Workers halt their labors on a timber retaining wall near Eleven Shed in Rogers Pass. Note that this is the era before specially-designed work clothes, and the workers wear old conventional clothing. Due to a prevalent fear of sunstroke, all the men are wearing hats.

*Above:* A cut was made through the nose of Sailor Bar Bluff, 7 miles above Yale. The navvies are dwarfed by this huge rock outcropping.

*Left:* This photograph shows one of six tunnels that were to be constructed in the Cherry Creek bluffs. The south shore of Kamloops Lake was a region of deep coves which were marked by these rocky buttresses.

*Left inset:* A pile-driver operated by Onderdonk's men is at work on the trestle over the Nocola River in 1884. In the background can be seen the barren hills of the upper Thompson Valley.

near the quiet waters of the Columbia. At Christmas, 1884, the crew, which had become 'just like members of one large family,' ended their party with a shout of 'Hurrah for the CPR.'

Bone, an engineer who had walked the three miles back and forth to school at the age of seven, typified the hardy men who saw in the building of the CPR the moral equivalent of war. Taking the line through the mountains set man against nature in a titanic struggle. The Reverend R G MacBeth knew many of the railway men and claims that these contractors 'did not, by any means, always make money. But . . . very few of the contractors or engineers cared for the money end of it in any case. They felt that they were engaged in a work of

*Left:* Eagle Pass, British Columbia, on 7 November 1885, about 9:20 am. Honorable Donald A Smith, later Lord Strathcona and Mount Royal, faces the camera as he prepares to drive the ordinary iron spike completing the Canadian Pacific Railway transcontinental main line between the Atlantic and the Pacific Oceans.
*Below:* Donald A Smith drives home the last spike. To his left is Stanford Fleming (white beard and top hat). To his right stands William C Van Horne (black beard and bowler hat). Just out of sight to the left stands Major Rogers: his Scottish hat rests on the tie to the left of the spike. The youth behind Smith is Edward Mallandaine.

significance, not only to Canada and the Empire, but to the world, and that was an inspiration worth while.'

Those like Bone who were employed by the CPR enjoyed the benefits of being skilled specialists in a large, dynamic company. The contracted labour had a much tougher time, and these largely illiterate men left few records of their life on the line. Melchior Eberts fell to his death above Kamloops Lake in 1881. But most of those who died building the line remain nameless. Such men were buried in the mountains under a cross bearing the words 'Died on the Railroad.'

Morley Roberts, a man of education, wrote a song: 'Some of us are bums, some of us are farmers.' But all, he claimed, were 'jolly fellows.' The crews drilled, blasted, broke up stones and smoothed the way for the coming of the rails. In the mountains, they worked on three benches, the safest being at the top where no stones and other debris showered down from above. Day began with breakfast, then the foreman shouted 'Hook up!' The men worked for five hours before 'unhooking' for dinner and then put in another five hours work, often in rain and mud in a gloomy river valley. The contractors and the bosses lived above the huddle of tents and shacks that housed the labourers.

MacBeth caught the essence of the work when he wrote: 'In the grey half light of early morning . . . but little imagination would have been needed to believe that dimly-seen forms which peopled the rocky river banks were the advance guard of an army making its laborious way towards some naturally fortified stronghold.'

Sam Steele, in charge of the Mounties on the CPR line in the mountains, had a less romantic view of the work. With a few men he had to protect the work crews from the gamblers and the crooks who arrived at the camps to fleece the unwary. Forbidding the sale of liquor for ten miles on each side of the line did not prevent the flow of booze to the crews. The Mounties had also to intercede on behalf of the men when sub-contractors did not pay their wages. On 1 April 1885, when the CPR ran out of money and the navvies struck, Steele pleaded with their leaders to be patient. As Turner Bone put it: 'It was not a strike in the ordinary meaning of that word.' The money was needed to support homesteads in Manitoba, Minnesota and Dakota. When the strikers tried to stop tracklaying, Steele rose from his sick bed and threatened to fire on the mob approaching his police post. But he also brought the workers' plight to the attention of the government.

The line reached the British Columbia border on 25 May 1884, and the first station beyond it was named Stephen. By July, a tote road reached the Columbia at Golden, and grading was well under way along the difficult stretch of line bordering the Kicking Horse River which dropped steeply down towards the Columbia. Between Hector and Field, seven miles apart in a direct line, the road descended 1141 feet. The gradient of the track down the 'Big Hill' exceeded 4 percent, but Van Horne explained this was only a 'temporary measure.' Uphill spur lines on to which trains could be run to slow them down were built. Four locomotives hauled short freight trains uphill during the first years of operation. Westbound freights arrived with smoking wheels as engineers clamped on the brakes to slow their descent.

The Selkirks trapped the moisture laden clouds as they moved east, blanketing the slopes with snow. Avalanches and snow slides roared down the mountains at speeds as high as 200 mph. James Ross wrote to Van Horne on 19 February 1885: 'The men are frightened. I find the snowslides on the

*Above:* Revelstoke, British Columbia, was reached by the CPR through the tireless efforts of many men.

*Left:* A ballast train pulled by a former Virginia & Truckee locomotive approaches the south portal of Tunnel No 4, two miles above Yale. This is a typical steep-sided river valley of glacial origin.

Selkirks are much more serious than I anticipated, and I think are quite beyond your ideas of their magnitude and danger to the line.' Seven men had been buried under slides, and two had died.

Ross built the line beyond Rogers Pass to avoid the avalanche slopes and steep grades, using a series of trestles to create 'The Loop.' A peak named after him broods over this part of the line. Then Ross took the line through Eagle Pass in the Columbia (or Monashee) Mountains, and met Onderdonk's men coming from the west.

The final last spike was driven on 7 November 1885 at Craigellachie.

In Canada's most famous photograph, Donald Smith taps the spike home at 9:22 am Pacific time. Sandford Fleming, with a square white beard, stares four square into the camera. He had invented Standard Time after missing a train in Ireland, and this method of marking the hours would prove invaluable in running the railway of which he had been so much a part. Van Horne, hands in pocket, stomach well out front, looks on benignly. The last spike, he had said, would be 'just as good an iron one as there is between Montreal and Vancouver and anyone who wants to see it driven will have to pay full fare.'

As Smith bends to hit the spike – he bent it on the first try – a confident 17-year-old casually cocks his head behind him. That boy, Edward Mallandaine, had wanted to fight Indians.

Instead, he had gone into business for himself, running a freighting service to supply the railway. Mallandaine died in Creston, BC, in 1951. The triumph of the last spike that linked Canada together seems almost near enough to touch at times.

After it was driven, the cry went up: 'All aboard for the Pacific!' Sam Steele attended the ceremony, then rode from Kamloops to the sea in Onderdonk's private car. The train raced through tunnels at 57 mph, 'our short car whirling around the sharp curves like the tail of a kite.' By the time dinner was served, Steele was one of only three people unafflicted by 'train sickness.' He wrote: 'I think this was one of the wildest rides by rail that any of us had taken, and was, to say the least of it, dangerous.' On the following day, a train rushed out of the tunnel towards a trestle on which stood a handcart loaded with section hands. They jumped off, clung to the edge of the bridge, and watched the train smash their cart into the river below.

Turner Bone did not see the last spike driven. He and his crew packed up, and got ready to leave on a work train. It chugged down the line towards them – and passed the group without stopping.

The excitement and the enthusiasm of the construction phase – and the sheer, hard, backbreaking work and worry that had gone into it – had become part of Canada's history and image. The act that brought the CPR into being stated: 'And the Company shall thereafter and for ever efficiently maintain, work and run the Canadian Pacific Railway.'

Now the Company began to grow into a national force almost as strong as government and to rouse in Canadians that sense of ambiguity about its activities that persists to this day.

# Spreading the Net:

## 1885-1896

'The CPR, though it had connected with the Pacific Ocean, was like a poor man with a large and growing family, who finds his boys pushing their legs through their breeches faster than he can conveniently cover them . . .'

David Hanna, *Trains of Recollection,* 1926

Although Van Horne claimed during the last spike ceremony that 'the work [had] been done well in every way' the railway had many rickety and dangerous places.

One earlier traveller reported that his train has been stopped by a blizzard. He had been put in a common coach, although he had sleeping car tickets. At Banff the only food available was cheese and crackers. Rocks came through the windows and forest fires licked at the coaches as they passed through the Rockies. In the winter of 1885-1886, avalanches roared down the mountain slopes, closing the line. And the winter snows proved to be a major problem over the years, despite the work of men stationed in the mountains charged with ensuring that the trains got through on time.

When Van Horne took over as chairman and president in 1888, he set about making the line a first class transcontinental railway, building feeder lines, upgrading the track, and ordering locomotives and rolling stock. He also established the CPR style of management, combining efficiency and frugality during a period of economic recession.

Within a year of the last spike being driven, the CPR had cleared its debt with the government. The Syndicate also gained control of the Canada Central Railway, extended it to Ottawa and Callander, and ran its tracks into Toronto and Montreal. Between 1885 and 1890, the CPR moved into the Maritimes, assembling and building the 'Short Line' from Montreal through Maine to tidewater at Saint John. Windsor, Detroit, Duluth and St Paul were tied into the expanding network. Short eastern Canadian lines that made no economic sense – or money – became part of a national system that turned a profit. Out west, 'the CPR had everything . . . and, as a natural process . . . gobbled everything in the way of feeders and rivals . . .' as David Hanna put it. But, he added, 'every sane Canadian is proud of the CPR.'

This pride found expression in the reception the first transcontinental train received as it travelled across Canada. The

The original station at Port Arthur, Ontario in 1884 or 1885, constructed of unfinished pine. Well-dressed townspeople wait for the train to pull in. Others, perhaps having nothing better to do, pass the time of day.

special poster that trumpeted the departure shouted in red 'Our Own Line.' In smaller print, at the bottom of the poster, were spelled out the benefits of the new line – 'No Customs,' 'No Delays,' 'No Transfers.'

Promptly at 8 pm on 28 June 1886, as the Montreal Garrison Artillery fired a salute, the *Pacific Express* eased out of the station. A fractured coupler delayed its departure from Ottawa by two hours. At Carleton Place the express connected with the train from Toronto which had departed that city without a demonstration.

Residents turned out in full force at stations along the line and were allowed to inspect the luxurious diners and sleepers. From its beginnings, the CPR sought to create an aura of luxury and comfort, touched with a hint of imperial grandeur and exoticism, around its passenger cars. Dining cars carried the names of British royal palaces, sleeping cars those of remote and romantic cities like Honolulu and Yokohama. No expense was spared to maintain this aura: The silver service in *Holyrood* cost $3000.

At Sudbury Junction some well-dressed, good-looking girls greeted the train; evergreens and inscriptions such as *Vive La Confédération* decorated the station. At Winnipeg, the train received a salvo of artillery. The city now had a population of 20,238, but much of the nearby prairie re-

*Right:* A CPR water tower is pictured near Fife, British Columbia.

mained empty and unsettled because of marshes and the activities of speculators. The train sped through green pastures and wheat fields to Brandon, with its population of 2348. The railway had created this town. Many of the lonely stations on the prairies would become the nuclei of new communities, dependent on the railway for their lives. The locomotive had to be replaced just beyond Broadview, so passengers strolled on the prairie, organized foot races and picked wild flowers – 'a jolly break in our ride across the plains,' as one passenger put it.

At the station named after him, passengers met Crowfoot. They presented him with a speech, passed the hat, and handed him a few dollars 'for the trouble he had taken in accepting our invitation' and went on their way through the Rockies. These mountains impressed and overawed the first travellers as they would all future ones. The train passed gangs of Chinese: At one camp, their cook took one look at

the passengers and then went on preparing a meal. The people of Victoria came to Port Moody to greet the train on its arrival there on 4 July. It had taken 139 hours to travel 2892.6 miles – and arrived on time.

The second *Atlantic Express,* which left Port Moody on 7 July, passed through blazing forests and valleys down which strong winds blew during an exceptionally hot summer. Derailed by a toppling wood pile, the cars caught fire. This disaster, and other minor derailments and collisions, did little to dampen the enthusiasm of early train travellers. And they helped to build an *esprit de corps* among railroaders as they learned to work together as part of a vast national system. The west had begun to wake up. By 1886, 163,000 people lived in Manitoba and the North-West Territories. Despite poor economic conditions, a sense of excitement suffused the air and the new railway enhanced it, heightening feelings of national unity and of a shared destiny.

*Below:* This picture was taken on the occasion of the arrival of the first Canadian train from the Atlantic to the Pacific at Port Arthur, Ontario, 30 June 1886.

*Above right:* A typical small town scene with octagonal water tower and station building. This is East Coulee, Alberta, as photographed by Stan Stiles in June 1969.

Sir John A Macdonald left Ottawa on a special train on 9 July. He'd expected to be looking down on his railway 'from another sphere,' he said, adding: 'My friends in the Opposition kindly suggested that I would more likely be looking up from below.' He had, however, 'seen both friends and foes travelling over the road.' Lady Agnes Macdonald had already become an enthusiastic supporter of the railway after travelling on the uncompleted line to the Rockies in late 1885. She had been thrilled by 'the most interesting and delightful trip I ever made in my life.' She caught the enthusiasm of an age when she wrote to a friend:

What astonished me was the comfort and ease of the railway, its strict punctuality, its quiet and prompt management and its little motion. We read, played cards, wrote letters, all generally with great ease and this on a line far away in an almost uninhabited country and in the depths of a Canadian winter.

She also noted the contrast between the two Canadas that the railway now joined together:

Ottawa seems so dull and tame and stupid and *old* after that new wonderful western world with its breadth and length and clear air and wonderfully exhilerating atmosphere that always seems to lure me on.

The title of a book published in 1872, *The Great Lone Land,* caught the essence of the west at that time. In 1886, the *Lethbridge News* reported that an American had referred to this region as 'God's Country.'

The remarkable Lady Macdonald wanted her fill of this new land, and chose an unusual way to see it. She sat on a box secured to the cow catcher when she travelled west with her husband in 1886. Through Kicking Horse Pass, down the Big Hill, across Rogers Pass and on to Port Moody she went. 'Every possible sense of fear is lost in wonder and delight,' she wrote in an article in *Murray's Magazine.* Spring water sprayed the train in a 'wet' tunnel, so Lady Macdonald doffed her bonnet and put up an umbrella. Then she rode, unafraid, through the Fraser valley, 'black with wild rugged rocks, and awful with immense shadows.'

Lady Macdonald provided Van Horne with the sort of publicity for the line that money could not buy. In 1882, the CPR had net earnings of about $400,000. By 1885, these had risen to almost $2.4 million. Railway mileage expanded from 3998 miles in 1885 to 6476 in 1896, and the line was continually improved and well maintained. In 1890, over 200 wooden bridges were replaced by permanent structures, and an equal number built in 1891. A photograph from 1894 shows a section hand setting out on an inspection trip in a boat after heavy rains flooded the track.

The Company made money any and every way it could.

Van Horne had a vision of Vancouver in 1884 as 'a great city there with steel tracks carrying endless trains of freight and passengers, an all-year port with fleets of vessels trading with the world.' The Company received 6000 acres in government land grants in 1885; its townsite covered much of what is now the city's central business district. A plaque at the corner of Hastings and Hamilton streets in downtown Vancouver states: 'Here stood Hamilton. First Land Commissioner. Canadian Pacific Railway. 1885. In the silent solitude of the primeval forest. He drove a wooden stake in the earth and commenced to measure an empty land into the streets of Vancouver.' When Turner Bone visited the townsite in the following year he saw only 'burned stumps.' A careless CPR slash clearing crew set fire to the primeval forest, and destroyed the infant settlement and the older townsite of Granville.

The first transcontinental train reached Vancouver on 23 May 1887, decked out with a picture of Queen Victoria on the smokestack. At that time, the city had a population of only 2000, but by the following year the Company had made $868,000 from land sales in the new community.

In 1886, trains began to cross Canada with tea from China and Japan. Then came the silk trains that delivered silk from Japan to New York in 13 days. These once-famous trains, dull-painted and windowless, had priority over all others, and flashed from Vancouver to Montreal in 80 hours. When the prairies yielded a bumper harvest in 1891 and labour became scarce, the CPR advertised for workers, offering transportation from any station in Ontario to the west for $15, and harvest specials began to run in July.

To westerners, and especially to Manitobans who had an elected government, the new railway proved to be a mixed blessing. In his 1923 *History of the Canadian Pacific Railway,* Harold Innis wrote that the completion of the main line was a 'significant landmark in the spread of civilization throughout Canada.' But, he added, 'western Canada has paid for the development of Canadian nationality.' The Manitoba legislature passed several bills to give charters to other railways to build lines, only to see them disallowed by the federal government. Thus were they constantly reminded of the power of the CPR and of their own lack of control over their own destiny. In the east, competition kept freight rates reasonable. But the CPR seemed bent on making every cent it could from its operations, and the monopoly clause in the government contract caused endless discontent among westerners. In vain did the Company plead that it had recognized a 'moral obligation' and spent $6.7 million on branch lines south of Winnipeg. By the end of 1887, George Stephen had become the most unpopular man in the west, with Van Horne running a close second. But Van Horne calmly noted that when Winnipegers burned Sir George in effigy, one mattress sufficed while it required two to do him justice.

Under political pressure, the federal government cancelled the Company's monopoly clause on 18 April 1888. But it guaranteed payment of interest on a new CPR bond issue of up to $15 million. In the fall of that year, another company built a line between Winnipeg and the border and then had the temerity to build a feeder line across the CPR track. The 'Battle of Fort Whyte' ensued as CPR crews ripped up the crossing and were confronted by the government's special constables and militia. A standoff ended with the replacement of the crossing, but the Company tended to treat any threat of competition as *lesé-majesté* rather than as an attempt to serve the travelling public through better service and lower rates.

Van Horne, knighted in 1894, set the tone of the CPR when he upbraided a trainman who had argued with an irritable and unreasonable passenger:

You are not to consider your own feelings when you are dealing with these people. You should not have any. You are the road's while you are on duty; your reply is the road's: and the road's first law is courtesy.

Thirty-one snowsheds were built between Bear Creek and Ross Peak sidings. This view shows the complex structure of timbers which was necessary to protect the tracks from the enormous snowdrifts. Without snowsheds, winter passage would have been impossible. The project, begun in 1886, took two seasons to complete.

# The Golden Years:

## 1897-1918

'We are not paupers. We can build the Crows Nest line without Governmental assistance if we see fit. But in view of what the Company has tried to do towards building up the interests of this country it is disappointing, to say the least, to be treated as a public enemy or a public menace.'

William Cornelius Van Horne, 1897

In 1893, a financial panic swept Canada. In that year, Van Horne wrote to his solicitor: 'The present times are the worst I have ever experienced, and I can see no sign of the better.' During the early 1890s, incomes and the price of wheat and other commodities on the prairies remained low.

But the railway continued to pay dividends. And it expanded its network. As mines opened in southeastern British Columbia, the CPR saw the danger of their output moving south of the border. James Hill built his Kaslo and Slocan line to carry ores to Kootenay Lake. From there, steamers took them to Bonner's Ferry, Idaho, the railhead of Hill's Great Northern Railway. The CPR leased and completed a 37-mile line, the Naksup and Slocan Railway, in 1894, to serve the mines in the Kootenay. The Company built a station and freight shed at Sandon. On 16 December, 1895, a special 'K & S' train drew into Sandon, carrying men hired by James Hill. They levelled the new freight shed, wrecked a trestle, pulled down the station and dumped it into a nearby creek.

The CPR had considered linking southeastern British Columbia with Fort Macleod to the east in 1889. In 1896, Laurier's Liberals came to power, and soon realized how vital to the nation's economy, especially in the west, the Company had become. Clifford Sifton, the Manitoban Minister of the Interior, believed that a railway from the Kootenay to the prairies had to be built to make 'every miner in British Columbia . . . a customer of the merchants of Winnipeg, Toronto and Montreal. Then we shall have taken one major step towards securing Canada for the Canadians.'

The CPR received a subsidy of $11,000 a mile to build the 182-mile line from Lethbridge to Kootenay Lake. It also agreed to cut its freight rates on the prairies. The Crowsnest Pass Agreement, passed on 29 June 1897, initially worked no hardship on the Company. When the rates bit into profits after the First World War, the CPR tried to raise them, with little success. For western farmers considered the 'Crow Rate' as unchangeable as the mountains through which the new line ran. The 1899 rates for grain, one half cent per ton mile,

*Above:* Between trains at the CPR station at Ottawa, Ontario in 1899. The pace slows down briefly near midday. Cabs await their next fare. Note the two shop girls taking a break by the side door.

*Below:* A grimy locomotive No 931, a 4-6-0, takes a breather near Brandon. Five hundred and two of these workhorse engines served with CPR and remained on the roster until 1960, the end of the steam era.

*Below:* Colonist sleeping cars are stopped in the Glacier House station, British Columbia. Snowsheds can be seen in the distance.
*Right:* CPR locomotives No 5760 and 5920 puff through the wooded hills and mountains east of Golden, British Columbia.

*Above:* Lord Shaughnessey was CPR's president and chairman of the board.
*Far right:* The Ten-Wheeler type 4-6-0 has to be the 'typical' CPR steam locomotive. Also called 'D-10,' built between 1905 and 1915, these sturdy, reliable engines formed the backbone of the CPR freight locomotive fleet.
*Below:* The CPR station at Lethbridge, Alberta, was quiet on a day in 1899. Note that the hand car at left appears to be loaded with baggage.

still held in 1982. The railways' loss in 1981-82 came to $641.1 million because of the 'Crow Rate.'

The exploitation of the workers who built the railway through the Crowsnest Pass led to a House of Commons enquiry. One man earned $387 for a year's work – and kept only $5.10 after contractors deducted expenses. Wages were fixed in camps, and men forbidden to leave – or even to talk at work in some places.

The depression began to lift in late 1896. In the following year, the Company's land sales doubled. George Stephen had recognized that a railway needed a populated west. As early as 1881, the Company stationed a land agent in London, and located a Land Commissioner in Winnipeg. A letter by Stephen in the London *Times* of 1 March 1883, suggested settling 10,000 Irish farmers in the northwest. In that year 100,000 immigrants had moved into the west, but no flood of newcomers followed the completion of the line. Droughts, early frosts, floods, grasshoppers and Riel scared them away. And there was plenty of free land left south of the border. Through the 1880s and early 1890s, a few people trickled into the Canadian west from Eastern Canada and the United States. In 1892, William Saunders developed Marquis Wheat, greatly extending the range of grain growing and the 'last best west' began to boom.

Van Horne told shareholders in 1898 that 'practically no mistakes have been made in the development of the system as far as we have gone.' He retired as president in the next year, handing over to Thomas Shaughnessy, a quiet man who expanded the CPR as Canada's economy boomed. In 1893, James Hill had completed the Great Northern, and the CPR had competition for freight. But the Company's land

policy began to pay off, and the CPR had the whole west to itself. CPR land went for $2.50 an acre, with a rebate of half of this if it came under cultivation in three to four years. The Company set up model farms, sent settlers back to their homelands to tell of the bounty and promise of the west, and toured display cars filled with crops around the country. In 1904, a large-scale irrigation scheme covering 220,000 acres began near Calgary. Wheat acreage almost tripled between 1905 and 1915. The railway also pioneered the use of film to promote development and issued pamphlets about the west in 40 languages. The federal government also launched a massive advertising campaign during these golden years, and it may be that many people say the Company as an agent of the government – or *vice versa*.

The railway provided steady income for immigrants as they struggled to establish themselves, and helped them to identify with their new country. D E MacIntyre, a Montrealer, supervised a gang of 30 Doukhobors in 1904 as they worked in a foot or two of cold water, straightening old rails and trimming them so that they could be relaid on branch lines and sidings. MacIntyre wrote:

> Every morning at about 10 o'clock, the CPR's crack passenger train, No. 1, appeared in the far distance. Standing on a rail pile [the Doukhobors] watched as it grew larger and larger. Then, when it was directly opposite us, it gave a long blow on its bull-throated whistle and the Douks as one man would stop and say 'Number One,' which was about all the English they knew.

The CPR strove valiantly to be all things to all people during the golden years between the end of the century and the close of the First World War. MacIntyre recalls the Company erecting tents and supplying cooking and sanitary facilities to immigrants stranded at a washed-out bridge in Saskatchewan. A burning trestle halted a train on Lake Superior. Some stubborn people refused to walk across the gap, claiming they'd paid to ride. Railroaders carried them over to the waiting train.

Other workers were less enchanted with the CPR, claiming that it paid low wages for long hours and operated in a feudal manner. The 'running trades' – engineers, conductors, firemen and trainmen, the aristocracy of the line – had a separate union which concentrated on gaining insurance and other benefits. The 'non-operating employees' made up the bulk of the labour force, caring for the track, the rolling stock, the stations and the passengers. At first, separate unions among these groups of workers came into being. In 1901, the Brotherhood of Maintenance of Way Employees organized a nationwide walkout and succeeded in raising their daily rate for a ten hour day from $1.25 to $1.50. Unions won minor concessions from the Company whose managers often fired those who joined them.

In November 1908 the Canadian Brotherhood of Railway Employees came into being in Moncton, and tried to obtain an agreement with the CPR. As the union's official history puts it: 'The Canadian Pacific management, from the very start, adopted a bitterly hostile attitude towards the Brotherhood.' They wanted only a union they could control. The Company fired members of the new union, and debarred clerical staff from joining it, 'because confidential records and reports might become public property.' A 1910 strike by CPR machinists for better working conditions failed. But on 4

*Below:* Joseph W Heckman took this photograph of the old wooden station at Sudbury Junction, Ontario around 1900. Note that the 'Sudbury Jct' sign above the Dominion Express Co door gives the distances to Montreal and Vancouver.
*Right:* The Sudbury station in 1915 was made of stone, replacing the previous wooden building.

November 1912, the Brotherhood organized a walkout as the grain traffic reached a peak. The strike forced the federal Minister of Labour to set up a board of conciliation so that disputes between workers and managers could be referred to a third party. The union called off the strike in January 1913.

Unionization disturbed the growth of the Company very little as it strode to greatness. The CPR had realized an Imperial dream – 'the all-red route to the Orient' – with its ships on the Pacific. In 1899 the crack new *Imperial Limited* linked Montreal and Vancouver in 100 hours. Luxurious hotels contributed to Company profits. The Scottish-baronial style of buildings favoured for the Chateau Frontenac in Quebec City, the Empress Hotel in Victoria and 'Windsor Castle,' the railway headquarters in Montreal, projected a solid image that hinted of noble origins.

An enterprising American decided to share the railway's wealth. Bill Miner stopped a CPR train near Mission, BC, on 10 September 1904, stole $7000 and lived quietly in nearby Princeton for two years, well liked by all. In 1906 he held up another train with the help of two companions, but found only $15 and a bottle of liver pills in the safe. This time he was caught, and the Grey Fox went to the British Columbia penitentiary but escaped over the border in 1907.

An anecdote from 1908 illustrates the style of the CPR. Charles Gordon, secretary to Thomas Shaughnessy, stuck a two cent stamp on an envelope, made an error, and threw the envelope away. Donald Smith came into the office, saw the envelope, retrieved it, and lifted off the unused two cent stamp. He slapped it down in front of Gordon, saying, 'That's not how we built the CPR.'

In 1882, the line had carried 388,785 passengers. By 1890, this number had risen to 2,685,730. In 1899, the CPR logged 1.373 *billion* passenger miles. Many passengers were tourists from Britain and the United States, come to see the wonders of the railway and the Rockies. Van Horne quickly grasped the tourist potential of his railway. The mountains that had made life so miserable for surveyors and construction crews became objects of romantic admiration when seen through the windows of one of the CPR's first class cars.

*Left:* This Joseph W Heckman photograph shows the CPR station at Winnipeg, Manitoba in August, 1899 as seen from the west.
*Below:* This Pacific type 4-6-2 was photographed at Calgary, Alberta in July 1946. The type was first produced after the turn of the century for use in New Zealand.

This view of the old and new stations in Québec City, Québec, taken in 1916, shows a contrast in size and architectural style.

'Since we can't export the scenery,' said Van Horne as he began to market the landscape, 'we'll import the tourists.'

Macdonald had stopped at the hot springs at Banff on his way home in 1886, and became a wilderness enthusiast. In June 1887 Parliament passed an act creating the 260-square-mile Rocky Mountain park to preserve the hot springs and the surrounding area.

Van Horne went on a promotional binge, designing some unusual advertising slogans to attract the right kind of tourists. 'How High We Live,' said the Duke to the Prince, 'on the Canadian Pacific Railway' linked aristocracy, good living and the Company. The first CPR pamphlet, issued in 1886, reproduced an article by the Marquis of Lorne, the former Governor-General. It claimed: 'Nowhere can finer scenery be enjoyed from the window of a car than upon this line.' The CPR built a hotel in Banff that stands out in the Bow Valley like a miniature mountain range, erected other hotels that resembled Swiss chalets, and imported guides to match, invited Edward Whymper, the famous mountaineer, to Canada, and issued a pamphlet on fishing and shooting that went into 30 editions. When the Bow River washed out the track in June 1894, local guide Tom Wilson suggested that the stranded passengers be entertained by the Indians. Thus began the annual Banff Indian days.

With wheat being exported by the railway from the prairies and tourists being imported into the Rockies, the CPR generated large profits. Net earnings rose from $12,230,165.49 in 1899 to $46,245,740.15 in 1913.

An American wrote in the late 1890s: 'Indeed I can say *Eureka* (I have found it), the gem of all my travel in four continents.' Another traveller asked if the picturesque glacier on the nearby mountain was real – or had it been put there by the CPR?

If the mountains attracted visitors they also created problems as crews, rotary and side plows worked to clear the winter's snow, and locomotives struggled to haul freight trains up the Big Hill. Between 1885 and 1911, avalanches killed over 200 people. Thirty-one snowsheds had been built along a 12-mile stretch in Rogers Pass. On 1 February 1899 a slide wiped out the station there, killing seven people. On 4 March 1910, as a crew cleared one snow slide, another overwhelmed them, burying and killing 62 people. In 1913, the Company began construction of the longest railway tunnel in Canada to bypass Rogers Pass. When completed in December 1916, the five-mile long Connaught Tunnel eliminated ten miles of hazards.

The war ended the Company's golden years. Never again would it dominate the west as it did during that time. In 1913, it carried 15,480,934 people. During the First World War, trains carried troops to the Atlantic ports – and contingents of Chinese labourers to support the armies in France and Flanders. CPR management and workers went into uniform and organized the railways there to supply the war fronts.

The CPR carried away to war the men of Walhacin, an Indian word for 'land of plenty.' They had irrigated land near Kamloops and made it fruitful. Storms destroyed the flumes while they were at war, and the town died.

On 11 September 1915, Van Horne died.

*Saskatchewan,* the car that carried the railway builder to Craigellachie 30 years earlier, formed part of his funeral train.

And on that day, every wheel on the CPR stopped for five minutes.

When they began to roll again, they moved into a very different and much more competitive world than the one in which Van Horne and Shaughnessy had nurtured and expanded the CPR.

*Below and facing page:* Indians show off their finery for Banff Indian Days held near CPR's Banff Springs Hotel.

World-renowned for its breathtaking location, the Banff Springs is by far CPR's most famous hotel.

*Overleaf:* Matthew Park photographed Canadian Expeditionary Force troops ready to entrain at Calgary in 1915.

# Competition
## and the
# Depression Years:
## 1918-1939

'The shareholders and Directors of the Company have always been impressed with the idea that the interests of the Company are intimately connected with those of the Dominion, and no effort or expense has been spared to help in promoting the development of the whole continent.'

Lord Shaughnessy,
President and Chairman of the Board, 1918.

The dreamers and doers who built and ran the CPR during the high tide of Empire risked much – and gained much. George Stephen, Donald Smith, William Van Horne retired wealthy and laden with honours. Stephen, created Baron Mount Stephen, died in 1921 at the age of 92.

He and the others had found in the railway a holy cause that combined profitability and the national interest. In throwing two bands of steel across the continent they had helped to build a nation.

Writing in 1916, Keith Morris claimed that the economic history of Canada since 1885 had 'fundamentally' been the history of the Canadian Pacific. The company then operated 18,000 miles of track and 100,000 miles of telegraph line, and employed 6000 people at its Angus workshops in Montreal. In all, the Company had 120,000 men on its payroll, and about half a million people dependent on them. Another million had some concern with the Company's activities.

The Company, once viewed as a hair-brained scheme liable to go broke any minute, now represented an excellent and solid investment. In 1921, almost half the shareholders lived in Britain, and another quarter in the United States. The dividend, declared sacred, gave good, if not spectacular, returns. And the shareholders also had the feeling of being part of some great Imperial scheme for national and inter-national development.

In 1915, J B Harkin, Commissioner of Dominion Parks, illustrated how successful Van Horne's marketing of the mountains had been. Rocky Mountain National Park had 90,000 visitors. Harkin estimated that foreign tourists spent over $16 million – $13.88 an acre. Wheat exports yielded just over $74 million – $4.91 an acre of wheatland. Thus, con-

*Below:* This is the competition: This Canadian National 2-8-2 with a tender heaped with coal is similar to (Santa Fe) Baldwin Class Q 2-10-2.

*Below:* A 4-6-2 poses for its picture at Windsor, Ontario on 2 September 1954. Number 2625 would be a G-2 (light Pacific) of the 1912 series.

*Above:* CPR crane 414330 is parked at Coquitlam, BC, in 1952.
*Below:* Engine 2203 is a doughty 4-6-2 shot in Ontario, June 1942.

*Below:* This interesting piece of rail equipment is a CPR pile driver.

cluded Harkin, 'our export of scenery per acre . . . was equal to almost three times the acreage value of our exportable wheat surplus.' The CPR, through its irrigation schemes, had made the desert bloom. And through its tourist promotion it had made the very rocks yield dollars.

The war cut off the British tourist traffic. And when the United States entered the war in 1917, the American trade dwindled.

When anyone travelled west by train after the war, they had a choice of three transcontinental lines. The booming west and the influx of immigrants had strained the CPR system. And the Manitoba government, still concerned about the dominance of the Company and the arrogant ways of its agents, helped William Mackenzie and Donald Mann to string together railway lines in Manitoba and to expand their Canadian Northern Railway. By the end of 1902, these two men had extended their line to Thunder Bay. Then they reduced their rates for grain, forcing the CPR to do the same.

The Grand Trunk Railway under general manager Charles M Hays also eyed the bustling west. It formed a subsidiary, the Grand Trunk Pacific, and reached an agreement with Laurier's Liberals. The government would build a National Transcontinental Railway from Moncton to Winnipeg, and the Grand Trunk Pacific would carry the line from there to the Pacific. The first train on this new line reached Prince Rupert, BC, on 9 April 1914, and the National Transcontinental line between Quebec and Winnipeg opened on 1 June in the same year.

Meanwhile, Mackenzie and Mann went their merry way across the west, building the Great Northern, picking up charters and grants from anyone who wanted a railway. The last spike in their transcontinental line to Vancouver was driven in January 1915.

It soon became obvious that traffic could not sustain three lines across Canada. The *Grain Growers Guide,* no friend of the Company, noted on 9 May 1917:

The CPR is one of the finest railway systems under the sun. It is well financed, well operated and gives good service with enormous profits to its shareholders, totalling last year [1916] $49,000,000. The loss on all other railways was only $20,000,000.

*Below:* This dramatic shot depicts a 4-6-2 in Winnipeg, Manitoba. The cloud of smoke pours from the locomotive just behind.

*Bottom:* This CPR excursion car was photographed in Vancouver, BC in July 1952.

*Opposite bottom:* Two CPR workers, apparently at their leisure, peer at the photographer of a passenger car at Cranbook, British Columbia.

*Above:* Sir Edward Beatty, Shaughnessy's successor, originally joined CPR as a lawyer who fought to keep CPR a privately-owned corporation. A lifelong bachelor, he dedicated all his time to the railroad.

A cartoon portrayed the CPR as a fat, bejewelled pig; the other railways appeared as scrawny porkers. Shaughnessy had a simple solution to this problem. The government should nationalize all three railways – and let the CPR manage the combined venture.

Shaughnessy retired on 11 October, 1918, handing over the presidency to Edward Beatty, the first native-born Canadian to hold the post. Son of the first manager of the Company's Great Lakes steamers, Beatty had joined the CPR as a lawyer and risen rapidly through the ranks.

A photograph of Beatty, probably taken in 1919, shows him standing next to the Prince of Wales on the deck of a ship. The prince looks withdrawn, standing with hand in pocket, heels together. Beatty has a prizefighter's stance, feet apart, hands at side, hat tipped over his right eye, a slight smile on his face and a cigar clutched firmly in his left hand. It's almost as if the Company had wrested dominion over Canada from the Royal Family, its rightful rulers.

Beatty, a Presbyterian, liked the 'idea of a one man organization.' A lonely man, Beatty filled the bachelor day of his life with the Company. 'It's too bad that Ed married the CPR' one of his few friends observed.

The Company needed all the attention that Beatty could offer.

In 1922, the government had created the Canadian National Railway out of the bankrupt messes of other lines. The CPR now had a rival with access to the public purse. During the reign of Beatty, many governments took over their national railway systems to protect the public interest. But Beatty remained a foe of state ownership of industry. In one speech he claimed: 'Canadian corporations are good citizens, and so long as they are guided by men of ability and with ideals, they will not only continue to be good citizens, but will develop from within themselves thousands of men whose standards of citizenship are unconsciously elevated through that association.'

Allied with this rather mystical approach was an increased stress by Beatty on attracting traffic to the line. In 1919, the *TransCanada Limited,* a luxury, all-sleeper train, began its run, and in the 1920s, the *Toronto Express* and the *Mountaineer* from Chicago whisked travellers west.

Beatty encouraged settlement, assisting returning soldiers in Alberta and Saskatchewan to set up 320-acre farms. In 1922-23, the Company settled on their lands 2400 'clean, hard-working, thrifty 'Menonnites who had fled from Russia. In the same year, Beatty helped a group of Scottish Catholics

*Opposite left:* This 1912-series ten-wheeler type 4-6-2 was shot at Lambeton, Ontario, in March 1947.
*Opposite right:* Locomotive 2716, a 4-6-2 G-5, was photographed in Vancouver, British Columbia in 1951.
*Below:* This photograph of the Revelstoke station, British Columbia, was taken on a hazy day in the 1920's.

to establish the Clan Donald settlement in Vermilion, Alberta. He also tampered with the Crow Rate, receiving a blast from the *Manitoba Free Press* when he issued new rates about 'this conspiracy to break the law, rob the people and bulldoze Parliament.'

Through the 1920s, automobiles cut into the Company's short-haul traffic. But they also brought guests to the CPR hotels. For those who could not afford to stay in these hotels, the Company started mountain camps at $5.50 a day. The first, at Wapta Lake in Kicking Horse Pass, was set up in 1921. Three years later, the first annual trail ride, another tourist attraction, set out from Yoho Valley Camp.

A remarkable public relations man put a new face on the Company during the 1920s as it sought to attract travellers. John Murray Gibbon promoted the CPR with style and elegance, basing his approach on a concept of Canada far removed from the Imperial Dominion favoured by past presidents. Educated at Aberdeen, Oxford, and in Germany, Gibbon came to Canada in 1913 to work for the CPR. He devised slogans like 'The Canadian Pacific Rockies' and 'Canadian Pacific Spans the World.' He commissioned posters and pamphlets of grace and taste. He encouraged Canadian culture, urging the CPR to involve more French Canadians in its activities. At the opening of the new wing of the Chateau Frontenac in 1926, traditional folksingers performed at a dinner for newspaper editors. In the following year the hotel was the site of the first Annual Folksong and Handicraft Festival. In 1927 Gibbon also organized a Highland Gathering and Scottish Musical Festival at Banff Springs Hotel on Labour Day. It featured a kilted clergyman, the Reverend Charles W Gordon (the novelist Ralph Connor) preaching an outdoor sermon.

At the celebration of the 50th anniversary of Confederation in Britain in 1927, Beatty heard Stanley Baldwin, the Prime Minister, claim that: 'The glory of the Canadian Pacific is that it is a corporation with a soul.' It also had lots of money, some of which it spent on purchasing ships in Britain for its fleet.

Baldwin's lofty rhetoric and the supply of ready cash that the Company seemed always able to command did little to help the CPR in a world plunged into depression in the 1930s. In November 1931 the Canadian Government set up a Royal Commission on Railways and Transportation which reported in September 1932. The CPR and the CNR, the Commission concluded, had engaged in costly and unnecessary competition with 'duplication of passenger trains . . . identical schedules . . . wasteful practices . . . establishment of a standard of passenger travel beyond the requirements of the country.' The report rejected nationalization of amalgamation, in case it created a railway monopoly. Beatty stumped the country proposing that one system under one management could solve the economic problems of the railways. He pointed out that personal income taxes had yielded the federal government $249-million over a ten-year period – 'less than half the deficit of the government railways.' The government suggested that the survival of Canada's railways lay in co-operation if necessary, but not necessarily in co-operation. The CNR continued to be propped up by the federal government while the CPR had to meet the tests of private enterprise.

Railways had been the symbol of progress in the past.

Now, as rootless, unemployed men clung to the freights, they became symbols of depression and economic stagnation. On 28 September 1930 the CPR station on Yonge Street in Toronto, completed in 1916, closed. This elegant building had marble-covered walls and a 140-foot high clock tower – but not enough passenger traffic to justify its existence. The Company had its worst year in 1932, showing a deficit of $42,000. In 1933, loans of $40 million fell due, with a further $20 million due in the following year. The banks, including the Bank of Montreal, of which Beatty was a director, demanded security to renew the loans. The president asked Prime Minister Bennett for a guarantee of a five-year loan at 5 percent in May 1933, and the government provided this under the Railway Relief Act in that year.

In the winter of 1932, the CPR closed its shops in Calgary. But the Company, in the words of James Gray in *The Winter Years,* 'stood out like a gigantic gas flare' on the prairies because of its enlightened land policy. Mortgage companies evicted farmers, then sold their farms for a fraction of what the owners owed. The CPR did not foreclose, and even cancelled interest on its loans in two years when the crops failed. The Company paid its workers as much for a day as government relief programs did for a week's work. But it demanded that the federal government enforce the Railway Act and remove the 'On-to-Ottawa' trekkers who had hoped to ride the Company's freights from Vancouver to Ottawa in 1935.

In the early 1930s, the CPR and CNR co-operated in providing work to alleviate unemployment. They also abandoned 517 miles of track, and saved $1,771,635 through joint efforts between 1935 and 1938.

In the late 1920s and through the 1930s, the CPR ran special ski trains in Ontario and Québec. But in 1937, despite increased attendance at the Canadian National Exhibition in Toronto, the number of railway passengers declined.

*Canadian Pacific Facts and Figures,* issued in that year, named the cause of the railway's difficulties.

Within the past few years, and particularly the last decade, there has been a decided change in the sources from which emanate the movement of passengers by rail, due to the advent and development of new modes of transportation, chiefly that of the private automobile.

Beatty, knighted in 1935, saw the CPR experience one brief shining moment of glory before the world descended into war. In 1939, King George VI and Queen Elizabeth crossed Canada by CPR. The king, impressed by the powerful Hudson locomotives that hauled the royal train, permitted the Company to rename them 'Royal Hudsons' – and to carry crowns on the runningboards of 45 of them.

A stroke felled Beatty on 17 March 1941, robbing him of speech. News of the stroke was kept from the public as he struggled painfully back to health, trying to keep on top of company business. Vice-president D'Alton C Coleman took over more and more duties, becoming CPR's fifth president in May 1942.

Less than a year later, Edward Beatty, who had made the Company his life, died in March 1943, aged 65.

*Left:* Sicamous Station in British Columbia, built of wood in a board and batten style, has an air of tranquility.
*Below:* A CPR baggage car is parked between two boxcars in Sutherland.

# The End of an Era:
## The Second World War and the Passing of Steam

'A railway is a republic and a monarchy. It is a republic because there is no pre-emption of high office for any favoured class among its servants. It is a monarchy in the virtual dictatorship of its President.'

David Hanna, *Trains of Recollection,* 1926

Only too often the history of the CPR emerges as the story of businessmen like Stephen and Beatty battling against great odds to complete a transcontinental railway and to keep it running. The thousands of men who built and operated the line, and those whose lives it touched and changed are more than footnotes to these 'great lives.' For the most part they have remained faceless and mute.

One pioneer called the CPR 'the mighty monster of the west,' and described the railroad big shots as a 'bunch of pirates.' But he added that they got the job done. Another man took over a station in 1906, receiving $35 a month, plus a house for $5 a month and free oil and kerosene. When he retired in 1947, he was earning $165 a month. Railroading ran in the blood in some families, all of whose members worked for the CPR over five generations. One man recalled the time he wanted to become a railroader. He went out to Medicine Hat on a railway pass to a job as a wiper at the roundhouse in 1903. He was expected to work for 11 hours for $1.21. When he found that his room and board would cost him $1 a day, he decided to seek work elsewhere.

The Company provided steady work, and treated its workers well. It created a social structure in which everyone knew his place, and its workers took pride in belonging to such a famous company. At midnight on 5 August 1925, engineman Seth Partridge's train, on its way up the Big Hill, ran into a rock and clay slide. He ran down the hill to Yoho station, and warned the occupants, who left the building a few seconds before the slide wiped it out. The grateful Company named a sliding after Partridge.

David Hanna, the first president of the Canadian National, summed up another appeal of railroading as a way of life when he claimed that any of his company's 100,000 person workforce would find 'the highest executive office is open' – if

*Below:* Brute force clothed in steel: this locomotive, a 4-6-2, is a Pacific type of the heavier G-3 or G-4 class.
*Bottom:* The sun sets at Midway, British Columbia. The peaceful and glorious view is on the Kettle Valley Route.

A vacationers' train arrives at Banff, Alberta.

he 'entered the service young enough.' In the 1920s, D C Carleton, who started with the CPR as a clerk in the baggage department in 1887, had made it to vice-president.

Women did not play a significant role in the all-male world of railroading. Kate Reed, wife of Hayter Reed, Manager-in-Chief of the Company's hotel department in the first years of this century, decorated the hotels with quiet elegance. And a faithful secretary helped Edward Beatty to handle Company affairs after his stroke in 1941.

An ex-employee reported that there was 'a paternal approach mixed with authoritarianism' in the Company's management style, adding that it resembled being in the military: 'Everyone knew their rank and the guy above was God.' Even fairly recently, an executive was told by the president that 'we own you twenty-four hours a day.'

On the line, the gods at the top of the pantheon were the conductor and the engineer. As early as 1895, a commentator noted:

> Like Japan and ancient Sparta, the cars are subject to a species of 'dual monarch,' the parallel potentates being the conductor – who generally retires with a fortune nobody knows how, for he doesn't get tipped – and the Negro conductor.

Blacks found jobs with the railway as porters and sleeping car attendants, but seldom rose above these ranks.

A CPR passenger train became a world unto itself as it crossed the country. The conductor, the 'captain of the ship' and the 'Lord Mayor' of a 'city on wheels' wore a watch that might cost a month's pay as his badge of office. The conductor looked after the paper work, wore a suit, and ensured that the train arrived and left on time. Tensions often developed between this white collar worker, the supreme authority on the train, and the engineer, known as the hogger and always addressed as 'Mister.' The engineer also earned a top wage, but he wore overalls and worked with his hands.

In 1931, conductors received the highest wages in Canada. In Moose Jaw, another CPR creation, in which it invested $5 million for railway facilities, conductors and engineers lived in big houses. But the railway superintendent occupied a mansion.

Hand in hand with autocracy went paternalism.

Beatty heard of an engineer who was due to retire without ever having seen him. He arranged to travel on the man's train. At the end of the section, Beatty went up to the cab, introduced himself, and wished the engineer a happy retirement.

The railroad created new skills, rituals, symbols.

A man known as the 'bank' fireman started a fire under the engine in the roundhouse: It took about an hour and a half for a locomotive to raise steam. The engineer would arrive an hour ahead of time to fuss over the locomotive, wiping it down with a piece of waste, polishing the bell. The CPR took great pride in its shining engines. The engineer controlled the locomotive with throttle and brake, from the right side of the cab. The fireman looked out of the left window for any signals, and rang the bell. Some firemen could not talk to their engineers – unless they spoke first. A fireman might work for ten years or more before being promoted to engineer. He had to handle the scoop to keep an even fire burning. A run of 120 miles would consume 12 to 15 tons of coal, depending

A CPR 4-6-2 puffs out of Winnipeg, Manitoba, heading west.

on track and weather conditions. On the 150 miles between Revelstoke, BC, and Lake Louise, one CPR fireman emptied the tender three times, shovelling 30 tons of coal on an eight hour trip.

Working in the yards that began to spread over the landscape at certain places in Canada required other skills.

The yardmaster could locate any car on the miles of track, even though they changed daily. A freight conductor would watch a long string of cars move past – then take out a notebook and pencil and jot down all their numbers.

The authoritarian structure often led to casual cruelty.

One cold night in a CPR yard, a shivering young man climbed into the cab of an engine to warm himself. The engineer demanded to know what he did. When the man said that he worked the switches, the hogger told him he belonged on the ground – not in the cab – and that he should 'git.'

The passing of the trains in rural areas marked the hours of the days. 'Milk trains' stopped at every flag station through which the 'moonlights,' the crack expresses, roared. The caboose was called the 'van,' 'crummy,' 'dog house.' Local

railways received nicknames from irate travellers. The T H & B (Toronto, Hamilton and Buffalo) became 'To Hell and Back.' That line vanished into the CPR in 1977.

But no one seems to have mocked the mighty CPR with a nickname that stuck. That other great Canadian institution, the Royal Canadian Mounted Police, generated scores of movies that distorted its real world and embarrassed its officers. The CPR's activities gave rise to only one Hollywood film – *Canadian Pacific* – made in 1949, and starring Randolph Scott and Jane Wyatt.

The CPR developed increasingly powerful locomotives. To haul a 15-car train up the Big Hill took four heavy engines. This problem was eased in August 1909, when the spiral tunnels between Field and Hector doubled the length of the track, and halved the grade.

The 4-4-0 locomotives (four wheels in front, four driving wheels, no wheels under the cab) dominated the first decades of the railways. In 1889, the CPR, which had used a wide range of locomotive types, built the first *Ten-Wheeler*, a 4-6-0, and over the years operated almost 1000 of them. Competition among transcontinental lines led to the develop-

ment of faster and faster trains. The *Atlantics,* acquired by the CPR, had 84-inch driving wheels. Between 1906 and 1946 the Company used the first modern steam locomotives, the *Pacifics,* with large cylinders and boiler capacity and powerful traction to haul trains weighing up to 500 tons. Then came the *Mikados* that proved to be outstanding successes at hauling heavy loads up steep grades. The handsome *Hudsons,* later streamlined, came into operation in 1929 as did the mighty *Selkirks,* used extensively in the Rockies. The first *Jubilee* with 80-inch driving wheels, was 'outshopped' by the Montreal Locomotive Works in 1936.

The fast and stopping trains that crossed Canada changed the lives and perception of many people. The luxury trains had electricity, running hot and cold water, elegant restaurants and parlour cars — comforts conspicuously lacking in most of the houses and communities through which they roared. The trains broke down the isolation of settlers, as the stations became the focus of community life. Time and the hours took on a new meaning. The comings and goings of the trains drew businessmen and idlers to the station to see who was arriving — and who was leaving town.

People came to pick up the papers and the mail, to hear the latest gossip from inside and outside the community. The Morse and telegraph keys chattered away, sending messages across the land, passing the signals that kept the trains running on time. The train stopped for a minute or two to drop off the mail, express parcels and passengers. Then the lordly conductor shouted 'All aboard,' and swung on to the train which steamed away, driving rods flailing, wheels turning, steam escaping.

To youngsters, the train represented power, escape and excitement, reminding them of faraway places beyond the horizon. It brought the city to small communities and lured away their youth. Everyone knew the language of the locomotive's whistle. A short shriek meant that brakes were being applied to stop the train, a long one that the train was nearing a station, junction or crossing. On the prairies the whistle broke the isolation of farmers: some people could tell the temperature from the way the whistle cut through the cold air. People set their watches by the trains as they became symbols of regularity and reliability.

People on the local lines developed an affection for 'their'

trains and 'their' crews. One CPR railroader recalled that they'd let people off at their homes, stop for dinner and even sit on a bridge and fish. An old couple in Ontario waited at a stop with turkey legs for the CPR crew one Christmas Day.

In December 1937 an event cast its shadow over the CPR. It acquired its first diesel-electric unit for use in rail yards. These power units cost more to buy – but less to operate.

During the Second World War, freight tonnage rose as trucks, gasoline and rubber shortages developed. The Angus shops in Montreal turned out Valentine tanks as well as Hudson locomotives, and the government took over 22 of the Company's ships; twelve were sunk in action. Passengers returned to the trains. In 1939, the CPR carried 7.2 million passengers. In 1944, the number had risen to 18.4 million, the highest ever reached by the system. Overall railway revenues doubled between 1939 and 1945. The war effort strained the CPR system. In 1939, it had 48,689 employees. By 1945, they numbered 70,775, despite the enlistment of 20,742 in the Canadian forces.

In 1941, the government froze wages and freight rates. Not until 1944 did it grant railway workers a six cents-an-hour wage increase, and a bonus. Operating expenses on the railway soared, and after the end of the war, highway carriers began to compete for freight. Price and wage controls ended in 1946, but rates and fares on the CPR remained at the old levels. In 1948, the Board of Transport Commissioners granted a general increase in tolls, but could not raise the rates on export grain because of the sanctity of the Crow Rate. Wage rates, material costs and, after 1957, interest rates, rose steadily while it became apparent that freight and passenger traffic had almost reached their ceilings.

The Company responded to these new stresses by modernizing and diversifying.

The grumbling, growling, hooting diesel replaced the shrieking, thundering steam locomotives under the direction of Norris 'Buck' Crump, Company president from 1955 to 1964 and chairman until 1972. His very name sounded like the slamming of a door on the romantic era of railroading.

At one time, railroaders had been the élite of the Canadian labour force, and their unions became very conservative. But

Locomotive No 5310 pushes a snow plow in East Coulee, Alberta.

Ian Sinclair, who reigned as president from 1966 to 1972, the Company showed how innovative and inventive it could be in responding to change. It installed computers, bought and ran dayliners, built container terminals, developed 'unit' and 'robot' trains, studied railway electrification west of Calgary, introduced piggybacking (carrying highway trailers on flat cars), automated its marshalling yards, acquired modern locomotives and new rolling stock for many specialized uses.

As machines replaced men, the old sense of pride and identity of the railroaders began to crumble. One complained that standardization of equipment, computerization and the use of radio communications had taken responsibility out of the hands of engineers. Before modernization, the CPR workers — and especially the engineers — felt they were in charge. The loss of autonomy was reflected in an increased feeling that somebody was looking over people's shoulders, checking up on them.

In 1948 a national railway strike appeared inevitable. The unions wanted a 25 cents-an-hour wage increase, and the companies offered 10 cents. Crump, apparently swayed by the argument that only Russia would benefit from a railway strike, compromised at 17 cents. In 1950, Canada suffered its first national rail strike over the issue of wages. Technological change triggered other disputes. On 2 January 1957, 65,000 CPR employees walked out in support of 2850 firemen who felt threatened by dieselization. The union claimed that firemen were indispensable for safety reasons, the government ordered the men back, and the resulting enquiry showed that firemen were reduntant on diesels. The firemen struck again in 1958, but received no backing from other unions and swiftly settled for what they could gain from a company bent on preserving its profits.

On 3 July 1971, the Company changed its name from the Canadian Pacific Railway Company to Canadian Pacific Limited to accommodate its varied transportation and natural resource activities.

The Company had already changed its symbol and its slogan. Through the years it favoured a simple shield with the words 'Canadian Pacific' on it. From 1886 to 1929 a strange-looking beaver sat atop the shield. The beaver dropped off in 1929, and the slogan 'World's Greatest Travel System' appeared on the shield. The beaver made a comeback in 1946, with a new slogan; 'Spans the World.' In 1963, the Company motto became: 'Diversification is the key to Canadian Pacific's progress.' In 1968, the shield and the beaver gave way up to abstract symbol still in use. The initials 'CP' were stylized, and the symbol combines 'a triangle, suggesting motion or direction, a segment of a circle suggesting global activities and a portion of a square suggesting stability.' (See pages 10 and 11.)

The Company no longer has its former clear-cut identity. It now engages in many activities. It has dumped its passengers. And a generation has grown up unaware of the Company's history and of the great power it wielded.

Throughout its history, the Company has played a significant role in uniting Canadians. A writer in the 1920s pointed out another feature of the Company — its sense of 'high moral purpose.' He told of Gideon Swain, the general custodian at Winnipeg, who rounded on two 'smart men' who were swearing in his station while women and children boarded a train.

In a speech in 1980, Ian Sinclair, CP's president, neatly summarized the Company's priorities: 'The first corporate obligation is to earn a profit.'

after the war, discontent arose among the CPR workers, who realized that past glory and company spirit offered no recompense for rising living costs. Crump, son of a CPR employee in Revelstoke, BC, joined the Company as an apprentice machinist at 16, and claimed he'd worn overalls longer than most union leaders. He wrote his thesis in engineering on diesels and presided over their widescale adoption by the railway. The first road (main line) diesels went into service in 1948-49. By 1954, about one third of freight and passenger trains were being hauled by diesels. By 1960, 'dieselization' had been completed, and in that year the last steam locomotive to pull a train on CP rail lines hauled a special from Montreal to St Lin and back. It was a 4-4-0, built in 1887.

The diesels allowed runthroughs. They had no need of coal and water. So communities built to serve the steam trains simply lost their reason for being and began to vanish.

During Crump's tenure, and that of his successor, lawyer

A big 4-6-2 steam locomotive, engineer peeking from the cab, standing in
Abbotsford, British Columbia, on a crisp March day in 1943.

3611

IAN PACIFIC

# Canadian Pacific's Ships and Planes

'The CPR was on the Pacific shore; but there was no traffic with the orient . . . The first CPR steamer from Vancouver to Asia carried two carloads of shingles and the bodies of several Chinamen piously being returned to their ancestral sepulchres.'

David Hanna, *Trains of Recollections,* 1926

From the beginning of his involvement with the railway, George Stephen had a vision of an all-British route to the Far East, a transportation system stretching from Liverpool to Hong Kong. In 1882 the Company issued a map showing steamship connections to Japan and Hong Kong from its western terminus. Three years later the CPR tendered a bid to the British Post Office to carry the mail fortnightly between Vancouver and Hong Kong for £100,000, but the offer was rejected.

Despite this rebuff, the Company chartered seven sailing ships to carry cargo from the Far East to its Pacific railhead. The first of these, the 800-ton wooden barque *W B Flint,* docked at Port Moody on 27 July 1886, with a million pounds of tea consigned to Hamilton, Toronto and New York. The connecting train sped across the country to deliver the tea to New York only 49 days after the ship left Yokohama. Between August 1886 and January 1887 the other chartered ships did the 'tea run,' providing 4000 tons of freight for the new railway.

The Company then acquired the *Abyssinia, Batavia* and *Parthia,* ex-Cunard steamers, under charter. The *Abyssinia,* out of Hong Kong and Yokohama, tied up at the new CPR wharf in Vancouver on 14 June 1887. It carried 22 first class passengers and 80 Chinese in steerage, three sacks of mail, 11 packages of newspapers and almost 3000 tons of cargo, most of it tea consigned to Chicago and New York. Later in the season, the chartered ships carried the British Minister to Japan and the brother of the King of Siam. From its beginning, the Company strove to attract distinguished travellers to its ships.

The first season resulted in a loss for the Company.

But it plunged on into the shipping business. In 1889 it placed orders for three 6000-ton vessels – the first *'Empresses'* of India, China and Japan. With graceful, yacht-like lines, and excellent service, these fast passenger vessels soon gave the Canadian Pacific the same reputation on the

ocean as its passenger trains did on land. And they proved profitable.

The *Empress of India* ran her trials in January 1891, decked out with the red-and-white checked flag that Van Horne had designed (see illustration, page 10). These new ships carried mail between Vancouver and China and Japan under a £60,000 contract secured by the Company in 1890. The contract carried a penalty clause that was never invoked in the first 15 years of operation.

David Brown, the Company's representative in the Far East, showed the same aggressive drive that marked so many of the CPR management. He secured connections with Australia and New Zealand – 'hands across the sea and let the kangaroo shake hands with the beaver.' He lured traffic from Ceylon by telling a senior government official: 'I represent the Canadian Pacific Railway, and I can give you transportation right into the exhibition grounds in Chicago' so that the country could participate in the World's Fair there in 1894.

The Company made plans in 1884 for a link across the Atlantic. On 29 January 1886 Stephen wrote to Sir John A Macdonald, after talking with Andrew Allan of the ship-owning family.

He now knows that nothing but the very best and fastest ships will be of any use to us, and that whoever owns them, the CPR must have a substantial control over them so as to ensure a unity of action . . .

Quality, integration of services, and unity of action became the marks of the Company style as it entered the golden years. As the railway penetrated the lake country of southern British Columbia, the CPR built steamers to connect branch lines. The first of these, the *Aberdeen,* came out of the CPR's own shipyard at Okanagan Landing in May 1894. In 1901 the Company secured control of the Canadian Pacific Navigation Company, and the red-and-white flag went up on a fleet of 14 steamers that plied the coastal waters of British Columbia. In 1903 the *Princess Victoria,* the first of the new company's specially designed ships, began to win the hearts of the people on the west coast with her grace and speed.

In the same year, Shaughnessy bought 15 passenger and cargo ships from the Elder Dempster Lines. The Company also moved into the emigration business, offering steerage passage between Liverpool and Quebec and Montreál for £5 10s; the immigrant ships carried cattle to London on the return trip. In 1906 the *Empress of Britain,* the first of the

The *Abyssinia* was launched on 3 March 1870 by J & G Thomson, Clydebank, for the Cunard Line and taken over by the builders in 1880 as partial payment for the *Servia & Catalonia.* S B Guion bought the vessel and installed compound engines in 1882. Ownership was transferred in 1885 to Sir William Pearce. On 11 January 1887 the *Abyssinia* was obtained for the CP Pacific service. On 28 January 1887 she departed Vancouver on her 17th, and last, CPR voyage. In October of 1891 she reverted to the Guion Steamship Co Ltd. On 18 December 1891 she was destroyed by a fire at sea, but, happily, her passengers were picked up by the Norddeutscher Lloyd steamer *Spree.*

A sizeable crowd gathers to welcome the Duke and Duchess of Connaught as they arrive on the *Abyssinia* in May 1890. This Vancouver Harbour scene also includes the CP Navigation Co's *Premier*, docked on the left. Note the dismounted cannons lying on the quay in the lower left corner of the picture. To the right carriages wait to drive passengers to their hotels.

Atlantic 'Empresses,' began its run on that ocean. Three years later, the Company absorbed the Allan Line in a secret deal.

The very high standards set by the Company for its ships proved to be a liability when the First World War broke out. The fast ships of the Atlantic and Pacific fleets were taken over by the government for use as transports or auxiliary cruisers. When the first Canadian contingent sailed for England in October 1914, 13 of the 31 liners in the convoy had once sailed under the flags of the Company or the Allan Line. About a dozen CPR ships were lost to enemy action during the First World War. Immigration, of course, dropped considerably. In 1913, 400,870 people arrived in Canada. Two years later, the number of immigrants had dropped to 36,665.

In the 1920s, the Company profited by meeting national needs in Canada, which wanted to fill its empty spaces, and in Britain, which wanted to empty its crowded cities. Reduced fares attracted British immigrants seeking to start a new life in a new world. The Company carried 11,000 'harvesters' across the Atlantic and Canada to work on the farms in the west.

The ships, like the railway, created their own social structure.

In 1927 the company built the four 'Duchess' passenger ships. They tended to roll and were known as the 'Drunken Duchesses.' A man who served on the *Duchess of York* wrote later about the lives of the 200 crew who served the needs of

*Above:* The *Empress of Canada III* steams proudly. The 650 foot liner was launched on 10 May 1960 by Vickers Armstrong Ship Builders Ltd, Walker on Tyne. The ship served with CP from 1961 to 1972 when she began service with the Carnaval Cruise Line as the *Mardi Gras*.
*Right:* A CP Ships container ship plows ahead with a full load. Containerization has revolutionized shipping since its introduction. A cargo can be shipped intact in a sturdy container from its point of origin to its final destination.

the 1570 passengers these ships could carry.

Kitchen boys received slightly more than £3 a month, and assistant cooks slightly more than £7. Uniforms were not supplied nor was laundry done free, except when the ship was in Canada. The chef had his private room, and the senior staff lived above the water line in 'Tin Town.' The rest of the catering and service staff crowded into a honeycomb of 'glory holes' near the ship's bows. The working day began at 5:45 am and ended at 11 pm when the chef said, 'the rest of the day is your own . . .' The night before the ship docked, everyone stayed up to clean and polish everything, for in those days, 'you never took a dirty ship into port.' If the ship tied up at one minute to midnight, everyone lost the next day's pay.

Despite these conditions, the spirit on board was 'fantastic.'

Over the years, the Company operated a wide range of ships from luxury passenger liners to tugs. Many came to grief. The *Empress of Ireland*, rammed by the Norwegian collier *Storstad* in the St Lawrence on the foggy night of 29 May 1914, took over 1000 people to their deaths when she

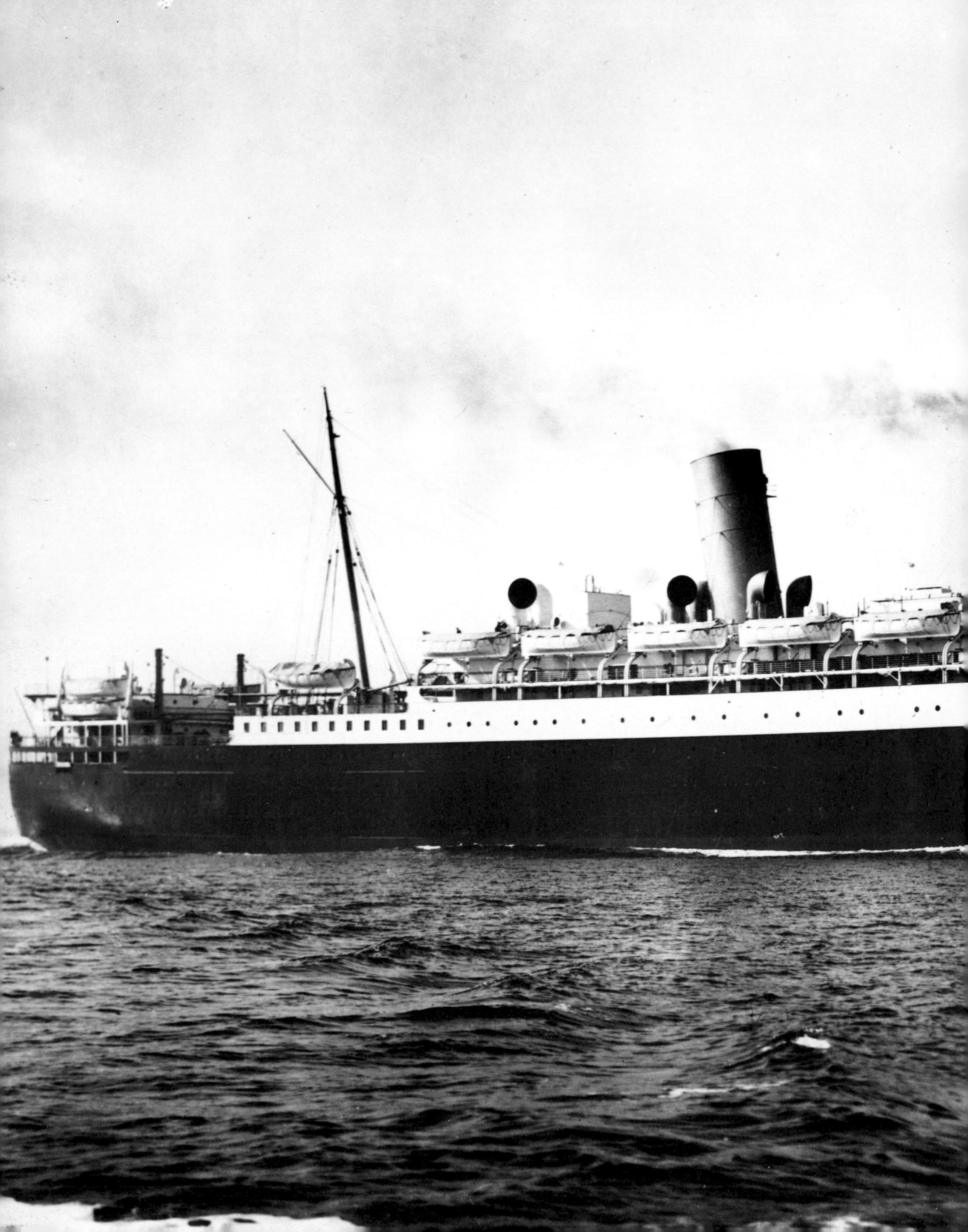

*The Duchess of York* was launched by John Brown & Co Ltd, Clydebank on 28 September 1928. On 22 March 1929 she sailed from Liverpool on her maiden voyage. In 1940 she was requisitioned to serve as a troopship and on 11 July 1943 she was sunk by enemy aircraft off the coast of Morocco, joining the roll of stout CP ships to be lost in her country's service.

The CP tanker *Fort Garry* steadily plows toward her destination. Note the safety warnings painted on the bridge superstructure which are necessary given the highly flammable nature of her cargo.

sank in fifteen minutes. On 23 October 1918, the *Princess Sophia,* southbound from Skagway down the Inner Passage of Alaska, went aground on the Vanderbilt Reef. The ship seemed securely wedged on the rocks, so most of the 343 passengers and crew went to bed. A sudden gale lifted the ship's stern, and she slid off the reef into the water, taking everyone to their deaths. Only a dog survived.

In October 1940 the largest and most luxurious ship in the Company fleet, *The Empress of Britain,* sailing alone off northwestern Ireland on military duties, was attacked by a bomber. The blazing ship, towed by a tug, became the target of a U-boat, which sank her with two torpedoes.

By the early 1960s, air travel had cut into the Company's transocean passenger trade. The third *Empress of Britain,* commissioned in 1956, ended her service with the Company eight years later by being sold to a Greek shipping line. In 1960 the Company launched its last passenger liner, the *Empress of Canada.* Although the CPR generated money by using its passenger liners on cruises during the winter, the fate of the *Empress of Canada* showed that such ships had no future. Only 20 people – including three CP officials – saw this beautiful ship leave her pier at Montreal on 18 November 1971. She carried 300 passengers in a space designed for 1000. Sold to an American cruise line, she became the *Mardi Gras* in 1972.

Cargo carrying proved to be more profitable – if less glamorous. In 1964, the Company ordered the *Beaverbrook,* a 6000-ton cargo carrier, the first CP ship specifically designed to carry containers. Seven years later the first of the new 'cellular' ships with the 'CP' designator came into operation. Displacing 14,000 tons, the *CP Discoverer, CP Trade* and *CP Voyageur* could carry 700 containers.

In 1964, as its ocean shipping activities contracted, the Company created Canadian Pacific (Bermuda) Ltd to own, operate and charter oceangoing bulk carriers. The new company's fleet expanded rapidly in the 1970s. Tankers and VLCC (Very Large Cargo Carriers) carried the names of *R B Angus, Lord Mount Stephen* and *Lord Strathcona.* One was christened with the name of that bulky railway builder, *W C Van Horne.* They sailed into troubled waters in the 1980s as more and more ships chased fewer and fewer cargoes. The Company learned the hard way that big was no longer beautiful – or even profitable. The bulk shipping operation turned a profit of $44 million in 1981 — but lost $40.9 million in 1983. In that year, CP Ships lost a total of $74.3 million.

Poor economic conditions forced the Company into joint ventures. At the end of 1983, it reorganized its container operations, and withdrew from service between the United States East Coast and Western Europe. On 1 January 1984 Canadian Pacific and Compagnie Maritime Belge formed a joint venture to compete more effectively in the container trade between Montreal and Western Europe.

\* \* \*

Although the Canadian Pacific Railway received permission from the government in 1919 to own and operate commercial aircraft inside and outside Canada, it did nothing about taking to the air until 1930. Then it cooperated with Canadian National Railways and invested half a million dollars in Canadian Airways Ltd, which consisted of a number of local lines. When C D Howe became Minister of Transportation in 1936, with jurisdiction over civil aviation, he made it very plain that he wanted no competition for his new Crown corporation, Trans-Canada Airlines. So the CPR

looked north, and acquired 10 bush airlines with 77 aircraft in 1941-42. Canadian Pacific Air Lines thus came into being on 1 January 1942.

Blending together a wild crew of northern pilots who flew by the seat of their pants (and ran their companies the same way) and a staid and conservative railway gave the Company both flexibility and stability. It was thus able to make an effective contribution to Canada's war effort in the air. The Canadian Pacific operated air observer schools for the British Commonwealth Air Training Plan, overhauled aircraft for the RCAF, and helped to establish and operate the North West Staging Route for planes flying to Alaska and Russia.

Along with one of the companies it bought, CP Air Lines acquired Grant McConachie, president of Yukon Southern. McConachie did for the Company, in the air, what Van Horne did for the railway on land. He had the energy and instincts of a maverick, disciplined by first hand knowledge of flying in Canada's north where a single mistake could be fatal. Born in 1909, the son of a CNR railroader, McConachie grew up in Edmonton. An unruly youth, he ran away from home at 16 to join the Canadian Navy. Then he worked for the railway until he found an outlet for his energy in flying. By 1931 he had accumulated enough time in the air to qualify as a commercial pilot. McConachie had an uncle who started out to be a fireman. The engineer had told him to shovel more coal, whereupon the uncle had opened the fire door, thrown in the shovel and left a career in railroading for the life of a huckster selling magic medicinal remedies. This uncle

agreed to provide the capital to put his nephew into the airline business. Soon McConachie was piloting the single Fokker aircraft that made up the fleet of Independent Airways through the Rockies, hauling freight between Vancouver and Edmonton. The business did not thrive, so McConachie flew fish out of northern lakes, founding Yukon Southern in 1939. He survived a bad crash, never made much money from his planes, but sustained himself through incredible luck and a great deal of nerve. A man with a perpetual grin, McConachie combined the skills of a bush pilot with the vision of an international entrepreneur. He became the prime mover of CP Air Lines' efforts in supplying the North West Staging Route, the Alaska Highway, and the Canol Project which took oil from the Norman Wells field in the Mackenzie Valley to Whitehorse in the Yukon.

In 1946, McConachie moved to Montreal as assistant to the President of CP Air Lines, helping to turn it from a string of bush lines into a major scheduled international and domestic carrier. On 11 February 1947 he became president of the company — and convinced Canadian Pacific to move the airline's headquarters to Vancouver in the following year.

Canadian Pacific Air Lines made its inaugural flight from Vancouver to Sydney, via Honolulu and Fiji, on 10 July 1949. The Labour Government in Australia had been reluctant to grant landing rights to a capitalist corporation. McConachie showed the Prime Minister, a former engine driver, his union card, told him he was a 'brother of the plates,' and secured the rights.

The airline expanded its services to Tokyo and Hong Kong in September 1949, just in time to cash in on the immigrant traffic from the Crown Colony. The Korean conflict also generated a great deal of traffic for the airline; its reputation

*Below:* The CP Ship *Voyageur* was launched by Cammell Laird & Co, Birkenhead on 19 August 1970.
*Opposite:* CP Air's DC-10s were built in Long Beach by McDonnell Douglas.

for good service and quality attracted American officers who wanted to fly across the Pacific in comfort. In the 1950s, Canadian Pacific Air Lines began scheduled flights to New Zealand, Mexico, Lima, Buenos Aires and Santiago, and then to Lisbon and Madrid. The planes, called *White Empresses,* maintained the tradition of service and comfort of the Company's great ocean liners.

In a strange reversal of history, Canadians began to praise the airline's service, comparing it most favourably with the government's airline that had a monopoly of scheduled passenger flights across Canada. The Canadian Pacific had struggled hard to link Canadians by rail. It had been criticized for becoming a monopoly. Now it came up against a firm government monopoly of air traffic across Canada. The Air Transport Board turned down the airline's applications to launch a transcontinental service on the grounds that it was not in the public interest to have competition.

McConachie persisted. On 4 May 1959 CP Air Lines initiated its service across Canada, giving up some of its northern routes outside the Yukon to a regional carrier. In 1961, however, the airline lost $7.6 million. It slowly moved into the black, earning a profit of $7.2 million in 1965.

McConachie had burned his candle at both ends – and in the middle – to make a success of CP Air Lines. He died of a heart attack in Long Beach, California, on 29 June 1965, but he had lived to see his airline become a power in Canada. He had heard the federal government name it as official Canadian flag carrier in the South Pacific, South America and Southeast Europe. In the same month in which he died, the government had referred to Air Canada and CP Air Lines as their 'chosen instruments' in the international aviation field.

To retain its competitive edge, the company acquired Boeing 747 jumbo jets in 1973, the same year in which it took the name CP Air. At that time, it had about 6500 employees, and flew over 50,000 miles along routes that radiated out like a large X from its headquarters in Vancouver. To the west, the airline served Hong Kong and Sydney. The line reached south to Santiago and Buenos Aires, and east to Tel Aviv. From Vancouver its planes flew south to Los Angeles and north to Whitehorse.

Stars among CP Air's galaxy of jetliners are the twin engined Boeing 737 used on short runs (above) and the huge Boeing 747, which is used on intercontinental flights (opposite).

In 1984, CP Air finally became a truly transcontinental airline. It showed its old expansionist urge by absorbing Eastern Provincial Airways, a regional carrier serving Atlantic Canada. It bought the airline from Newfoundland Capital Corporation, after a pilot's strike and intransigent management had generated a loss of $8 million in 1983.

The energy crunch of the 1970s, and the economic downturn of the 1980s, raised the airline's costs and lowered its revenues. CP Air lost $39.2 million in 1982, but cut its losses to $16.4 million in the following year.

During 1983, CP Air introduced the 'hub and spoke' system to provide greater efficiency and a more convenient schedule for passengers. It exchanged some of its aircraft for shorter-range ones. And it integrated the airline's operations with those of CP Hotels to make the division more profitable and to enhance the airline's presence in the travel and tourism market.

A Transport Department audit of CP Air, released in the summer of 1984, concluded that it is generally a 'good airline' with dedicated employees. It did have some minor problems and the audit recommended 'increased company quality control, surveillance and enforcement throughout the system,' better employee training and the development of maintenance and engineering procedures. But these problems afflicted other major corporations in Canada, the audit noted.

CP Air has become just another Canadian corporation, struggling to adapt to rapid change.

Grant McConachie was the last of Canadian Pacific's originals. He gave the airline – and the Company – a sense of flair and adventure as he struggled to establish new routes and to secure permission to take his planes across the continent.

And he gave the Company a human face – something that it lacks today. And yet its activities probably touch the lives of more Canadians than at any other time in its history.

# The Canadian Pacific Today

'We don't go after major successes in this company but we avoid major failures too.'

Ian Sinclair, President of Canadian Pacific, to a questioner at the Company's Annual Meeting in 1973.

**J** Lorne McDougall's history of the Canadian Pacific Railway, commissioned by the Company, appeared in 1968.

In his introduction, 'Buck' Crump explained why the CPR had commissioned the work to avoid the alternative – 'something which represented the work of many hands, all striving to extract what was controversial, so that it ended up a bland, flavourless mass of facts; every fact verified and most of them of no importance.'

Such defensiveness sounded odd coming from the president of the Company. The changes in the name, slogans and logo also revealed a certain nervousness about CPR's image. During the 1960s, the state began to play an increasingly important role in the lives of Canadians. It also began to take on that air of moral righteousness that marked the CPR's attempts to help Canadian unity and development. At one time, and in many places, the CPR had been 'the only outfit in the world,' as one oldtimer put it. Now the bureaucrats looked askance at private enterprise, distrusted its ways, and became suspicious when it turned a profit.

And the Company had competition in many areas. But, as McDougall noted in a masterly understatement, the 'Canadian Pacific has never been a tidy little business.' In 1962, the Company organized Canadian Pacific Enterprises Ltd (CPE), which ran its oil and gas, mines and minerals, iron and steel, forest products, real estate and agriproduct operations. Between 1970 and 1980, the Company's assets rose sixfold and its profits increased twentyfold. In 1982 CPE moved its headquarters from Montreal to Calgary – about the time the western boom burst. By 1984, the conglomerate had $12 billion in assets. But it also had suffered from the recession.

The *Globe and Mail*'s 'Report on Business 1000' for 1984 noted that the 'sagging fortunes' of Canadian Pacific and Canadian Pacific Enterprises – 'a combination considered by many to be a fitting proxy for the entire Canadian economy' – showed just how badly the recession had hit Canada. CPE's

*Above right:* Two types of trucks from the vast CP Express fleet pull into a parking lot. The CP Express/CP Transport trucking empire stretches from Halifax, Nova Scotia to Nanaimo on Vancouver Island. The lines reach north to Flin Flon in Manitoba and Dawson Creek in British Columbia.

*Right:* Triple diesel locomotives in 'action red' haul a string of tank cars out of Montréal, Québec. Montréal is the CPR headquarters city, and also has the distinction of being the easternmost part of the railroad's line that is double-tracked.

236

profit fell 58.4 percent in 1983, coming to only $62.9 million on revenues of $8.7 billion. On a compounded basis, CPE's profits had declined more than 30 percent in each of the past five fiscal years. In its thrusting, expansionist way, CPE had acquired the Canadian International Paper Company for $1.1 billion (US) in 1981 – and lost $101.8 million on it in 1982.

The parent company, CP Ltd, did little better than its offspring. CP Rail earned $184 million in 1983, but CP Ships lost $74.3 million and CP Air $16.4 million. CP Ltd's profit fell 24 percent over the previous year to $143.6 million on revenue of $13.1 billion. But the Company's five-year return on capital came to 16.8 percent, a reasonably decent showing for tough economic times.

And the Company ranked first in Canada in 1983 in revenues, seventh in assets, and 19th in profits. CPE Ltd ranked fifth in revenues, tenth in assets, and 47th in profits according to the *Globe and Mail*'s survey of the top 1000 companies in Canada.

To some extent, though, the Canadian Pacific has become simply another large Canadian corporation. The various companies have about 127,000 employees and 62,000 shareholders. CPE owns a major part of over 150 companies and has interests in over 100 more. One story claims that during negotiations with a union, company officials failed to report the profits from a line which CPR owned – they had forgotten about it!

The Company's activities extend into the US, Greenland, Spain, Australia and South Africa among other places. At the end of the last century, it acquired a small mining company to provide traffic for a branch line in British Columbia and to rid the region of a man who might have proved a nuisance to the Company. Then it acquired smelters, and in time Consolidated Mining and Smelting (Cominco) came into existence as a major Canadian base metal producer. In 1961, the Canadian Government, bent on developing the north at any cost and employing its native people, built a railway to Pine Point in the Mackenzie District of the Northwest Territories. The majority interest in the mine belonged to Cominco. But it was Canadian National, the railway line that built and operated the highly profitable mine. Ore from Pine Point went to the Cominco smelter at Trail as nearby deposits were exhausted. The mine shut down temporarily in 1982, a victim of poor lead-zinc prices and international competition.

*Opposite:* The *Dayliner* builds up speed outside the town of Ellerslie on the Alberta prairie.
*Below:* The CPR *Dayliner* makes the Calgary to Edmonton run, taking on passengers at Wetaskiwin, Alberta.

Red locomotive 1802 idles on a snowy day in North Bay, Ontario. This E-8 unit is one of only three diesel-electrics specifically designed as passenger units. The 1800s operate out of Montréal.

In 1955, the CPR introduced the scenic-domed, stainless steel passenger train, *The Canadian,* on its run between Montreal/Toronto and Vancouver. But the Company realized that it could no longer make money on passengers. In a presentation to the MacPherson Commission on Transportation in 1960, CPR vice-president Robert Emerson stated that the railway planned to scrap $64 million worth of passenger equipment. He doubted 'whether it is fully realized the extent to which Canadian Pacific is a freight road . . . passenger train service on Canadian Pacific is no longer required for the economic well being of Canada.' In 1973, passengers on the Dominion Atlantic, a CPR subsidiary that had once thrilled local people with its dark red, gold-trimmed locomotives, had to sign a curious document stating that they were travelling at their own risk between Windsor and Truro. Their train took 2½ hours to cover 59 miles, while they sat or stood in the caboose at the end of a freight train.

Save for some lucrative commuter services, CP Rail left its passengers to be cared for by the state in January 1977 when VIA Rail came into being. By October this new state-owned transportation corporation had acquired most of CP Rail's passenger equipment for $18 million. But Canadian Pacific still owned the tracks over which VIA's trains ran and leased them to the corporation. It also maintained ownership of stations. In 1984 the federal minister of transport announced that the government would be purchasing these stations from Canadian Pacific.

In the same year, CP Rail announced that it would eliminate cabooses on trains — and the conductors. Electronic devices could do their job just as well. Predictably, the unions objected at this increased substitution of machines for men.

The Company has been quick to grasp at new technology to improve productivity and maintain profits. During the 1960s, the term 'intermodal' came into use to describe the integrated nature of the Company's activities. Piggybacking had been practised as early as 1855 to carry coaches by train in Nova Scotia. CPR revived the concept in 1957 to compete with truckers on the highways. In 1977 a Company vice-president stated that the average capacity of freight cars had risen from 39 tons to 64 tons in 40 years. The CPR's 100 ton grain hopper cars could be loaded in 12 minutes and unloaded in three. At that date, railways in Canada carried 37 percent of all goods transported — but consumed only seven percent of the fuel used in transportation.

The CPR experimented with winter sailings from the lower St Lawrence river ports as early as 1962. Five years later, when the St Lawrence opened for winter navigation, the CPR built a container port at Wolfe's Cove near Québec, the former site of its ocean passenger terminal. At Saint John, which has the advantage of the 'Short Line' across Maine to the heart of Canada, CP Rail, municipal and provincial agencies joined with the National Harbours Board to move the port into the container business. The Board built a container terminal and leased it to Brunterm, owned by CP Rail and a private company. The decline in general cargo tonnage out of Saint John was offset by the increase in container traffic in 1970 and 1971. Containers swing from the decks of ships on to rail cars, and solid container trains head for Montreal, 480 miles and 18 hours away. With 16,500 miles of main line track in Canada, and 5000 in the United States, CP Rail can deliver cargo throughout Canada and the US midwest. The

A gorgeous shot of *The Canadian,* brilliant chrome against the snow, now in VIA Rail service, continuing a proud tradition.

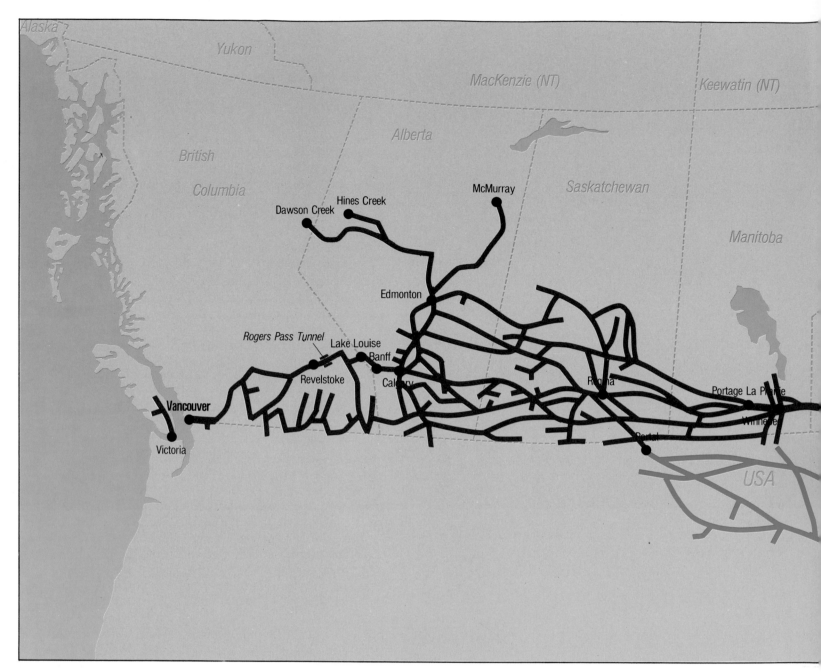

Road switcher 8163 as seen in July 1976 (below) with the old CPR colors, and one year later (opposite) with the new 'action red' scheme.

# Canadian Pacific Rail Activities

━━━━━━━━━━ Canadian Pacific (CP Rail)
━━━━━━━━━━ Soo Line

The CP Rail system is single track except for the section between Portage La Prairie and Thunder Bay, and trackage in and around the cities of Vancouver, Sudbury, Toronto, Ottawa and Montreal.

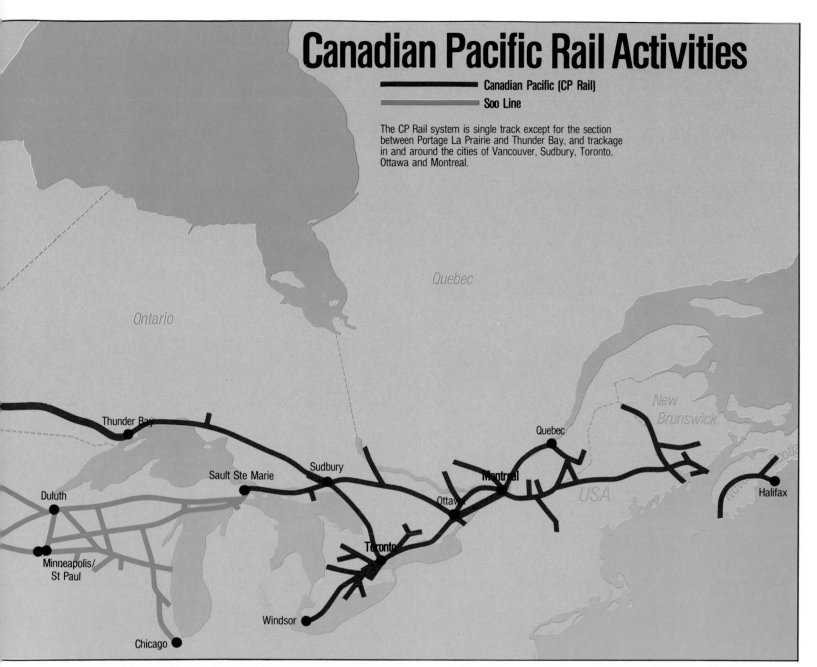

company has developed containers that are smaller and lighter than the standard one but carry the same load.

The Company initiated 'unit trains' in 1967. These carry single commodities; the first took 3700 tons of sulphuric acid to a plant in Ontario. In the same year, CPR Rail began testing remote-controlled 'slave' diesel locomotives for use with these unit trains. The locomotives sit in the middle of the freight cars, and respond to radio signals. In 1968 and 1969, the Company's subsidiary, Fording Coal, together with Kaiser Resources Ltd began to ship millions of tons of coking coal to Japan. Unit trains, hauled by 3000 horsepower locomotives pulled 88 hopper cars between the coal fields in the Kootenay region and the deep-sea bulk terminal at Roberts Bank, south of Vancouver.

The Company's Public Relations Department issues a sheet which lists the dates of the significant achievements and events associated with the railway. Not unexpectedly, the list fails to include the date in November 1979, when a CPR freight with cars containing toluene, propane and chlorine derailed and caught fire in the Toronto suburb of Mississauga. About 250,000 people had to leave their homes. The evacuation was carried out in a calm and efficient manner, but the Company was still sorting through damage claims in 1984.

The derailment resulted from a 'hot box' – a bearing overheating where the wheel joined the axle. Most freight cars are now equipped with ball and roller bearings that prevent this problem. And electronic scanners at 25-kilometre intervals pick up any 'hot boxes' and warn the enginemen.

In November 1983, after a long debate, the Western Grain Transportation Act cleared Parliament. It achieved a goal towards which the CPR had long struggled – the abolition of the Crow Rate. For years the Company had lost money by carrying grain at rates below those charged in 1897. Under the new system, the Federal Government will pay the railways a 'Crow Benefit' which will reach about $650 million a year by the 1986/87 crop year. The government will also pay the railways for any cost increases for the movement of grain over and above designated percentage increases borne by shippers. Thus while grain growers and shippers complain that the end of the Crow means economic disaster for them, they will simply be paying a more reasonable tariff to have their crops exported. The government of Canada, or, more correctly the Canadian taxpayers, will still be subsidizing the carriage of grain to markets by a state railway and a privately-owned one.

The abolition of the Crow and the provision of greater incentives for moving grain to market meant that CP Rail has been able to raise capital to improve its system. It is upgrading its track, acquiring new equipment, building new facilities. And it is undertaking the largest single project since the original transcontinental line was built a hundred years ago. When 'Hell's Bells' Rogers discovered the pass named after him and received his $5000 bonus, neither he nor any of the Syndicate could have realized how much money it would cost to keep the trains running through Rogers Pass.

The Rogers Pass project now under way will cost $600 million, and be completed in late 1988. It involves the construction of about ten miles of tunnel through two mountains, the building of six new bridges, and the addition of 20 miles of second track through the Selkirks.

The project will employ 800 people. Where it took hundreds of men to lay track on the original line, a machine

*Left:* Mt Ogden towers over diesel locomotives at Field, British Columbia, on the CPR main line, just west of Lake Louise.
*Bottom left:* Long strips of 1440-foot continuous welded rail are being laid near Revelstoke, BC.
*Below:* CP Rail diesel locomotives haul the big gondolas of Canadian Pacific's Fording Coal subsidiary.
*Bottom right:* A CPR freight train stops at the quaint old Lloydminster station on a sunny April day in 1978.

246

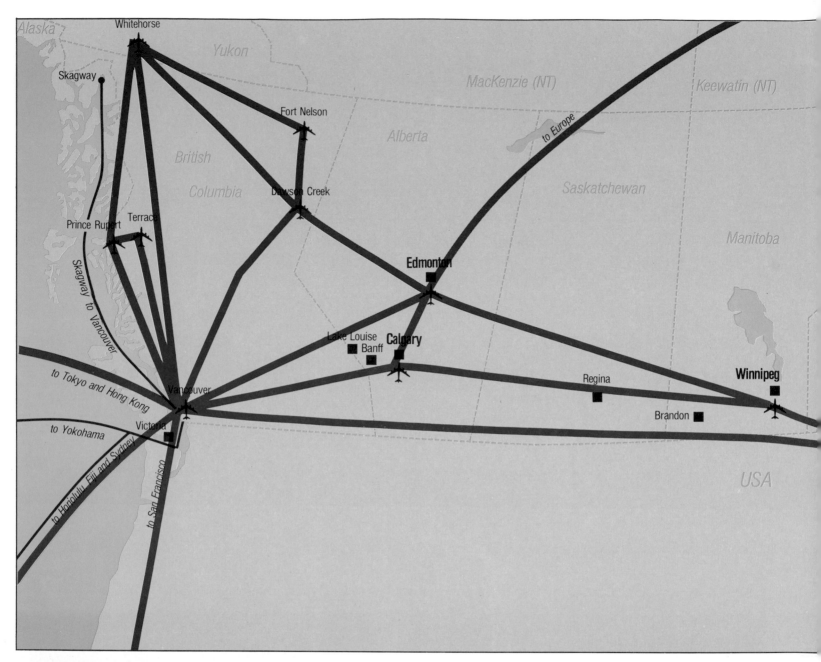

# Canadian Pacific Non-Rail Activities

▬▬▬ CP Air     ■ CP Hotels

───── CP Ships, CP Bermuda     ✈ Airports served by CP Air

Boldface indicates cities with CP Hotels which are *also* served by CP Air.

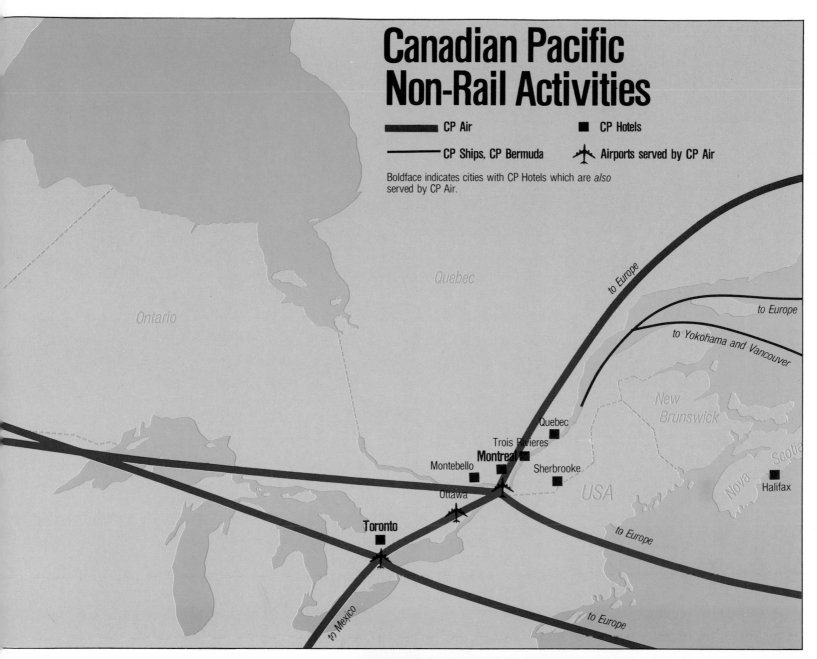

Quebec

Ontario

to Europe

to Europe

to Yokohama and Vancouver

New Brunswick

Nova Scotia

Quebec

Trois Rivieres

**Montreal**

Montebello

Sherbrooke

USA

Halifax

Ottawa

**Toronto**

to Europe

to Mexico

to Europe

*Left to right:* Some of the more famous hotels operated by CP Hotels include Chateau Lake Louise at Lake Louise, Alberta; the Royal York in Toronto, Ontario; Le Chateau Frontenac in Québec City, Québec; and The Algonquin in St Andrews-by-the-Sea, New Brunswick.

*Left:* Le Chateau Champlain towers over the Place du Canada in Montréal, Québec. Many of its 614 rooms boast arched picture windows.

and an operator can do it all now. Five routes were examined to determine the most feasible one, and many geotechnical and engineering studies done. Unlike the first time the line went through Rogers Pass, the Company also had to undertake environmental impact studies. Modern machinery will strip away 15 million cubic yards of overburden and 520,000 cubic yards of rock. At present as many as six 3000-horse-power diesels have to be added to heavy freight trains for the nine-mile haul up the steep grades near Rogers Pass. The project will reduce the 2.2 percent gradient to one percent.

The accommodation for workers is a far cry from the tents and log cabins that housed the workers on the original line. Two camps to house 400 workers feature single bedrooms, snow protection and bear-proof garbage disposal. And the wages are better, too. A woman working as a carpenter in the summer of 1984 reported taking home $600 a week, and a formerly unemployed father and son team building retaining walls cleared $1200 a week. The West is again depressed, as it was in 1884, and working on the railway has provided welcome employment for many people.

Even in these tight times, the Company still dreams of big projects – and takes new initiatives. In the fall of 1981, it opened its $162-million Polaris venture on Little Cornwallis Island in the High Arctic, the 11th largest lead-zinc mine in the world. Cominco built the mill on a barge that was towed to

*Above:* The Polaris Mine on Little Cornwallis Island in the Arctic. Note the icebergs and the buildings on stilts in the background.

*Below:* Cement roadbed foundation is continuously laid as part of the Rogers Pass project in British Columbia's Selkirk Mountains.

the heart of the Arctic. Insurance alone cost $1 million.

As early as 1931 Canadian National and Canadian Pacific discussed merging their telecommunications network, but the formal partnership did not occur until 1981. The two companies have issued a proposal to develop a 'city within a city,' the Metro Centre of Toronto on railyards, at the cost of $1 billion.

But when the Company celebrated its centennial in 1981 and threw a party, it provided only hot dogs and chips for its employees at Montreal's Windsor station. In the same year, the world economic summit was held at the luxurious Chateau Montebello, near Québec City. But the Company will do business with anyone. The Chateau hosted a conference on poverty in 1973.

The Company still has to live with its history – and sometimes to suffer from having too much of it. In November, 1982, the Company received criticism for demolishing its 71-year old station in west Toronto, without municipal or federal permission.

Frederick Burbidge, president between 1972 and 1981 and chairman after that, once claimed that the Company 'made its own luck by being receptive to change and alert to new opportunities.' This approach becomes both more difficult and easier as governments continue to regulate *and* deregulate transportation in Canada. In July 1984 the Canadian Transport Commission ordered CP Rail to main-

*Above left:* Hamburg Plaza is one of several CP Hotels in Europe.
*Above:* Banff Springs Hotel rises like a great castle in the Alberta Rockies.
*Right:* Le Chateau Montebello, nestled amidst a private 65,000 acre estate, was the site of the 1981 Economic Summit.

tain service on a line between Mont Laurier and St Jerome in Québec, on which it had lost $450,000 in 1983. But the Federal Government agreed to subsidize future losses on the line. In the same month, a decision of the Quebec Transport Commission allowed a freight operation of CP Trucks to expand its operations in the province, and to move into rural areas.

Like many other old Canadian institutions, the Canadian Pacific is often appreciated abroad more than it is at home. The Company packages and sells its knowledge through Canadian Pacific Consulting Services Ltd. In July 1984 the Chinese Government signed a $1.6 million contract with this arm of Canadian Pacific to undertake a feasibility study on the storage, handling and loading of coal into unit trains in northern China.

In a sense, the history of this innovative, ingenious company has now come full circle. Chinese came to Canada a hundred years ago to serve the Company and to build the line. Now the Company has moved to China to help the people there to apply modern technology in solving problems of railway building and operation.

## SOURCES

The Canadian Pacific's Public Relations and Advertising Division (P.O. Box 6042, Station 'A', Montreal, P.Q., H3C 3E4) issues a short bibliography, a chronology and facts and figures on the railway, as well as other material. Books on the Canadian Pacific fall into three categories – standard works, reminiscences of railway builders, and recent attempts to demythologize the railway and the company. The most comprehensive treatment of the Company and its operations is W. Kaye Lamb's *History of the Canadian Pacific Railway* (1977). J Lorne McDougall's *Canadian Pacific – A Brief History* (1968), commissioned by the Company, is strong on financial and economic aspects, but contains little on the human dimensions of the railway's development and tends to be defensive. Harold Innis published his *History of the Canadian Pacific Railway* in 1923. It contains masses of data and a number of insights on the relationship of the railway to hinterland development. Keith Morris wrote a somewhat bombastic history of the railway, *The Story of the Canadian Pacific Railway* in 1916, when the Company was at the height of its power. It contains material from a range of sources that are not identified, and the book was reissued in 1981. The Reverend R G MacBeth, an imperialist to his fingertips, knew many of the men who worked on the railway, and produced his *Romance of the Canadian Pacific Railway* in 1924.

The early history of the railway is covered in Omer Lavellée's *Van Horne's Road,* an illustrated account with 460 photographs. Lavellée, Canadian Pacific's Corporate Historian and Archivist, has brought together some rare material and information not found elsewhere. Pierre Berton's *The National Dream,* covering the years from 1871 to 1881, stresses the personalities involved in launching the railway. *The Last Spike,* described as a 'historical novel' in the CP Rail bibliography, tells of the construction of the line between 1881 and 1885. Both books were condensed as *The Great Railway Illustrated* (1972). The two books, abridged, appeared again in a separate volume in 1974, with colour illustrations from the CBC television series based on them. The television series, incidentally, was sponsored by Royal Trust – not by the Company. Books by other writers add a human dimension to the railway's story. P Turner Bone, a Scottish engineer, came to Canada to seek his fortune, and wrote an interesting autobiography *When the Steel Went Through* (1947). D E MacIntyre worked on the railway before the First World War, and included stories about it in *End of Steel* (1973). Ken Liddell, a newspaperman who died in 1975, worked as a newsagent on the railways. His book *I'll Take the Train* (1977), contains much information on the CPR, and has nice touches of humour. David Hanna, first president of the Canadian National Railways, wrote his reminiscences in 1926, *Trains of Recollection.* Hanna has an odd style and a sardonic, admiring, attitude towards the Company. Allen Gibson's short book *Train Time* (1973) tells of the impact of the railways on a small town and its people in Nova Scotia. Elizabeth Willmott's *Meet Me at the Station* recaptures the feel of the railway stations, and their role in community life in Ontario.

Two biographies of key people in the Company's history deal with them from opposite ends of the spectrum of historical writing. Heather Gilbert's *Awakening Continent* (1965) is a life of Lord Mount Stephen in two parts. The first section deals with his activities from 1829 to 1891, contains a great deal of detailed information, but does not tell much about him as a human being. D H Miller-Barstow's *Beatty of the CPR* (1951), an anecdotal and readable account of the life of the first Canadian-born president of the Canadian Pacific Railway, brings this remarkable man alive.

Ronald Keith's *Bush Pilot with a Briefcase* (1972) is a breezy, readable life of Grant McConachie, the man who gave his life to CP Air. George Musk's book, *Canadian Pacific: The Story of the famous shipping line* contains a vast amount about the Company's shipping activities, with details of every one of its vesels.

Robert Chados' book, *The CPR: A Century of Corporate Welfare* (1973) concentrates on what the author thinks the Company has done wrong, rather than on its achievements. Susan Goldberg's *Canadian Pacific: A Portrait of Power* (1983) is as much a study of bigness as of the Company. It lacks a focus, but contains a great deal of useful information, including a list of the Company's holdings and interests. Roger Burrows' *Railway Mileposts: British Columbia* (1982), written by an enthusiast, also contains a great deal of useful information. And E J Hart's *The Selling of Canada: The CPR and the Beginnings of Canadian Tourism* (1983) shows how the Company set the style for Canadian tourism – and created an image of Canada. It also rescues from obscurity that remarkable man, John Murray Gibbon.

*Left:* The Canadian crosses Stoney Creek Bridge in August 1957, when CPR still had the passenger route.
*Top:* The caboose in the sunset signals the end of this telling of the CPR story.

# Index